A LUCKY LIFE

Being... White

Seeing... Red

Feeling... Blue

Kenneth Hugh Harrison

Lucky Valley Press
2016

A LUCKY LIFE
Copyright © 2016 by Kenneth Hugh Harrison
All Rights Reserved

ISBN: 978-0-9967802-6-1

Book Design and Pre-Press
by Ginna and David Gordon

Published by Lucky Valley Press
Jacksonville, Oregon
www.luckyvalleypress.com

Printed in the United States of America

CONTENTS

Preface	1
Saint Mary's Amazing Grace	5
Quiet Flows the Don	13
Skirmishes with Gertrude	21
Proverbs 13 and Interpretation	29
A Resolve from Ashes	35
Illusions Cleared Through Smoke	41
The First Step on the Long Ladder	49
Peace in Our Time	59
Delivering the Goods and More	65
War Opened with a Skylark	69
Illusions and Pretensions	79
The First Step to Independence	85
Daedalus to *Philoctetes*	89
The *Philoctetes* Chained in Freetown Harbor	93
The Wild Swan Song	103
My Name Was Posted on a List	115
Murmansk Memory: Revisited	119
HMS Vigilant	121
HMS Berwick and the Golden Fleece	133
A Norwegian Family Farewell	149

A Hasty Decision, Quickly Regretted	157
The *Queen Elizabeth*	167
The *Mauretania*	175
A Scotch or Two, With Hospitality	185
Two Queens	193
A Brief Encounter and a Brief Exit	203
Caesar of the Barclay	209
Grace Had Arrived in My Life	219
Two Princesses and a Dream Fulfilled	225
Phoenix Out of the Ashes	231
The Art of Seeing	235
Waiting for Godot	243
Mea Culpa, Mea Culpa	247
The New Teacher Learns American Spirit	257
From Cactus to Apple Orchards	265
Beads, Bangles and Bongos	271
Aptos Half-High	277
The Circle Has Been Mended	283
The Ship *Amazing Grace*	293
My Random Memory & Blood Type	299
Angels Who Appeared as People	303
Photographs	following page 311

PREFACE

When attempting to remember episodes, or periods, or one's words and actions and exchanges between individuals, the mind wants to recall particular people who were important in the past. It is like looking at old photographs and notebooks; time has faded the image and the words. At my eighty-ninth year today, I piece together what once was one day following the next, which became a week and then a month and eventually another year, and became my life in dates and times.

Of course, happy and tragic times and momentous incidents are available in the memory, and are indelible in the memory, like an echo or an image. I hope I have recalled friends and those who loved me, and especially the "angels" who appeared, perhaps fleetingly, or were pivotal in some way to solve an impasse or open a door I thought was shut.

No man by himself can solve his dilemma or his quandary or his impasse every time without help, in my case an "angel," an individual who seemingly appears out of thin air or, by Fate, came to solve the problem! As you read of my various escapades, incidents, frustrations, and dilemmas, you will note that Fate often brought me helpers who appeared at the right time.

I call them "angels" because they came at times when the "door" was locked and they opened it, or my despair had prostrated my courage and they lifted me up.

As a child, three years old, I was deposited in a Catholic Orphanage by my sailor father, who probably was at his wit's end when my mother died and he was about to leave on His Majesty's service on a battleship going to the Far East. But a three year old was not able to reason why his father or his mother would leave him in a strange and alien place. From this traumatic abandonment (from the child's point of view) what follows could be psychologically quite affective to the character.

I mention this only as a reason for what follows in the autobiography, particularly as you see the long trail from abandonment to belonging and being loved. Of course not everyone has the time and the luxury of picking up the pieces and putting the whole picture back again.

Like many others, my early life was as the son of a seaman, who appeared only on occasion whenever his ship happened to return to his homeport of Portsmouth, as sailors have done so over centuries, having been half around the world in His Majesty's service.

In fact, from the age of three, I only saw my father six times before I was seventeen: twice in the orphanage, and from seven to seventeen, four times between commissions. In those days, England was a sea power with ports and parts of the Empire spread all around the world. So, the life of a sailor in the Royal Navy was mostly somewhere other than his home! To give you the picture, the major ports were Gibraltar, Alexandria, Aden, Bombay, Trincomalee, Sri Lanka, Colombo, Singapore, Hong Kong and Shanghai. And of course, the Caribbean and many islands in those days were possessions of the British Empire spread around the world in the Atlantic to the South Atlantic, the Mediterranean into the Indian Ocean, the China Seas, even to the tip of South America to the Falklands.

Being the son of a young sailor, with letters from all around the world, one's imagination would project to so many far places strewn across the world map where one would hope to go one day. However, World War 2 changed things irrevocably. Though I got to sail to many places, sadly I was never to the orient in the far Pacific, where my father had traveled.

I have seen enough to know that this new electronic age and jet planes and allegiances have changed the world. It is smaller, with many more people sharing an electronic connection, Coca Colas and Big Macs! On my computer I can in a few minutes communicate with a place that would have taken weeks to contact when I was a boy! Since I have retired, I have taken cruises and journeys that I never dreamed of. The world is at our elbow.

As I look back to that beginning as a waif in an alien place, and I look at what I have and have been given by love and opportunities, I see how lucky I was, and who opened the doors and pointed the way.

I was blessed in my life in several ways. Having two loving, intelligent, talented wives who were personally instrumental in healing my heart and enriching my mind. Louise not only loved me as I was, but gave me two beautiful daughters, whom I'm sure healed my psyche as well as filled my heart and the house with joy. More, because they followed my footsteps, becoming teachers and giving to others their skills and their love and guidance. I love them dearly, and they sustain the love of their mother who nurtured their abilities and their spirits.

AMAZING GRACE

Amazing Grace, how sweet the sound,
That saved a wretch like me
I once was lost but now I'm found,
Was blind, but now, I see.

When we've been here ten thousand years
Bright shining as the sun,
We've no less days to sing God's praise
Then when we've first begun.

Amazing Grace, how sweet the sound,
That saved a wretch like me.
I once was lost, but now am found,
Was blind, but now I see.

John Newton

SAINT MARY'S AMAZING GRACE

I thought it best to start at a beginning. Not *the* beginning, which I don't remember, though I was told my mother's name was Hilda Gladdis, before she became Mrs. Harrison, my mother, in 1924.

My beginning was holding on to my father's big leathery hand as our feet crunched on wet gravel leading up to some grey concrete steps to a giant wooden door of weathered grey panels with an enormous key plate and handle.

At that time of year, possibly October or November, it was already into what the Scots called "the gloaming." The light was fast failing, and my father was a dark tall shape who was, in the best way, attempting to calm my rapidly increasing anxieties. "This is a nice place. You'll love it here. There will be other children. You'll see."

With that, he reached up to the great rusty metal knocker, which even to this day I can see: it was a crucifix, attached to the flange of the knocker. My father gave it a quick "rap-rap!" To my ears it sounded like the knell of doom! I began to bawl. The door creaked open, and a face appeared that seemed to float within a stark white frame upon a black mass. I broke free of the leather hand as words were exchanged; "I am Victor Harrison, with my son. I called this morning."

"Oh, yes. We were expecting you. Please come in."

I was lifted up suddenly and whisked into the reception room in my father's arms as the great door shut off my known world and enclosed me in an unwanted and, I suspected, less desirable future, which had already started. In the sparsely lighted room, the great gloomy shadows thrown by the yellow light became threatening bogie-men waiting to leap out as soon as my father left, which I intuited with ever-increasing fear.

The billowing dark cloud apparition with her floating white face led us into a darkening room whose only light came through the two large multi-paned windows heavily curtained in velvet. Since it was past early sunset, we were in the half-light, which with its shadows added to my rising anxiety and perhaps intuition, since I began to cry.

The Nun-witch came out of those shadows and, looming over me, reached forward with two long billowing arms with fingers like talons! I screamed in terror, and found myself placed on the saddle of a large carved wooden rocking horse with bulging eyes. It was an alien beast, not designed to placate me. Her bony hands sat me on the saddle and began to rock me gently as Dad kissed me and said, "Don't be scared. The nuns will take good care of you. Daddy will be back." He let go of the horse.

He addressed the nun as "Sister," whom I now knew in my terror as "Nun-witch!" She turned away from me to my father, whom I could see backing into the gloom as my short arms futilely reached into the void. As my father melted into the shadows, I screamed so hard. I believe it was for sorrows I could not express, for losses I could not understand. The great door opened momentarily and closed irrevocably on the outside world.

Now in my eighties, I know and understand what must have gone on in his mind, as no one in his family, his sisters, brothers or his mother or his father offered to take his son. Finally, as his several years of commission loomed, one can see him forced as a last resort to place his three-year old son in a Catholic Home called an orphanage.

As he sailed away in 1927 on His Majesty's service, to show the flag to some far flung possession, he was dispossessed of his family, but comforted by the fact that if God exists therefore charity and compassion still exist, and it would be there, in that Catholic orphanage. As retrospect and age, like wine, matures and understands, what could not have been palatable then, is now an elixir of love.

Circumstances force choices that are available, not necessarily choices one desires. A depression of sorts was already spreading like a sickness across England in the twenties. The aftermath of the Great World War had begun. So ironically, by putting me in the orphanage at the time, he was protecting me from total neglect or worse. *God works in mysterious ways...*

Though I was only in that orphanage four years, possibly my most impressionable age, I believe it probably had effects that remained for a lot longer. For instance, I now I believe that the seeds of my later rejection of Catholicism were sown there.

What happened during those four years is not readily available, since memory at this age is not easily to retrieve. But I can remember certain or occasional incidents. I do remember being given a square of floor to be scrubbed and cleaned as my responsibility.

I remember my first meal. We sat on benches at long tables, and the nuns and the priests sat on the raised dais at the end of the room. One younger girl novice, in a blue and white dress, carried a shallow basket containing slices of bread. She slapped one piece of bread onto the white empty plate in front of each inmate as she moved along the rows. As the second novice reached each plate with its slice of bread, she ladled the hot beef-fat onto the bread. This beef-fat was rendered from the butcher's odds and ends, scrags and lumps of fat, which we called "drippings." Bearing the poverty of the times, it was very tasty, but scarce. Keeping in mind that in the prevailing long depression of that era, we were considered lucky to be so sustained. On reflection, it reminds me of Oliver Twist: "Can I 'ave more... sir?"

Another instance after a short time there is etched in my memory because I felt I was again separated. A bus was brought into the grounds, and soon everyone was excited: "A visit to the zoo!" "We're going to the lions!" My imagination ran rampant! "Lions, tigers and rino'rosses!" I ran around the bus and almost ran over the sister, who was marshaling the line into the bus.

"What are you up to now?" I had my answer ready, "I'm going to the zoo!" I blurted out!" "No, you are too young. Not this time." She dismissed me with her bony hand as she stepped onto the bus in a cloud of dark blue.

The door closed and I was alone again. As I turned away to go to my sand pile or dirt, I could hear the others begin to sing as their voices drifted out of the open windows as the back of the bus receded down the gravel path to the gate and to freedom. A smattering of voices, not too musical but exciting, began to recite, "Amazing Grace, how sweet the sound... I once was lost and now am found..." The off-key singing dwindled in my ears and I was once again by myself. However, I gained an afternoon with the absence of supervision, and a rare freedom.

As I continued my random gardening, irrigating a channel I had dug in the clay soil, a sudden inspiration came upon me and so I transplanted weeds and an occasional dandelion. In the midst of my efforts, my ears were suddenly assailed by a roar that I could not immediately identify. "GROWL...YAY...GROWL!" In the imagination and fantasy that was my three-year-old mind, such as it was, I heard a giant roaring his rage about being kept within walls. As I listened more attentively, I thought it might be from the zoo!

Much later, I was ridiculed by older inmates for thinking it was the zoo. I was enlightened that it was the 20,000 fans celebrating their team's win, the Southampton Saints, which had a football stadium, the Dell, just about half a mile from St. Mary's.

Another incident impressed upon my memory is two boys who ran away from the orphanage. Rumors were spread around, but few facts. But a couple of days later, a police van brought the escapees back for the authorities to deal with them. At dinner that night, when a priest read their "sins," or offences according to the authorities, he ordered them each to flop over a chair, and the priest gave them three lashes on their bottoms from a Malacca cane.

You can understand why I remember that incident.

Another memory is etched in my mind: In the dormitory above my cot was a large picture of Jesus by an arched oak doorway studded with metal hasps and nails. He held a lamp in one hand and in the other, a shepherd's crook. The lamp illumined the doorway, and the description below said: *Knock unto the door, and it shall be opened to you!* I did not at first understand it. But like a mantra, I recited it every night, until one night I had a epiphany: I understood, in simple terms, *open this door, and ye will understand*. The *door* was a metaphor for enlightenment. I had connected with God, I believed.

A particular incident was a surprise on one of my father's rare visits. In fact, in the four years I believe there were only two or three visits, not counting the bringing of me to this place. It was in Christmas week, when he was in port after eighteen months of duty in the China station.

He was allowed to see me briefly in the doorway vestibule where there were a few seats and a table with a vase of flowers and a crucifix. After an awkward pause, as I inched closer to him, he proffered a brightly wrapped package with a ribbon. The ripping of paper and wrenching off the ribbon, lo and behold, revealed a Hawker Hurricane biplane with Royal Air-Force roundels, and a small pilot in the cockpit. But, more excitement, under the lower wings were slung two small bombs. If you turned the key, the mechanism released those two bombs!

My father saw my delight and more, and I suddenly let out a, "Wow! Dad, this is smashing!" I hugged his legs and he departed. But as soon my father was behind the closed door, the Sister Superior swept into the vestibule and snatched the airplane out of my hands, and with cold authority pronounced, "The Orphanage Rule: we cannot allow one little boy or girl have something when all the others have nothing."

I did not understand communism, or what her philosophy was. I clenched my teeth momentarily, but my final memory of that place was when I understood that, at last, I was to be released from the orphanage, my father was coming, finally, to take me away! I was to be bathed and scrubbed, (I thought, "Why do Catholics apply carbolic soap and rough brushes as though it would erase not only dirt but sin?) "Yes, Sister," when the novitiate asked me, "Does the iodine hurt when I put it on your chill blains?" My wince and moans, I thought, would be answer enough!

When she had finished, I gracefully smiled and said, "Thank you, Sister." I didn't know how to address a novitiate, but I thought it was better to err on the side of flattery. "Aren't you a lucky boy, to have a daddy," she said as she combed my hair and opened the bathroom door. "We will miss you, and I hope you will remember us!" She sounded like a postcard, with the signature anonymous.

The chilblains followed me, one on each toe, itch and all, out of Saint Mary's Orphanage. However, there were invisible impressions in my psyche that would not be exorcised in the near future. From the advantage of hindsight, I was given several chances to learn from my own mistakes, and to be given the best that humans can give to each other, above all love and charity no matter where it comes from. I stood in the vestibule nervously.

The grandfather clock in the hall chimed 12 noon.

Almost simultaneously at the last chime came a knock on the great door. It was opened and there he was! He was here! My father collected me and the Superior put her hand briefly on my head, for some reason crossed herself and said to my father, "May God guide him." My father offered his hand as a gesture of thanks.

As we went through that great oak door, I skipped down the two steps onto the gravel in a burst of freedom and grasped my fathers sun-burned leathery hand and said, "Let's go quick, Dad," perhaps not trusting the moment of freedom.

The railway journey to Portsmouth was only 25 miles, but the local stopped at four stations along the line. We finally arrived at my "new home." It was one of hundreds of drab slate roofs that long ago were red bricks but, with time and soil, were faded and grimy.

They were built at the turn of the century in order to house the dock and factory workers. They were built in rows connected to each other, and the back "yard" was only 18 feet wide and about 35 feet long. The WC was attached outside, so you'd visit it in rain and sunshine, frost and ice.

And, although the afternoon was still daylight, in the passage inside the little house it was gloomy. I was still gripping my father's hand: I was shy, and perhaps anxious. As we went into the sitting room, I noticed the table was laid and in the center of the table was a yellow Jell-O and a round cake and lemonade already in a glass I presumed was mine. I blurted out, "What Saint's day is it?" It was only on sacred days in the orphanage that we might get Jell-O! It was my first meeting with my stepmother, who was introduced, "This is your *new* mother."

The word *mother*, in some way, seemed alien and in my mind I mumbled the word, psychologically not giving my acceptance: *stepmother*, from that day, was my inside appellation, not *mother*. I was uneasy from the first meeting, though Dad seemed content.

"The winter evening settles down
With smell of steaks in passageways.
Six o'clock.
The burnt-out ends of smoky days
And now a gusty shower wraps
The grimy scraps
Of withered leaves about your feet
And newspapers from vacant lots;
The showers beat
On broken blinds and chimney-pots
And at the corner of the street
A lonely cab-horse steams and stamps

And then the lighting of the lamps."

T.S. Eliot
Preludes

QUIET FLOWS THE DON

Words have always fascinated me. It started with interest in the origin of names. Simple Anglo-Saxon mono-syllabics like Smith, Greene, White and so on, as compared to poly-syllabic Celtics like MacDonald, MacDougall, Mackenzie, and the names of the ports that my father was visiting in his journeys all over the world: Gibraltar, Malta, Alexandria, Trinidad, Shanghai, Hong Kong; all eventually led to tentative follow-ups in the reference section of the library, looking up such words as *apology* and comparing it to *apologia, appropriate* and *apropos, minestrone* to *ministerium* and so on, such fascinating sounds and mysteries of meaning along with the odd *felucca* or *dhow* which were mentioned by my father in brief letters or in cryptic statements upon his even briefer visits, which reminds me of where I was going.

I was intent on getting books back to the library or I'd be in trouble again. Trouble was a word I was very familiar with in those days: *a condition of distress, anxiety or danger; distress disorder, malfunctioning physical affect to cause pain or discomfort to somebody*, which somebody was mainly me, I concluded. So, I would use the public library as one of the legitimate ways I could spend hours away in perfect peace and safety from the naggings, bossings and put-downs with which I was so fed up.

Books can be opened or closed. They don't threaten, they don't put-you-down, they elevate, they empower, I found, as I retreated into them. The library became my refuge, but more than that, a quite state-of-mind that gradually fed my resolve.

That day was one November Saturday, with blustery winds and rain coming in off the channel, making it perfectly miserable for those poor sods who had to be out of doors, *like me*, I thought, as I struggled up the library steps on Fratton Road, cradling the two books I had to return inside my mackintosh. Wet books would mean a two-penny fine and where was I going to get tuppence, anyway? Once inside the shelter of the little lobby, I eased the books out and put them on the bench nearby as I struggled out of my dripping raincoat and hung it next to other wet coats and macs on the rack in the hallway.

"Due today? H'mm?" The librarian squinted up at the clock, "Running it close as usual, I see!" The critical commentary came like the rain, frequently and capriciously and sometimes without warning. He was a little dried-up prune of a man, with his steel rimmed spectacles balanced half-way down his thin, pinched nose and what remained of his hair slicked across his pink, rapidly balding head. He squinted up at me from his return desk. "Alright, my lad. In you go. Here's yer card. Watch out for the wet on my books."

His propriety was noted, but not remarked on since it was not wise to rouse his pettiness and get his spite against you. After all, I needed "his" books. I smiled as I recognized my own wit. "Yes, sir," I reassured the librarian, and mumbled, "Thanks," as I took my library card from his reluctant fingers and went on past his desk into the stacks, where I let out my breath and slowed my pace as I rounded the corner of "P" for poetry. I plunked down on one of the little worn stools that were sprinkled around the stacks and I began to scan the offerings packed tightly on the one small shelf given to Poetry.

I first noticed the wine colored covers of Byron, Coleridge, Pope, Shelley, Tennyson, and Wordsworth, vaguely familiar names I could recognize from my English teacher, Mister Gardner's, introduction to the English Romantics earlier that month. "Byron, I find a little pompous," he had said. "Shelley somewhat precious and effete for my tastes; Coleridge interesting, but narrative orientated; and, as for Pope, I find him verbose and, for my taste, somewhat mechanical and predictable. On the other hand, Wordsworth seems to be essentially English: his voice is that of reason arising out of Nature herself to whisper of that which hearts feel is in the very earth we tread on."

His words did not convey their meaning to my ear as much as give me delight in the sounds and an anticipation of my own discoveries to come. Mr. Gardner had become, I now realize, my model, a touchstone of taste and value.

At first, he seemed opinionated and aloof, but over that year he came to be a kind and supportive guide in my fumbling beginnings as an English student. I much later saw, when I was becoming a teacher, how much I may have been influenced subconsciously by Mr. Gardner, the first adult who found worth in my early work, and thus began my faint hope that I could one day find something to say, and say it well. To perhaps write and become an author.

But back to the library! That particular day, I turned away from the poetry shelf and found myself around the corner staring at a large (it seemed large then), red clothbound book with gold-glinting edges on the thin rice-paper leaves! I hardly looked at the title, *And Quiet Flows the Don*, which was embossed on the cover. I fingered the rich, incredibly fine rice paper. I opened randomly, and began to read:

Gregor Malekhov, a young Cossack, has doubts about the Communist revolution and for a time fights with the Bolsheviks, but then switches to fight with the Whites believing in this way he would be helping the Don Cossacks to retain their independence. A description of a Cossack charge, sabers flashing as they bear down on the entrenched Bolsheviks, was so vivid and so real that I was startled by the librarian's voice intruding surreally and sarcastically into my world of whirling sabers and the abruptly strangled screams of the already dead Bolsheviks crumpling to the bloody ground...

"Mikhail Sholokhov! What are you doing on the floor...? Don't you know what time it is? The library is closing!" he snapped, adjusting his rimless glasses for focus. "Sholokhov! What are you doing with Sholokhov?"

"I, I didn't know the time... I was jus... just reading," I stammered as I struggled up from the floor holding the gilt-edged book that had so absorbed me, sensing somehow that I was caught doing something I shouldn't, though it wasn't clear to me specifically what, in those days of wagging fingers and frowning faces turned in my direction. I readily assumed guilt, if it was implied!

Like other young Catholics, with rigid, ritual, repetitive dogma and regular warnings of Sin, Guilt, Damnation, Confession, Repentance and so on, I was not the most outgoing personality and brimming with confidence, I was not! It took many books, many experiences and time before I understood *mea culpa* was a bad habit and one that led me to hide my light under a bushel of atonements and other humbling devices that doused my spirit and cowed my soul. I would return many years later to a simpler Christian faith with a clearer understanding of *all mankind's* imperfections, and of my own, without undue guilt. But that is another story.

The librarian followed me to the checkout desk, mumbling something about the youth of today and the lack of respect, and begrudgingly stamped the check-out card and the pocket inside the cover, as I scrambled for my raincoat and squeezed through the already closing door out into the now dark street.

All the way home, I clutched that crimson colored book with the gilt-edged pages with one hand inside my raincoat, as though I'd stolen a treasure box from the Louvre. For two or three days I was lost in the Russian revolution and a world of wild words and happenings, with wild horse-charging Cossack attacks with slashing sabers and fierce cries that

I imagined were letting out their long suffering feelings of anger and suppressed indignation over the injustices and oppression to which they had been subjected. It completely enthralled me. The vivid description of the mayhem and chaos that hand-to-hand conflict releases was then like a charge of adrenaline surging into my heart and mind.

I now realize that I was *vicariously* slashing and lancing the invisible hurts and indignities that ignorance and circumstance had accumulated within me. I was, I remember, a rather shy asthmatic Catholic boy, with far too many sensibilities and imaginings for the rough, almost primitive streets of Portsmouth, with beer-sodden sailors brawling and hitting-out at their demons on a Saturday night around the pubs, and in the narrow gas lamp-lit streets formed by the dingy, crowded, slate-roofed hovels that once had been built to house the dockyard workers, fitters, carpenters and riggers in the industrial revolution.

It would take World War Two and thousands of German incendiary bombs along with high explosive bombs to demolish them, but that was in the future. In 1935, when I was visiting the library attempting to emancipate my ignorance and stumbling towards an unknown and uncertain future, the Portsmouth that I experienced daily was not far changed from Charles Dickens's time, and everything was older and more decrepit in the poorer districts around the dockyard and the naval bases, where His Majesty's ships often lay waiting their turn in the docks or being refitted before returning to some far off station such as Malta, Alexandra, Aden or even further east, to Shanghai or Hong Kong.

Other parts of the city were quite orderly, and there were many neat roads and streets where there were better terraced houses with little gates leading into small gardens or courtyards that crowded the pavement on either side, with a tree or two planted in those gardens that softened the uniformity of the houses. But those districts might as well have been foreign countries to us naval brats in the poorer sections.

I was nearly home, having walked about a mile and a half down Fratton Road to Lake Street, and was crossing over to the other side when I remembered that I was supposed to be home by 7pm. I didn't have a watch, but the big clock hanging up above Samuelson & Bros. (Jewelers to the

King) showed 9:20pm, and I knew the library closed at 9pm on weekdays, so what I'd suppressed unconsciously, I now had to face. I was not only late, but bloody late!

My anxieties began to accelerate and I rapidly became asthmatic and my breathing labored. I struggled into Baker Street, in a laboring, stumbling walk, bouncing off the old chipped brick sides of shabby houses that lined the sides of the street, until I came to 68, where I fumbled inside the letter-slot drop for the key string hanging inside and finally managed to open the grimy, paint-worn door and stumble into the corridor.

I was gasping pretty hard at that point, wheezing in and whistling out. I stood or leaned there for a moment, realizing that no angry voice had called, "Is that you, Ken?"

The silence was so penetrating that for a moment, I could not even hear my own wheezing breath. I was holding it! Ah, the sudden realization that I was alone! I was alone! I went into the living room and immediately spotted the often expected but never so fervently wished for note telling me that she had gone out and would not be back until midnight, probably, and there was a sandwich in the bread box. My joy and relief were so immediate that even the dying embers of the last of the fire she had lit earlier were a small comfort. The tick-tock of the clock and the faint sound of embers falling through the grate were company as I sat eating the cheese sandwich and the last of the day's milk I found still in the bottle in the kitchen.

It wasn't until I was undressed and in my bed reading Sholokhov's *And Quiet Flows the Don*, that I realized I was breathing freely. It wasn't long before the leftover candle spluttered and the book fell with a thud to the floor. Why I remember this night comes clearly to me now seventy five years later as I reflect: It was my first gilt-edged, rice paper paged book, and it was my awakening to the power of words that set imagination on fire in the mind. It was, I believe, the beginning of understanding myself. I was beginning a long path to travel and understanding, but I had *started*.

SKIRMISHES WITH GERTRUDE

Gertrude, my stepmother, claimed to be Belgian, born in Aix la Chappell and lived, she said, in Cologne as a young girl. She was in her late thirties, tall, blonde, blue-eyed, and spoke three languages fluently: French, German and English.

The neighbors were somewhat wary of her. They considered her *interesting* but *definitely from the continent*, as they would put it in those days of ethnic nationalism and bias, which was particularly evident in pub conversations and among neighbors in the fiercely pro-British Naval atmosphere.

After the visit of a German battleship one year, she could not wait to rush down with Eric and me in tow to meet the German sailors as they came ashore. She cried, "See how smart and handsome they look in their uniforms! Look at those ribbons flowing from their caps! They are so... German!"

After she engaged a group in German conversation, fluently and excitedly, the word got around that she *definitely* could be a German Spy, which probably accounts for the unexpected visit from Scotland Yard just after the Battle of Britain ended in September of 1940.

Two plain clothes men supposedly from Scotland Yard arrived one morning after a particularly long night raid with a stream of German planes continually flying overhead and occasional whistling bombs dropping close to the dockyard, therefore on our streets, adjacent as we were to the Naval dockyard.

They were informed by telephone, it was reported, "strange flashlight beams had been spotted emanating from our backyard." Since rumors suggested that my stepmother was from Germany and spoke the language fluently, and she was observed chatting freely to visiting German sailors just before the war, you can understand the quick response to the neighbors' suspicion and gossip.

They questioned her extensively, discovering that she actually had been born in Liege, Belgium, at that time our ally, and not Germany, even though she had lived in Köln (Cologne) where she had been married and had two sons. They asked to be taken to the shelter in the back garden where they discovered bits of a broken mirror and dirt piled on top of the shelter! Gertrude *remembered* doing this while excavating in the garden. Needless to say, the neighbors were not convinced that the pieces of mirror were *accidentally* reflecting the searchlights and whatever else skywards! They had seen too many Agatha Christie movies!

But back to this particular day in 1937, when we were on our way downtown to watch and wave in Dad's ship after a year and a half absence overseas. Eric, my stepbrother, was with us, holding his mother's hand as we crossed Baker's Street to enter Stanley Road, which lead us to Commercial Road. There we caught the tram that went downtown to the old part of Portsmouth, near the entrance to the harbor and the sally port, the arched gateway which lead to stone steps down to a landing, where Nelson boarded his gig that took him out to the Victory, in those days anchored just offshore.

The imposing granite and flint-stone walls of the harbor fortification ran alongside the channel, leading into Portsmouth Harbor, further protected by a massive round fort guarding the entrance to the naval harbor.

The harbor was large with extensive piers and docks that stretched for miles up to Whale Island, the naval gunnery school. The prison ship hulks from Nelson's days still lay rotting on the mudflats of the upper reaches of Portsmouth and the old Norman keep, built in the first century on the ruins of a Roman fortification and where two schoolmates, Stan and John, and I scratched our initials on one of the stone blocks at the arched entrance to the tower. Not having the necessary respect for history that a better education might have provided, we made our mark for posterity.

There was a plaque on the bottom of that same wall, commemorating the building of the castle by the Normans in 1157. The Roman fortifications, worn down by time and tide, were now only a broken foundation with little to show but soil embedded slabs and worn, almost smooth moss-covered blocks of what once might have been formidable walls, dating back to the first century A.D.

We got off the tram at the sally port and made for the arched gate in the wall that accessed the inside walk, leading to the steps Nelson walked down in 1805 to his waiting gig that took him to *HMS Victory*, Trafalgar, the defeat of the Spanish Armada, and his death.

We arrived on the inside walk and jostled around before we could find a space to stand, since there were quite a few others already there looking for an advantageous spot from which they could clearly view the narrow sea lane into the harbor.

Already an air of excitement was developing as snatches of questions and comments arose above the crowd in a continuous buzz, which reached a higher pitch as someone sighted the long gray battleship gliding past one of the block-houses out in the Solent. As she came closer we could see lines of sailors drawn up on the foredeck and lining the rails as she made her way towards the harbor channel and us.

Everyone strained to see the recognizable features or stature of their father, husband, brother, friend or fiancé which for the most part, was difficult since we could see only 500-600 of the total port or starboard watch, out of a crew of close to 1800 men. Many would be invisible to the onlookers on shore since they were still inside the ship at their stations, such as the engine rooms.

However, every porthole, every hatchway, every possible vantage point was filled with an eager face hoping to glimpse his wife, perhaps with a new baby born a few months after his departure eighteen months before! Or for a quick sight of father, mother, girlfriend or an old shipmate come to welcome home a mate and share a few pints of beer and their latest stories.

These returns to home ports after long commissions were exciting and emotional times that spilled over into the city itself, where the news of all capital ships was closely followed in each district, each house, each hotel bar, and each pub! And don't forget the girls and women who were by circumstance and economics forced to provide what sailors across the seven oceans search for in every port. The generosity and largesse provided by sailors was often the only income available to those unfortunates in those days.

In the thirties, the shout, "The Fleet's In!" became a big London Review, followed by a musical, "The Fleet's Lit up," in 1938. Sailors and *broads*, as Sinatra might say, were mutually reliant on each other, like pepper and salt.

But back to the welcome home gathering at Portsmouth harbor wall at the entrance to the harbor at the sally port. Since the *Nelson* had been in commission 18 months and was returning to her home port for the first time after being on the China station based in Hong Kong, her pennant was very long and trailed aft from the mast head, rippling and snapping in the wind like a long, long ribbon from a kite, even occasionally touching a crest of a wave in her wake.

Occasions like that are long remembered and emotions were evident on the faces of the wives, mothers and sweethearts, children and others who gathered to welcome their husbands, sons, fiancés, fathers and brothers!

As for me, I would be seeing a comparative stranger, my father, who was a mystery to me rather than a well known and loved parent. By the time the ship had docked we had returned to the little house in Baker's Street to await my father's arrival which, according to his duties and whichever watch was released first, might be that day or might not be for several days.

The waiting was a brooding calm for me. For my stepmother, I'm not sure. But I noticed a heightened tension and excitement as she bustled around the rooms to get everything ship-shape for my dad's arrival, not that there was much to arrange or a lot to do, for a seaman's pay did not afford much more than basic necessities.

The house was like thousands of others in Portsmouth, Plymouth or Chatham, the three main homeports of His Majesty's Navy (HMS was on every sailor's cap band. In my dad's case it was *HMS Nelson*). These *houses* were what might be called *apartments* more correctly or *condominiums* more grandly. They were connected on both sides in rows of

8 to 15 or more. In the industrial north these kinds of structures were mass-constructed for minimal space and convenience, row upon row of grey-slated rabbit hutches as measured by today's standards. There were common fences enclosing a narrow space often measuring 12 feet by 20 feet and included an outhouse toilet, the only *convenience*, other than a cold water sink in a scullery and a cast-iron stove in the living room. No toilet inside the house and no refrigerator, dishwasher, hot water system or wall-to-wall carpet, just wooden floors with a mat or two were the order of the day, and linoleum, if you were lucky.

For instance, only enough money was available to place a yard-wide strip of linoleum at the sides and bottom of my bed. No electricity was laid in those houses but we did have three gaslights, one in the front room (for some reason called *the sitting room*, though very seldom was anyone sitting in it) one in the living room, the other in the front bedroom.

They all used a small mantle, the size of an egg cup, made of white fabric mesh. I learned much later this was made of thorium or cerium compound, which glowed, white when placed over a gas flame from a jet. When turned low (in order to conserve the amount of gas purchased by a couple of copper pennies in a meter) it gave a weak glow after being lit by a match. The light was effective up close but in general, the gas lamp only threw a diffused yellow glow, probably due to the dingy glass shade covering the mantle. This created shadowy shapes over much of the room, suggesting to one's imagination all kinds of grotesqueries.

These moving, menacing shadows that were animated by the drafts and at times by the howling gales that blew in off the channel were more threatening than the absence of all form in the blackness of dark when the gas shut off or the candle spluttered out. Sometimes in my more anxious nights alone, with my step mother out attending a whist drive or some other social entertainments, the wind whistled through the cracks, holes, and loose slates on the roof, moaned in the rafters and, combined with the sometimes incessant rain sweeping across the window and rattling the panes, would stir up the haunting fears of possible retribution from a Catholic hell, or visitations from dimly recalled horrors. These were impressed upon my overly imaginative mind by the latest Boris Karloff movie seen at the Globe, our local cinema, which I often raced to with the sixpence I had diligently and prayerfully hoped for on Saturdays. I clutched the sixpence so hard it would often leave the image of King George V impressed upon my palm.

On such nights, with only my three-year-old stepbrother left in my care as my *companion*, I would smuggle a candle upstairs and hide it under my bed. I would retrieve it after my stepmother left for the evening, or the night or whatever and, having lit it, I would shush my stepbrother to sleep and open my latest acquisition from the treasures of the public library.

I sailed many an ocean, camel-backed over many a desert and struggled over mountains during those lonely but adventure-filled nights. Those furtive, secretive hours of flights into the make-believe world of literature allowed me an exciting, albeit vicarious world through the various characters, heroes, larger-than-life people of the stage and screen, adventurers, explorers and even villains who introduced me to a far greater world, where accomplishment and discovery were unlimited.

I found a better world than the one of Oliver Twist and the sordid, squalid Victorian streets that Dickens described so well and which in Portsmouth still existed in a poorer part of town, near the old dockyard. Like my father and his father, my eyes began to turn away from the familiarity of my own poor environment, from the dull, impoverished drab fading bricks of those grey slated hovels, left over from the industrialization of such cities housing the workers close to their war-oriented drudgery for the unknown world beyond the far horizons.

But all that was a deep subconscious desire that would need unexpected turns of events and in fact, a war to awake this youth from his world of make-believe and fictionalized fantasies. In 1934 to 1937, the looming Second World War was a distant rumor, an expected but vague possibility given the Germans and their history and the need to protect the empire and our army and navy, particularly in important naval ports like Portsmouth, Plymouth and Chatham.

The sounds of martial music were never too long absent, often wafting over the breezes to remind us of our history of constant military preparedness and of heritage born of necessity, and our ever-readiness to say goodbye.

I somehow felt there was a different world out there and a different role for me to play. I did not understand how it would be possible, but I never doubted that it *would* happen.

Thus I fed my yearning for eventual flight away from the circumstances that I could accept but hoped to modify at a future time, when travel, constant movement, and change would become my modus operandi and my great escape. One day I might find myself a place in the greater scheme of things where I would be free at last and belong. In the back of my mind was the ever-present shadow of my stepmother who had become my bête noire from whom I wished to flee one day.

That became my mantra, which I wished on and prayed for and which, after a long torturous way, became a reality.

> "Hope deferred makes the heart sick,
> but a desire fulfilled is a tree of life.
> He who despises the word
> brings destruction on himself,
> but he who respects the commandments
> will be rewarded.
> The teaching of the wise is a fountain of life..."
>
> The Proverbs of Solomon,
> Proverbs 12 & 13
> Son of David, King of Israel

PROVERBS 13 AND INTERPRETATION

From across the rooftops, wafting on the offshore breeze, the sounds of a military band drifted in fragmented notes through the grimy window, opened to let some air into the fetid living room.

My house was one of hundreds built in rows on each side of the narrow streets for the labor pool crammed into the towns and cities where there were factories and, as in Portsmouth, a dockyard where thousands were employed, from laborers or shipwrights, painters, pipe-fitters, electricians, carpenters to every type craftsman and menial labor. Young girls were employed in factories such as textiles, clothing or manufacturing.

I opened wider the grimy little window that looked down on the back yard with the WC so that I could better hear the band instruments! I could hear the cornets, and the tubas oomphing, and once in a while even the big drum. I could imagine the squads marching, *hep two three four*, as I lay in my narrow bed with its thin blankets.

I thought of my father, who after twenty-two years or more would be one His Majesty's subjects pensioned off, to be one of those retired in the middle their life to fend for themselves after giving their all to His

Majesty's interests all over the world in peace or war. After sailing around the world, visiting various stations in the Indian Sea, the China Sea, the North Sea, the Arctic Sea, every bloody sea you can name he has sailed, I mused.

As I got up and yawned and scratched my head and as I dressed, I wondered what mood my stepmother, Gertrude, would be in this morning. *Well, here goes*, I thought, as I came down the stairs into the living room.

"'Morning, Mum," I mumbled, not really feeling the "mum" part. She was, after all, not my real mother. I'd always felt awkward even saying it.

"Washed your face and hands?" she snapped.

Oh, Oh, I thought, *She's in one of those bad ones.*

"No, not yet," I mumbled, "the water's too cold."

"It's not going to get any warmer. It won't kill you," she said, pushing him toward the scullery basin, turning on the one cold water tap as she did so.

The shock of ice cold water on my face immediately shivered me into the harsh reality of early morning and the lack of amenities in a squalid English house built in the industrial revolution.

As I slicked back my hair and pulled up my socks, I sat down at the living room table to spoon down the porridge that was put in a bowl for my breakfast.

As I sat down, I noticed that the milk pitcher was empty. It was not my favorite thing to eat thick oatmeal without milk, so I asked my stepmother, "Is there any milk?" My stepmother snapped, "There's no milk left and the milkman didn't leave any this morning. So you'll have to do without."

Warm, sticky oatmeal is a poor breakfast. I found the concoction almost gagging without milk, and even the sugar I put on it hardly helped to get it down. At least it was something to put in my stomach.

I wondered what it would be like having breakfast early in the morning in the West Indies, for instance? I bet I would have papayas, mangos, coconuts and bananas, and a swim in that warm water.

"Come on Ken, you'll be late!" She broke through my day-dreaming with such suddenness that I slid off the chair and ran down the passage to the front door, pulling my one jersey over my head as I did so and stuffing a worn tennis ball into my shorts pocket.

As the door closed behind me, I felt a surge of energy and spirit and I burst into the frost-laden air with a sudden, "Yahoo!" I ran then, leaping and jumping sporadically like a freed animal from captivity, which I often did, perhaps remembering that not so long ago I felt so restricted and isolated.

When I had traversed several streets, Baker, Livingston Terrace, and Cherry Garden Lane, I slowed and finally dropped to a fast walk as I neared Flying Bull Lane Senior Boys School, the place where I first began to know hope. I could actually trace my father's odysseys on the large Hammer-Wagner Projection map on the back wall, just behind my desk. Mr. Gardner's large map showed the British Empire in pink, spread all across the east and west of the flattened halves of the globe of the whole world.

It looked like one third of the world was pink!

As I crossed the road and entered the schoolyard, I took the worn tennis ball out of my shorts and, dropping it on the ground, began to dribble it soccer-style with my feet. As I approached, a group of three boys waved me over. "Hey, Ken, bring it here. Let's 'ave a go, mate." John, Stan and Eric began to move into keep-away positions, tapping the tennis ball from one to the other, as I tried to intercept.

It deteriorated into a laughing, jostling, free-for-all chase of the ball, until they, became a four-on-four wrestling melee. It came to an abrupt halt when a tall, balding middle-aged man with rimless glasses and a ruddy complexion came striding through the gate, just as Mr. Parker, the art teacher, acting as duty time-keeper, rang the bell for school's beginning.

The tall man stopped for a moment to survey the onrushing students' response to the bell and, nodding to Parker, said, "Good! Right on time. That's the ticket!"

Then he continued his stride into the building with military precision. I stuffed the scuffed tennis ball into my pocket and followed the back of Stan into the assembly hall. The principal, Mister Hitchins, always held an assembly in the main hall, where he read a passage from the bible and discussed the gist of the meaning or its import. Before reading a passage from the King's Bible from Proverbs 13, he looked at the assembly and said, "Let us bow our heads in morning prayer." His sonorous voice droned in my ears as I, fighting dizziness and a desire to lay down, struggled with focus.

"Lord, look down with favor on us, your servants, as we begin another day. May we act with honor, learn thy word, teach the ignorant and fulfill our duty to you, God, and King and country. Amen." The headmaster's mind was an amalgam of military memories and foggy understanding of his role as headmaster in a senior boys school. He thought two unarguable things vital to a young boy's guidance: discipline, as understood by any man privileged to serve in His Majesty's service, and, of course, a daily reading from the King James, with his humble opinions liberally interjected to assure clarity.

"All sit!" He gestured to the rows of students.

They flung themselves willingly and with relief onto the floor, squatting and lolling around. Some others with short legs and more room sat with their legs spread out. Some sat back on their heels holding one wrist onto the other wrapped around their knees. I could never squat on my heels, like natives do, as I had found in books about India and Africa. They seem to untiringly wait in that way, patiently, I thought.

"The reading today is from Proverbs 13, verses 1 through 3 and 12 through 15. Now, pay attention!"

Old "Itch's" voice broke through my musing. "A wise son hears his father's instruction, but a scoffer does not listen to rebuke...."

What was it that my dad had said in that letter? Something about coming home soon? After nearly eighteen months absence and my stepmother's constant manipulative authority, my father's impending return would solve a few problems, I mused.

"He who guards his mouth preserves his life, he who opens his lips comes to ruin." The headmaster's voice droned in my ears. Having missed verse 2, I rubbed my eyes, and tried to focus and pay attention.

"Hope deferred make the heart sick, but a desire fulfilled is a tree of life. He who despises the word brings destruction on himself."

I hoped my father wouldn't listen to everything my stepmother said. She lied so much, I didn't understand why my father couldn't catch on. Boy! If I could tell my father what I knew! That would teach her a lesson alright.

I sat up straighter. I'd better pay attention. Old "Itch" would be bound to pick me out for a question.

"Good sense wins favor, but the way of the faithless is their ruin." The reading ended with a loud slap, as the headmaster closed the book forcibly. "Now then," he began, "What does a wise son hear?" he asked. He strode away from the rostrum, took a few steps to the edge of the stage, and sure enough, he gesticulated with a pointing finger, almost accusingly, right at me. "Yes, you, Harrison, what is your answer?"

What question? I thought, *I don't remembering his question.*

I blurted out what I could construe from whatever, "He keeps his mouth shut... Sir!"

The whole assembly either laughed or stifled giggles or gasped, and it was understood that the headmaster brooked no levity.

"Perhaps," the headmaster icily remonstrated, "it would better if you had! But what I want from you, Harrison, when I ask a question, is a specific answer that indicates your comprehension of the text. Do you follow, Harrison?"

My mouth became dry, I wet my lips, and I tried to recall something about father. In panic, I blurted with some bravado, "He hears his father's instruction... Sir!"

Realizing as he did the irony of not having any father's instructions about anything at home, he said, "Ah, so we have a glimmer of something, a beginning, perhaps a hope of things to come!"

The headmaster smirked to his audience, rather pleased with his repartee. As Hitchins turned his attention from me, the tongue unlocked and, turning to Stan Thomas nearby, I said, "Crikey! I thought I was a goner there!"

Stan elbowed me in my ribs as I sat down, "Yes, ruin and destruction almost!" Stan's friendship was an island of refuge and solace.

As the assembly was dismissed, I stood up and joined John and Stan as we headed to Mr. Gardner's English class. As we passed Mr. Teddington's science classroom with its strange smells, Mr. Teddington bent down from his six-feet three inches to smile as he said, "Don't shut your mouth too tightly!" as he straightened up and went into his room and shut the door.

I stood there for a moment, then strode to my favorite room: Mr. Gardner's English class. It was in that room on an ordinary day that I was given an epiphany of sorts, an insight or a ray of light or understanding that went beyond my normal perception.

Mr. Gardner had, as usual, put his coat on the back of his chair at his desk and, with his shirt sleeves rolled up, was writing some sentences on the board. At the same time he explained the significance of the adverbs he underlined at the beginning of the subordinate clauses, and the significance of the choice of the adverbs. At that moment it was as if a light had lit within my head and it was in that moment of lucidity that everything became clearly understood.

From that day and that time I became a writer and fluent with my thoughts in writing. In fact, by the end of term, I was given the chance to go to a prep school to prepare for a scholarship in English, leading to college perhaps.

However, as events unfolded, my stepmother said that she could not afford a blazer for the prep school, that she needed more money, and I was getting big now and I cost more. Oatmeal was expensive?

A LITANY

Drop, drop, slow tears
And bathe these beauteous feet
Which brought from Heaven
   The news and Prince of Peace:

Cease not, wet eyes,
   His mercy to entreat:
To cry for vengeance
   Sin doth never cease.

In your deep floods
   Drown all my faults and fears;
Nor let His eye
   See sin, but through my tears

Phineas Fletcher
1580-1650

A RESOLVE FROM ASHES

My father returned from a far east commission on the *HMS Nelson*, a battleship with nine powerful sixteen inch guns in two turrets on the foredeck and one abaft of the bridge in series of three per turret. Her twin sister ship was the Rodney, but because of the post-World War One limitations, her after-deck behind the bridge was abruptly shortened because of the treaty restrictions on size. Otherwise, they would be two of the most powerful and handsome battleships in the navy.

   Though the *Hood* was admired as the handsomest battleship on the seas, ironically, in the coming war she was exposed as faulty in her armored decks, which ended with her destruction during a shoot-out at the hands of the *Bismarck*, a modern German battleship off Greenland.

But back to my father's return from a year and a half absence in the China seas and other parts of the Far East. I was resolving to leave as soon as possible from the oppressive presence of my stepmother when my father arrived at 68 Baker Street, strode in the front door and entered the small living room with his duffel bag on his shoulder. Pausing to light a cigarette dangling from his lower lip, he cupped his hands, lit the end of his fag (as all sailors called their cigarettes) and inhaled deeply. He untied the neck of his duffel, reached inside and hauled up a saffron colored tissue bundle and casually tossed it to Gertrude.

She flashed him a special smile that I had not seen for a long time. She kissed his cheek and said, "Vic, you shouldn't. It must have cost a packet." She unwrapped the saffron tissue, revealing a slender box with an amber necklace, which she dangled in front of him with "oohs" and "ahs" accompanying her delight.

Dad had presents from different places abroad. An amber bead necklace from Singapore, a red silk kimono from Yokohama, frangipani perfume from Bali, a sandal-wood junk for me from Hong Kong, a carved wooden camel with mounted driver from Alexandria for Eric and pearls for Gertrude from Japan.

The room soon filled with little eddies of exhaled grey blue smoke curling up to the ceiling and tangling in the shabby lace curtains hanging on a rod in the window. A thin tendril of smoke crept out of his mouth up to his nostrils and then emitted as a smoke ring. I'd seen it in films, particularly from Bogart (who could talk and smoke with ease, though we learned that the big "C" got him in the end).

My father was reminiscing, "The Balinese with their chimes and bells and gongs, a real rummy lot... small too!" He lifted his head and shoulders as if to punctuate the diminutive size of the Balinese, thinking of his six feet four inches as he towered over them!

"Do yer like the Junk, son?" he asked as he lit another cigarette. I gazed at the ugly brown alien shape with its battened sail. It resembled nothing in my head full of sleek cutters, yawls and ketches, or any other boat I'd seen in any harbor.

"Oh, yes!" I reassured him. "It's interesting, Dad."

I lay it aside. *A piece of Junk, alright!* I thought.

"Now, them Japs." He could switch from one spot on the globe, from Bali to Tokyo, between puffs of acrid blue smoke, like a conjurer materializing rabbits or doves. "They know colors and they could carve anything in ivory or sandal wood. They know silk, Son... them Kimonos are something else." Suddenly he got up, took his fags and was out the door to the pub, to dream on over a pint of mild and a chain of cigarettes.

These gifts were soon forgotten in the days that followed. For one thing, my stepmother had not yet brought my father up-to-date with her versions of things past, and I was in daily apprehension of what her tales might bring on me. My father was not likely to want to hear my side of things, not that I could really say much without further antagonizing her.

Tomorrow, he's got to stand duty and he won't be back until the day after, so maybe by then she'll be more relaxed and might have forgotten the last time I had balked at her commands or thwarted her wishes.

It was about a month before that I'd asked if it would be alright to go and play soccer with Stan, John and Mark and the rest of the kids over in the old wood yard at the back of Stanley Road, behind the billboards on Commercial Road.

It was an old yard that used to store timber and the acre it occupied had long since gone to dirt and weeds, but it had become our gathering place and our playing field, our pitch, where great matches between England and Germany or Scotland suddenly developed whenever someone appeared with a soccer ball!

That is, if it wasn't already fully in use for a new version of some battle, from a movie or perhaps a re-enactment of some vaguely remembered clash between our loyal, brave British regiment and some other wild, primitive tribe from distant streets that had invaded our territory and had to be routed. Whenever us *Navy kids* got there first, this magical playing ground became the North Sea, where German and British battleships blasted each other with stones thrown from respective trenches. Our dugouts came in our wild imaginations to represent the *Graf Spee* or the *Nelson* or *Hood*, or whatever fanciful dreadnoughts we might conjure up.

The appropriate noises were shouted as the imaginations flooded in with the adrenalin. "Boom!" A stone was fired from the *"Hood's"* awesome sixteen inchers. "Wee-ee!" as a stone ricocheted off the old, dilapidated, rusty sheets of corrugated metal functioning as the bridge of the enemy ship. "A direct hit!" would be shouted when the stone was seen to knock a possible hole or dent in the make-believe dreadnought.

Grand-dad's metal helmet, a souvenir from the First World War, and sometimes old discarded pots or saucepans, provided our head protection, but on occasion, an honorable injury was received by a stone bullet and duly acknowledged.

"Wow! I got 'im!" "Good thing you were only hit in the leg!" "It's just a bruise." "Yeah, that's alright for you to say!" A white rag was waved and a truce declared. We would all crowd around the *casualty* and, after casual inspection, after the *blood* was wiped off the scrape, the *wound* was declared not mortal, "Only a scratch! Bugger-all to worry about!" the truce was off, and the "Germans" and the "English" went back to their "ship," and took their stations in the dirt trenches under the dubious protection of rusty tin and sheets of thin rotting plywood and rusty metal now transformed into "the *Mighty Hood*," England's most powerful, and unsinkable battleship.

Little did we know how soon this mythical belief fostered by ignorance and national pride would be replaced with shock and disbelief. The *"Mighty Hood"* was sunk in five minutes of gunfire in battle with the German battleship *Bismarck* when direct hits penetrated her magazines and she disappeared in one huge explosion that engulfed her and 1,418 of her crew.

But this knowledge is in retrospect, since in 1936 it could not be even imagined that in five years our national pride would be so rudely shattered as the reality of war sunk more than fantasies. This fantasizing and associating our make-believe with the real in our minds was our way, I suppose, of yearning desperately to be more than were, to belong to something more powerful and important than our lowly existence would permit.

We became part of our historical mystique and heritage that somehow, in all that squalor and lack of things beautiful, enlightened and infused some invisible but extant spirit within us that raised our feelings and our sights up above the dirt, the lack of fortune, and the impoverishment to which we were expected to succumb.

We may have been scruffy, dirty, ragged and penniless, but we were English ragamuffins! I know that in the soil of that seemingly hopeless illiteracy and powerless poverty of my pre-war England, some small powerful seeds of self-respect and a glimmer of hope beyond my immediate prospects were planted. Ergo ego, perhaps? But that was to become apparent much, much later.

When I became fourteen years old on May 13th, 1938, I was informed by Mr. Hitchins, the headmaster at Flying Bull Lane Senior Boys School, that a scholarship would be offered to allow me to continue my education at a Prep school in Southsea, which might, if I studied well... "Who knows?" he had mused. "Might even lead to college, my boy!"

He gave me a note he had scribbled for my stepmother. I rushed home in high adrenalin, thoughts piling upon thoughts as my excitement rose to almost fever pitch.

She was sitting in the living room reading a letter from my dad, who was on his way home from Alexandria in the Mediterranean, where he had been for the last few months. He was telling her about being pensioned-off after ending his twenty-two years of service.

Apparently, Gertrude was not too pleased at the idea of her sailor husband dropping anchor permanently! She had a frown on her face when I approached with Hitchins' note to her. I noticed it was quite crumpled from my nervous clutching all the way home from school.

"What's this?" She snapped, as she snatched it from my reluctant hand.

"It's a note from the Headmaster." I tried to control my obvious excitement.

"What have you been up to now, then?" The tone was accusatory and the frown developed quickly into one of her all too familiar moods.

She scanned the note, looked up and snapped, "Oh, we are getting high and mighty aren't we? Prep school, indeed! Not for you, my lad! It's work for you! It's time for you to earn some money and pay your way. I've got no money to spend on your bloody higher education!" She waved me away and pointing to the cold ashes in the hearth said, "Make yourself useful. Clean the fireplace and build a fire!"

I remember to this day how I felt. The previous elation and anticipation left me as though a plug within me had been pulled and all had been drained. In place of the lightness of being that almost lifted me to flight as I walked the way home was a leaden heaviness that could hardly be born on my shaky legs. As I knelt in front of the hearth to shovel-up the grey mound, clouds of dust arose and I noticed tiny drops falling briefly upon the gray, cold ashes.

I remember feeling angry that I had shown her my feelings. As I stood up with the rolled-up ashes, ready to take them outside to the dustbin, I wiped the wet from my face with my fist and turned towards the back door so she wouldn't see, but when I opened the door to the back yard, I slammed it shut and threw the wrapped ashes into the open bin. That was that. It was never mentioned again, by either of us.

But within me grew a resolve that became a determination to become free of others' will to limit or control my destiny. Thus a small atom of independence began which in the future would guide me to make decisions that would change my world.

A CIGARETTE

A cylinder of thin paper containing
fine shreds of tobacco that one applies
a flame from a match or a lighter on one
end, while inhaling the smoke from the
other end in your lips, which comes
from the burning tobacco.

The illusion comes from the habit from
needing the nicotine, which if inhaled
long enough, will impair your lungs,
and you will develop cancer
or other obnoxious illnesses.

KHH

ILLUSIONS CLEARED THROUGH SMOKE

It was Saturday and I was looking forward to my sixpence and, more importantly, to the spending of it. All through the week while sweeping, scrubbing and filling the coal scuttle, running errands and whatever else she could think up for me to do to get the most for her sixpence, I was thinking beyond the tedium and the sometimes dreariness to the moment I would be outside the house with the sixpence impressed in my palm as I raced as I always did to the corner, so as to be out of recall, safe.

I came down stairs to the living room to find her in the kitchen making porridge as usual for breakfast.

"Mornin' Mum," I mumbled, hoping she'd had a good night and was in a decent mood. She didn't say anything and I'm used to that, but it wasn't good because she had a frown and stared out the scullery window as she stirred the grey mess in the pot.

"The sun's shining," I offered, as I tried to warm things up. She turned and her right eyebrow raised. "Oh, quite the gentleman this morning, aren't we?" she said. My attempted smile failed and I feared the worst.

"I suppose you're looking for your sixpence. That's why you're in such a good mood this morning," she said.

I knew by her tone that trouble was coming. My heart began to feel heavy. Actually, I had some trouble drawing breath. It seemed as if all my energy had somehow drained away.

"I haven't forgotten that you slammed the door on Wednesday after I told you couldn't play soccer after school." Her voice was kind of pretending like in the movies. She was speaking softly, but I knew she was going to be hard. *Oh, God. Why did my Dad marry her?* I'd thought that many times, wondering if he really knew her like I did.

"So, my boy, you won't be getting your sixpence. You don't deserve it. Perhaps, you'll behave in the future."

I hardly heard. I was a fool to trust her. My chest was heaving but something deep inside me got hard. *I'll show you.* I turned away and ran to the front door. Her shouted warning that followed me was lost in my now deaf ears and my desire to strike out at something, anything.

I heard the door slam bang shut behind me, but I didn't care. She wouldn't keep her word, so I didn't care. As I raced to the sanctity of the wood-yard, I hadn't even noticed that I was breathing freely.

Falling to a walk, I entered the alleyway on Stanley Street, pushed into a space that had been made in the wood with corrugated iron sheets erected to form an impassible barrier to the vacant wood yard. Once through to the weed-strewn derelict yard, I took several deep breaths and kicked a rusty old can lying in my path.

The can flew in a perfect parabola across a bunch of weeds and as I marveled at the trajectory the can landed right into one of the large, empty, rusty oil drums that had been part of the debris and odd bits of timber, iron sheets, and other stuff that made the yard what it was: a playground, with unlimited scenarios and props for the active imagination.

In the center, of course, was our cleared, dusty, flattened area with its four oil drums, two each end for "goalposts," weighted with rocks and cement blocks in their bottoms. England had played Germany, Ireland and Scotland but it was us English boys, and we played really hard there (I had bruises and cuts on my legs to prove it). Of course it wasn't the actual English team.

"Hi' Ken. What yer' doin'?" Stan's voice broke into my thinking. "Oh, hello, Stan. Nothing. I was jus' going over stuff." Not much good telling about how things really are, I thought. "Better watch it! It can get you into trouble," he said with a laugh, not knowing how true it was.

"Let's go down to the docks," he said. "There's a Norwegian coaster in today, my dad said. Unloading some timber." "Alright. Let's go," I was happy to have friendly company and I'd resolved to enjoy my stolen freedom that afternoon. We walked over to the Commercial Road side of the yard and crawled through the hole in the fence with advertising pasted on it and surrounded the huge hoardings. We strolled arm around each other's shoulders, as we whistled Colonel Bogey and snapped into a march. On to the Norwegians!

The Old Quay was how we named the one long quay at the bottom of Sultana Road, which ran between Commercial Road at the west end and Fratton Road at the east end, about half a mile apart.

On the harbor side of Commercial Road, Sultana Road ran a short way down to the water's edge and the gates of the power house, with its coke piles just inside the gate like gray pyramids. Every once in a while, we would be allowed to take our small wheel barrows, box-carts, bicycle-pulled two wheelers or whatever other thing we could rig-up to carry a sack of coke from the gasworks back up to our houses.

The coke, which had already been used when it was coal, would need coaxing in the little black wrought iron stove that was our only means of cooking and heating. You would have to chop wood into little sticks and arrange it on rolled-up newspapers to start a fire. This was one job I really hated in the bitterly cold mornings when the house was not only freezing cold but last night's ashes had to be scooped out of the grate. After heaping them onto a sheet of newspaper you had to wrap the ashes up, and the gray cloud rose up to choke you before you opened the back door and nipped out into the frost-covered yard to ditch them into the dustbin. By the time you got back in, you were stiff with the cold and wonderin' how you could get to the West Indies before you bloody well died!

I really hated having to clean out and start that miserable bloody fire. But, as I was saying, every once in a while during the winter the gas company would send out the message that coke was available. And down we would go to get our one sack. It was better than nothing, I suppose.

Anyhow, we arrived at the quay and found a small coaster with the last of the pine planks being unloaded by the derrick on her well-deck forward of her hold, which was open and almost empty. Her bridge and the small raised superstructure abaft of the bridge was occupied and crowded, with only a narrow strip of wooden deck that allowed access to both the bow and the stern.

There was a blond-haired woman hanging washing on a line, strung across from the port side to the starboard. A tall man in blue trousers and a blue coat with brass buttons was shouting in words I couldn't understand to the young guy on the winch. I guessed it was Norwegian. To me it almost sounded German but not, a little more lilt in it. I looked for Stan, but he was down at the bow, staring at it.

He was a nut on boats, and always wanted to build his own. A sailing boat, of course. In class, he would pass a rough sketch of a little 15 foot yacht and I would pass it back as a 35 footer ketch, with bird's eye plan to show two cabins, a galley, a toilet, main cabin, a back-up diesel and a dingy trailing aft! We'd grin at each other and it was understood that we'd do it for real one day. Maybe sail around the world.

His dad was an artificer in the Navy dockyard. He worked on the naval ships. He was always on about getting Stan apprenticed to a shipwright or something like that.

Boy, I wish my dad would get me apprenticed to somebody, maybe a draughtsman. I liked to draw and design things, you know, shapes of things like cars and planes.

The smell of the timber and the diesel oil brought me back, and I walked along the key admiring the trim coaster with her black painted hull, her white with blue trim superstructure and her bright blue cross on her red ensign, draped from the stern flag pole.

Flags interested me. For one thing the colors were interesting, and you'd be surprised what you could learn from studying flags. Take for instance the flags of Norway, Denmark, Iceland and Finland. They all have crosses. Different colors but still, crosses. Even little old Switzerland, tucked away in those Alps, has a little white cross in the middle of its red square. I wondered how flags were chosen.

"Look at her flare," Stan said as I got up to him. "She's built for the North Sea alright." "I bet she does 12-13 knots when she's in a fair sea." "Not with all that timber in her. I doubt she'd do ten," I argued. "But she is a nice ship," I agreed. The blue uniform came and leaned over the side and said with an accent, "Yorr' close," he smiled as he puffed smoke to one side of his mouth and pointed aft to the engines.

"She vill do ten alright 'n maybe eleven if ve poosh it." I looked at Stan, who grinned at me and whispered, "Yeah, but I bet when she was new..." The pipe came out and the Captain spat over the side into the oil-spotted water and added, "But ven she vas new, den she goes 14, maybe 15, I bet." Stan elbowed me in the ribs, his grin and raised eyebrows giving me the, "I told you so!" look. We both waved to "Sven" (that's what I decided his name vas) and he waved back with his pipe.

We often found ourselves hanging around this quay or at the old docks down by the sally port, mooching around and eying the different ships and boats, choosing as if we were buying, without a penny in our pockets!

It was a different thing when one day much later, I think I must have been 13; I was with my dad, who was posted temporarily at home. He took me to the *HMS Hood* when visitors were allowed to go onboard and admire the pride of the British Navy. Every English schoolboy knew from reading *Jane's Fighting Ships*, or just knew, I suppose, that the *Hood* was the biggest most powerful battleship in the world!

We were walking on the foredeck on visitors' day. I couldn't believe the size of those massive great 16 inch guns. I gazed with awe at them and, turning to my dad, I said, "She's the biggest, strongest one in the world, Dad, isn't she?" He pulled me away from further inspection as we turned to go back to the gangway ashore.

"Yes, Son, she is. But I'm glad I'm not going to be on her in this next war."

"Why not, Dad?" I was puzzled at his remark. After all, wouldn't you want to be on the most powerful ship in a war?

"Son," he said, "I don't have time to explain it now. But this big lady is a floating bomb." I persisted, "Why is she a bomb, Dad?" I was confused. The *Hood* was supposed to be the pride of the British Navy! "Why, Dad, is she a bomb?"

He stopped and bent down and said quietly, as we stepped onto the quayside away from the sentry standing at the foot of the gangway, "Look Son, take my word for it, but I'll tell you about it when we are home." He patted me on the shoulder as he looked back up at the officer peering down on us.

It came up again later when I was sitting at the table looking in *Jane's Fighting Ships* at a picture and detailed inventory of *HMS Hood*. I read the details with increasing awe and puzzlement. She had guns of every kind everywhere. There were the big sixteen-inchers, the four-inchers, the anti-aircraft and machine-guns. She seemed so awesome in every way. And beautiful, too. She was kind of balanced.

As I sat there in fascination, I felt my dad's presence in the room. He always smelled of rope and tobacco and kind of *salty-smoky, like an old boat,* I thought. He looked over at me from the chair by the backyard window. He was smoking his Player's Supreme Cut. He would go through two or three packs in the two day week-end he had off duty. "So, Son, you're still looking at that stuff about the *Hood*, eh?" As he spoke, blue-gray puffs of smoke drifted across the room towards me. My nose began to twitch, and rubbing it, I said," Yes, Dad. I'm puzzled about what you said on visitors' day yesterday."

"Well, let's see if we can explain it, Son." He inhaled as the tip of his cigarette winked red for a second and the blue-grey fingers roiled up, forming a drifting haze under the dirty white but yellowing ceiling. I rubbed my eyes, which were beginning to sting. I've got to get out of here, I thought. I closed the Jane's. "Tell me, Dad, about the bomb thing."

He cleared his throat and took another big puff on his cigarette. "You see, Son, when she was built years ago, she had her magazines down deep, like any other battleship. But every time they add more guns, to keep 'er the biggest and the most, they have to put more ammunition on 'er too. An' where do 'yer think they put it?"

By now he's puffed his cigarette down to a butt and so taps out a new one, which he lights from the end of the old one. Holding the old against the new he pulls in breath as he gets a good red glow going at the end of his new one. Looking up, he grinds the butt into an already full ash tray, and answers himself... "All over the bloody ship. That's why she's a bloody floating bomb, Son."

With that, he stands up, grabs the remaining Players and takes his ash tray with him out into the back yard, while I, knowing that my normally taciturn father has spoken his piece, head for the front door and fresh air. It's a good job he doesn't say much. I could be a goner if I'd have to take much more from that heavy broadside of his endless burning, smoking cigarettes!

I ran fast for a couple of minutes, the wind feeling good against my hot cheeks and blowing through my hair. That was another problem with having a father that smoked so heavily. When he was away, the smoke was away too. Though the smell was always there, as even occasionally Gertrude would light up, and then there was the fire in the winter. It was difficult to breathe. That bloody, shiny black coal would spew out little tendrils of sulfurous yellowish gray smoke as it burned and I would have to move as far away as I could from the fire. Then I would get cold. I hated the winter.

The wind was coming off the North Atlantic, blowing in a Sou' Wester, as the sailors would say; it would whistle and moan through the cracks in the bricks, and the loose slate tiles on the roofs.

Sometimes late at night, when I was younger, scrunched up alone under my bedclothes, I would imagine all sorts of Boris Karloff-kinds-of-monsters trying to get in through those cracks! Sometimes, the rain would come sweeping in off the channel in sheets of driving, stinging, soaking rain that would be like a water wall you couldn't go through. People would be literally blown along sometimes in a direction they didn't want to go!

That's when I would imagine what it must be like to be on a battleship plowing through giant foaming waves, pushing through to get to the German fleet off Jutland somewhere. As I slowed down into a walk, puffing a bit now, I found myself on Commercial Road near the Charles Dickens house.

I thought, *Oliver Twist would have liked that house*, but as I came to the gate, I remembered that he wasn't real. I was beginning to realize that I had better pay a little more attention to the real world. I was spending a lot of my time drifting and musing on the fictional characters and images from the world of books and films.

For instance, though I was barely twelve at this time, I was fascinated by the use of the cigarette by stars in movies. I observed that, whereas a smooth, impeccably dressed film star would put his cigarette between his fingers, gesticulating like a orchestra conductor, a poor laborer would keep his ciggy in his mouth, even when he talked. One day, I might have a cigarette in my fingers, waving spirals just like David Niven and others, as I punctuated the conversation like an actor. But, keeping in mind my aversion to my dad's acrid Player's smoke that stung my eyes and tickled my nose, I didn't think I'd be a future film star, like Humphrey Bogart, chewing the dialogue in the middle of a tobacco cloud. I'd probably sneeze right in the middle of a tense moment!

> "... Of when degree is shak'd
> Which is the ladder to all high designs,
> The enterprise is sick."
>
> Shakespeare
> *Troilus and Cressida*, Ib. 101

THE FIRST STEP ON THE LONG LADDER

The First Step on the Long Ladder began seventy-five years ago, when my stepmother, Gertrude, refused the scholarship offered by the headmaster Mr. Hitchins on the grounds that, "We cannot afford to pay for your cap and jacket or whatever you need to go to prep school," and she added, "I need you to get a job to help pay for things."

After a few days of walking around the city, I found myself knocking on doors and waiting interminably in shabby little offices or dingy looking shops for a brief introduction. This was my "résumé," my labor permit, the result of ten years of diligence:

This is to introduce Kenneth Hugh Harrison who has completed his four-year curriculum at Flying Bull Lane Senior Boys School. He has been honest, diligent, and attentive during that time. He showed excellence in sports, where he played soccer and field sports for his school. Other than absences due to asthma attacks, which I'm told occurred unexpectedly, his attendance on the whole was good. I believe whomever would find need for his service, would find him honest and diligent.

Yours truly, F.P. Hitchins, Headmaster

With this vague abstract of skills, abilities and aspects of character I may have evinced during my years at this school, hand-written upon this small piece of paper with the flying bull logo as the official school crest printed at the top (my design chosen out of ten submitted altogether) and the Headmaster's signature scrawled beneath it, I ventured out into the more cynical and harsher reality of post-depression, pre-World War 2, unemployed English workforce!

As I look back from my vantage point of eighty-nine years experience in the pre and post war eras, I see how naive and ill-prepared I was for anything more than menial or at best physical labor of the most rudimentary sort. Even so, I vaguely knew that my education was to be furthered in some mysterious but hopeful way.

My first attempt at pursuing further education (of a sort) was answering an ad in the local paper which stated briefly: *young ambitious lad wanted as carpenter's apprentice: phone 435 3357.*

I was agog with wild expectancies! I could immediately see myself blowing the sawdust of my neatly-done dovetail joint, running my finger over the tight joint, and smelling the fresh wood! Gathering my excitement, I headed for the nearest public red kiosk.

In those days, most of the poorer working (or unemployed) class had no phones at home. We also had no 'fridge, hot running water, inside toilets, nor indeed had we any kitchen, only a scullery with one cold water tap. We cooked on a stove that really was a Beall black cast iron heating-cum-cooking appliance with only a coal or coke burning fire to produce the heat for cooking or baking in the small oven.

In that red magical kiosk I became, like Kent Clark, Super-Ken! Confidence flashed into my suddenly supercharged self. "Yes, I am out of school. Yes, I did complete my studies. I am, yes, fourteen years and two months of age. Yes, yes, I can get my parents' consent! My dad is in the Navy, abroad now. Yes, sir. I can be there at eight-o'clock sharp on Monday. Thank you, Mister Davidson!"

My first interviews were depressingly short and unpromising. Always, I would leave eagerly, with high hopes that soon gave way to another disappointment. The interview would generally be terminated abruptly when asked for *references or experience*. It seemed no one was looking for a fourteen-year-old honest, occasionally asthmatic, skinny kid with no experience just out of senior boys school! But now, a carpenter's apprentice! It seemed magical, lucky beyond my normal expectations.

Monday morning came at 6am for me, because by then I was already fully awake! At 7:15am I was at the door, eager to be out and running for the trolleybus which would stop at the end of Stanley Street.

"Don't forget to ask about the money!" Gertrude's voice called out from the living room. My eyes rolled up. "Yeah, I will." I was about to be an employed person! For God's sake! I was not *little Kenny* anymore!

The door slammed shut, as if it had read my mind.

1134 North End Road. I arrived at 7:45am at the address given by Mr. Davidson. I suppose I was half expecting to hear the hum and whine of machinery and perhaps saws ripping through wood as I found a large building on the corner with the number 1134 on a brass plaque, raised on the brick wall in front. But the huge building seemed rather noisy in a muffled way as I walked its length past the front entrance marked Office and Accounts, looking for a back entrance. Around the corner I saw a large opening through which a white van had just disappeared. I followed it and found myself in a delivery yard with several loading docks and vans backed up to them loading and unloading laundry!

I stood bewildered for a moment, my expectations had been far from realized! Laundry? What had laundry to do with carpentry? Seeing my uncertainty, a welcome voice inquired, "Lost, mate?" "I was looking for a carpenter's... shop." I gestured with my folded paper, "The ad said back of..."

He cut through my fog and thumbed in the direction of the far corner of the yard where I could see a wooden shed, "Over there," he smiled, "Chippie Chalmers, that's 'im!" "Thanks, mate!" I was already in the adult mode. In spite of my uncertainty and new maturity looking for my first job, I felt quite grown-up calling an older man "mate!" As I approached the doorway of the shed, the smell of wood and varnish came wafting to my nose and with it appeared a large grey-haired man with red cheeks wearing overalls and a paint- and varnish-stained apron around his waist.

"I've come to apply for the apprentice job," I blurted out, presuming this was Mister Chalmers. In the ensuing questions and answers that fulfilled the interview part of the proceedings, I apparently met whatever qualifications Mister Chalmers wanted, because he abruptly said, as if he had said it before, "You understand it will be ten shillings a week for the first year and we'll see about things after that. You'll need overalls," looking at my flimsily shod feet, "and a pair of strong boots," he added. "Can you start tomorrow at eight o'clock sharp?" "Yes, sir!" I couldn't believe my luck. I was employed!

When I got home and told my stepmother, I came back to earth when she made a big fuss about the boots and the overalls. Same Gertrude!

"Do you realize how much those things will cost?" Why couldn't you have got a job without costing me money?" She was back in form. I wondered, *What's the difference between the cost of boots and overalls and a cap and coat for prep school?*

But, I said, "Well, at least I'll be earning something. And probably I'll learn carpentry." But somehow, I wasn't very sure of anything at that point. The overalls were bought, but the boots were deferred. She snapped, "I'm not made of money, you know!" Actually, I never did get those boots, after all. In fact, I didn't get much wear out of the overalls either, due to my sudden decision to terminate my *apprenticeship* as a carpenter's mate!

But that was later! At eight o'clock sharp, despite the pouring rain, I reported as directed to Mr. Chalmers at his little shed at the back of the laundry yard where I found him in his dripping oilskins and wet Wellingtons. "'Mornin' Son," he greeted me. "Nice weather fer' a duck!" "Yes, sir!" I said, happy to be inside, even a shed.

"Well, now. You'd best be puttin' on them oilskins, since what you're wearin' ain't goin' ter stop spit, never mind bloody rain!" He pointed to a black smelly oilskin hanging on a hook near the door. I put it on, which is not really descriptive of how it actually *felt*. Though I put my skinny arms into the sleeves and did the buttons up, it felt more like draping a tent on my shoulders! It was so big!

Mr. Chalmers tied a piece of rope around the middle in the general location of my waist and, handing me a bucket that had some nails and a hammer in it he said, "Right. We're goin' up on the roof to fix slates that 'ave come loose. You follow me, young Ken, an' I'll show you what to do."

What mind I had available began to question. *What has the roof got to do with carpentry? What the hell am I doing going out in this bloody weather fixing tiles on a laundry roof?*

"Come on son!" Mr. Chalmers pushed me out the door, grabbing an extension ladder as he left. "Take hold that end," he pointed, "and walk over to the roof over there," he nodded. I stumbled with one hand holding one end of the ladder and the other hand holding the rattling bucket. I was bundled up in that big wet oilskin wrapped around my puny waist, with the rain beating against my face as I struggled to keep hold of both the bucket and the ladder!

Mr. Chalmers seemed impervious to the elements. Rain was dripping from his moustache and dropping in rivulets from his oilskin hat. For a moment, he looked like a fisherman just coming through a wave! "Right!" He bellowed in my ear. "Up you go then, lad." He nudged me towards the ladder that was placed up towards the laundry roof where it rested, precariously. I eyed the length of the ladder and thought it to be way too high for a young lad to be climbing.

But I inched up and stood frozen on the second rung! I felt the wind and rain trying to topple me from the rung. The ladder leaned against the gutter, which to me seemed precariously balanced with the wind too!

"Give me the bucket!" He shouted, sensing my funk, blinded by the rain and my paralysis. I was somewhat relieved to lose the burden of the bucket. I wondered all the while whether I should give up carpentry for something infinitely less dangerous.

I willed myself up the next couple of rungs and, having now a firmer grip on the ladder, hauled myself nervously on to the next higher rung, remembering my role as a paid employee, when the roof appeared and, thank God, it appeared to be flat!

Actually it was a ridge that ran along the sloping roof and, as I discovered later, continued between the two roofs with rain gutters paralleling them. It seemed awfully narrow up there!

The rain was unending. It blew in from the Solent approaches, where it came from the Channel. It came in sheets, riding on a whipping South

West wind, the cold penetrating inside my wet oilskins and my misery increasing. "See this," he pointed to a slate tile that was hanging askew from one nail, threatening the water seal tightness. He swiftly took a nail from the bucket which had arrived with him behind me and skillfully tapped it firmly into the tile hole fixing the slate snugly in place.

"Now, see that one?" He pointed to another dislodged slate, "You fix it like I showed you!" I eased tentatively along to the faulty tile and took the cold, wet nail in my colder, wetter fingers and fumbled the slate into position, tapped the nail and, though my fingers unskillfully mangled them both, eventually I got the slate firmly in place.

"Right, Son!" he shouted, already moving towards his descent down the ladder. "Good! Now you fix all the ones that are loose. OK?" he shouted as his head disappeared below the gutter at the roof's edge. I felt like the captain had deserted his sinking ship, leaving me, an apprentice, at the wheel! Although I realized I was, after all, a working man now, I still felt fourteen years of inexperience, up on a perilous laundry roof, like a sailor, helpless on the bridge, in charge of a bloody sinking ship!

Shaking from the stormy wind and pelting rain, clinging to not only the roof but my oil-skinned dignity, I managed to conjure up an image of my father on the deck of his destroyer or cruiser, sloshing along in his oilskins as he fights his way to his gun platform, where he mans the gun that blows the enemy away!

And so I crawled my way among the loose slates and fixed them as best I could despite the howling Atlantic storm and the wildly tossing ship without a captain. I made it safely back to port and to the ground. I was an apprentice survivor. I left the skyscraper ladder to Mr. Chalmers, and as the twelve o'clock steam whistle sounded, I waddled to the carpenter's shed anticipating my cheese sandwich lunch and perhaps a cup of tea, which any survivor should be awarded.

The next *carpentry* I was introduced to came the next day, after an afternoon of drying out in the shed while cleaning out and generally re-organizing Mr. Chalmer's chaos of assorted wood pieces, four-by-twos, four-by-fours, sheets of four-ply, and odd bits of desks, tables and chairs, shelves and assorted fragments of cut off planks and just unrecognizable junk that Mr. Chalmers called my *back-up supplies*, which at the time I took seriously. I was not used to irony and missed quite a lot of Mr. Chalmer's dry wit.

I arrived damp and less enthusiastically as on my first day, which seemed more like weeks ago rather than twenty-four hours, so much going on in my head in the interim. As I walked into the shed, I was greeted by a hearty, "Ah! Mornin,' there, young Ken! You're back!" I missed the inference I would later understand, when I would not come back not far in the future.

"Pick up that gallon can there, lad, and that five pounder over there," he pointed in the general direction of his workbench and added, "You'll find two steel punches in the can." I looked at the bench and saw an old rust-spotted gallon can among the assorted cluster of cans, boxes and tins that yesterday we had moved around as we organized the shed. Sure enough it was heavy with two six-inch steel punches. I wondered, *Why the can?* So I removed them, and immediately was answered, as if he had read my mind, "Bring 'em in the can, lad. That way they'll not get lost." Then, seeing my hesitancy in selecting the five pounder, he solved my ignorance by grabbing the handle of one of the assorted hammers in view and passed it to me. "That's a five-pounder," he said by way of teaching his apprentice. I almost dropped it because I had no idea of its heft. He seemed amused but I was not.

My apprenticeship was not advancing in the way I expected. I had not yet used a saw, a chisel or a hammer and nail. My dovetail seemed to have flown away. I had not been shown a single dovetail or a mortise and tenon. The carpentry book that I borrowed from the library after I was given the carpenter's apprenticeship explained that learning how to make these two joints was basic to carpentry and a necessary skill. So it was with reluctance that I followed Mr. Chalmers out of the shed into what was to become my initiation into the concrete reality of harsh labor and the penalties of being naive and semi-ignorant.

As we came through the back doors leading from the yard into the laundry, a heavy damp smell of wet clothes mingled with bleach and soap hung in the air. I found it very oppressive and immediately felt the urge to get out of there. Down the passage from the dock to the swing doors leading into the actual laundry I stumbled, *a carpenter's apprentice*, carrying the hammer and the steel punches rattling in the can as I followed the back of my tormentor through the swing doors into hell.

If hell was heat, cacophony and chaos, then that's what the laundry was, with its rows of huge churning washers emitting deafening noises and women shouting to each other as intermittent waves of humidity and hot air assailed the ears, eyes and throats, making conversation impossible. It made shouting the only way to communicate over the pervasive thumping and swishing of the great wooden vats revolving in various stages of their cycles, and with the hum and whirring of the dryers as a background to all the hustle and bustle.

Countless young girls and older women, some like harpies, shrill in voices and cackles, added to the chaos. In their blue aprons and hats they cooperatively folded sheets or rolled baskets of washing between the washers and dryers.

I stood bewildered for a moment and suddenly it seemed as if all eyes were focused on me. I heard rising and falling whistles, which I had emitted occasionally as attractive girls passed by. Now the feminine, shrill whistles rose above the hum and rhythmic sounds of the machines, followed by giggles and laughter. I was initiated right then, into the boy-girl world of mutual and instant admiration of our differences. Though in my case, in that setting, and given my overlarge overalls and being new to this exposure, I was lacking self-confidence and self-image, but I certainly had admiration for the other sex, although they had not previously noticed. I was shy, but getting increased interest from girls, since I was not bad looking and tall.

A Catholic boy from an all boys school was perhaps somewhat retarded in the understanding of boy-girl flirtation, and of the parameters of sexual advancement and its place in the social scene. I was aware of mutual interest on several occasions and experienced a new excitement that, I must say, helped to make that laundry less of an ordeal.

But I was quickly learning about things they didn't teach in boys schools or even out of schools! In the 1930s there was a reluctance to communicate facts about sexual relationships, conception, birth-control or even basic knowledge of differences between men and women and their needs or desires relating to the sexual drive. Freud had long since published his first works including *Beyond the Pleasure Principle* in 1920, and earlier in 1898, *Studies in Hysteria*. His theories in his later works, *Hamlet and Oedipus* in 1949, and *The Sane Society* in 1955, would become the foundation of university courses in psychology and be taught widely as part of common concepts of human personality, but these were not widely know in the 30s by the ordinary person in the street. In 1938 only vague whispers were heard concerning "wild theories from a German nut," though he was actually Austrian, and we were all too ready to attribute *odd or strange ideas* to all Germans, our contemporary enemy. I recall from my childhood uncles and fathers referring to the unspeakable horrors inflicted by the "Bosch, those Jerrys" or "the horrible Hun," in the First World War (actually referred to as the Great War until World War 2 began in 1939).

But back to my lack of knowledge about females generally, and sex specifically, in that neo-Victorian period existing in England between the world wars, despite the impact of the *Flapper Twenties* on the more sophisticated. When I found myself in company with dozens of females of varying ages, with diverse proportions of anatomy sufficient to arouse even the sleeping libido of a virtual innocent, I was visibly disturbed and confused as to my role in the scheme of things!

My discomfort must have been visible and the whistles and remarks and occasional audible kissing sounds from puckered lips further embarrassed me as I followed my boss through the rows of revolving drums and hissing steam to the vacant patch of concrete, where a washing machine once stood and was about to be prepared for the installation of a new one.

"Right, then, young Ken. If you'll take your eyes off the young ladies and get back to work, I'll show you what you have to do!" I dropped the bucket down and he took out one of the cold chisels. He took the heavy hammer from me and knelt down in one of the corners of the concrete rectangular bed upon which the machine would be set, pointing to a blue cross painted on the floor. "See that cross?" He put the chisel in the center of the cross, "I want you to punch a hole like this," and he banged the chisel several times on its head with the five pounder, "three inches... deep...in all four... of the crosses," he grunted with the exertion, and only achieved a barely visible indentation on the hard concrete. A bloody hole was, in my opinion at that moment, a task that asked for brute strength way beyond my puny physique!

As if to read my mind, Mr. Chalmers stood up, laid his big hand on my shoulder, and pushed me downward towards the cross I had to deal with. "You'll get the swing of it," he said. "Just keep your eye on the chisel, not the girls!" He chuckled and blew his nose loudly into a red cloth as he turned away, leaving me to discover the intricacies of punching three-inch holes in hard, unyielding concrete. During that hand-blistering, bone-shaking, mental-dulling experience, I came to a firm conclusion that "carpentry" was *not* for me!

I momentarily hesitated before I told Mr. Chalmers of my decision to terminate my brief *apprenticeship*, but as I walked out of the shed for the last time my body was aching, my hands were blistered and I was out of work, yet I was not depressed. I actually felt exhilarated as though free from something. I had learned to exert my independence, if only to terminate my first job!

From that moment, I would never hesitate to come to my own decisions and act on them. I had become a self-willed young man. As for girls, I had even learned something from them. I'd learned that I liked them, and they liked me. I realized that they were mysterious but that I had some attraction for girls. For a previously *segregated* Catholic boy, that was a seminal discovery!

Even though I did not have a job, I felt a subtle change inside me. I did not dwell on it, but it made me look forward to the future, whatever it might bring, and it was not long before I began to whistle and feel quite happy, which was a strange experience for me!

"I believe it is peace for our time...peace with honour."

Neville Chamberlain
Radio Speech after Munich Agreement
October 1938

PEACE IN OUR TIME

One day after innumerable days of school, I was cleaning out the cold grey ash in the grate in the back of the cast iron stove, not only the one source of warmth in that bitterly frigid, drafty, and un-insulated linoleum-floored two storied rabbit-hutch of a house, but served as our *kitchen* whenever a hot meal was in the offing, which wasn't often. The stove had room for two pots on top and a small oven about a foot square in capacity. I had already finished the dishes and pans left for me in the scullery, which had a yellow stone sink and one cold tap to bring the only running water into the house.

I was told that morning by Gertrude, my stepmother, that my father was at last returning from one of his Far Eastern commission. He was expected to be docking in a few days.

My feelings were ambiguous at the news. On the one hand I desperately wanted to see my father again, but this longing was tempered by the knowledge that if Gertrude was in one of her moods, she might spill all kinds of vitriolic lies, near lies and fabrications to shame me in front of my father, if she had a mind.

All this ran through my mind as I washed the pans, cleaned out the ashes and built a small nest of newspaper with six inch, finger-thick sticks of wood circling the paper nest like the poles of a teepee. My father had shown me how to lay a fire long, long ago. My mind continued its musing as I brushed up the remnants of ashes into the dustpan.

It depended on whether she was in a good mood or a foul one. Little did I know then that she was full of guilt and pent up frustration from the double life she had developed based on my father's long absences.

These small mass produced hovels like the one we lived in were built during the industrial revolution to bring workers for the factories close to their employment. They were cheaply constructed brick houses with slate roofs in endless serpentine rows, crowding each side of the narrow dingy streets that formed the Mile End District of Portsmouth. It was just a few blocks from the ten foot high flintstone and concrete wall that encircled the town side of the Royal Dockyard.

We lived at the verge of His Majesty's dockyard, and in a sense, at His Majesty's bidding, whenever he needed to "show the flag," or to parade the gray steel guns to bolster up the fading image of the might and power of what I now know was a tenuously held Empire whose days were soon coming to an end.

So it was that one of the rare, short homecomings of my father was about to occur since retrieving me from the orphanage in 1932. It was now 1938. At that time, I did not know what those who had radios or read the daily papers knew. There was a crisis developing because of Germany's armament buildup despite the supposed treaties forged after the end of World War 1 in 1918. There were rumors. I did remember one day last year, when all of Portsmouth was agog as a great silver zeppelin glided silently and effortlessly across the sky from one end of the dockyard to the other and into the Solent. The gossip said it was Germany's Graf Zeppelin on a courtesy visit. But when I saw that black swastika on the fin, a little voice whispered to me that the Germans were spying on our defenses. I often read spy stories whenever I could get them, so it wasn't too odd that I had such thoughts, fanciful as they were.

Two days later, "Go and wash your face and hands, comb your hair and put away that book off the table! Your father is coming!" Such perfunctory remarks or *orders* were the normal thing from her. So I slowly closed the book, placed a fag card sticking up to carefully to mark the page and placed it on the sideboard before sauntering into the scullery to wash my face and hands under the cold water tap, drying myself with the thin worn towel that draped over the line fixed across the stone sink.

I felt a deep resentment not quite focused on anyone or anything. My slow actions to her orders were my small way of retaining a semblance of my fragile dignity that had been torn and tattered by her indignities and jibes over the years. She didn't notice my subtle recalcitrance. She was busy going over in her mind what tactic or wile she would employ to keep my father malleable and harmless and unaware of her social life while he was away.

There was a dull thud of a heavy object banging against the front door and a key inserted in the lock as a blast of cold air rushed down the corridor into the sitting room.

"He's here!" Gertrude let out, as she rose and rushed forward to the corridor! I heard the voices cease for a moment, then my father's deep resonant grunt as he shouldered a stuffed canvas bag and strode into view into the living room.

Dumping the bag onto the floor, he turned a lined and sunburned face towards his son, "Let me look at you! By God, you've grown like a beanpole, Son!" His great seaman's hands grabbed me and his steel blue eyes attempted to see in one glance what he had not been here to see for 18 months. I felt like a stranger to this tobacco and smoke emanating boom box.

I wanted... I was intimidated by his close physical presence, and perhaps communicated this as he said, "You need some meat on those skinny bones, Son," ruffling my hair and pushing me away at the same time as he switched his hold on my shoulders to a great bear hug for Gertrude, simultaneously kissing her with a loud, "My Gal!" and slapping her on her bum.

"Now, let's see what's left in the old bag, shall we?"

Taking a packet of Players cigarettes from his top pocket he tapped one out, leaned down and placed it in his mouth and, striking a match, he cupped it and drew the flame onto the end of his cigarette and drew the first of many puffs of smoke that in just a few days would coil up to the faded white ceiling, writhing like snakes into and around the curtains and filling every crack and crevice until the whole house reeked like a Shanghai Dosshouse (as my father would describe it). Years later, I learned my asthma probably was induced by my allergic reactions to tobacco smoke and perhaps some psychological conflicts developed during those years. But at that time, I was not aware of the insidious subtleties of human nature when repressed or subject to indignities or cruelty.

I sat on the floor expectantly eyeing the great duffel bag that had come from across the great China seas through the Indian ocean, the gulf of Aden, the Suez canal, through the Mediterranean, through the Straits of Gibraltar, out into the Atlantic past Spain across the bay of Biscay into the English channel and around the Isle of White up the Solent into Portsmouth naval harbor.

I knew every sea, every country and every port that His Majesty's ships sailed all these years to guard and protect the pink empire on Mr. Gardner's classroom wall behind my head. I sat at the back of his classroom, being one of the tall boys, as we were seated according to our heights: smallest in the front, tallest at the back. That was about the only elevation I experienced in those days.

Some said we sent Mr. Chamberlain to Germany to try to buy some time, and to appease Hitler in his aggressive stance. I heard that Chamberlain came back with a treaty of some sort. "Peace in our time!" was his message.

My dad, when he heard it on the radio, lit a fag, blew smoke up to the ceiling and said, "I hope I'm out before the Jerries start something!" He was expecting to be pensioned off in a couple of months. Actually, it was only a week later that he came home smiling and saying, "I'm paid-off, and I'm pensioned off!"

Gertrude didn't seem too excited and asked him quite a few questions, like what kind of payment he would get! My father was happy as a clam and couldn't wait to get out of his uniform and into his little garden and to plant his runner beans, potatoes, tomatoes and whatever else.

The little plot of black soil was no bigger than twenty feet by eight feet. There was a narrow path less than three feet wide leading to the WC. A brick wall four-feet high on each side separated both neighbours. At the end of the yard was a twenty-foot clothes pole strung on a pulley and fixed to the bedroom windowsill. The washing was pegged on to the line and hoisted up to dry in the wind!

I noticed Dad seemed very happy tending his *garden*. He built a bench against the wall so he could smoke his cigarettes in peace after he finished the string lines for the runner beans.

A month later, a telegram came to the house addressed to my father. He got dressed in his uniform, which had been put away in a box with mothballs. I asked him, "Dad, why are you dressed in your uniform?" He turned to me, stuck a cigarette in his lips, lit the end and said, "Son, I've been re-called to duty. You will have to take care of the beans and tomatoes. There's a crisis of some sort. I've got to report right away." He gave me a hand on my hair as a gesture of emotion and humped up his duffel bag. He gave Gertrude a perfunctory kiss, lifted up Eric, my-step brother, gave him a kiss, went to the front door and he was gone.

It seemed rather sudden, one moment he was here and the next moment he was gone. It seemed not fair, he was happy for a short while. Gertrude stood looking out at the garden and I noticed she had a smile on her face, which I thought was not appropriate. It was as though she had been reprieved. My feelings were sad, as though something was not right.

That evening, she left at seven to go to a whist drive, leaving me to take care of Eric, who was seven, so I got him into bed and lit little a candle so I could read my Charles Dickens book, *Great Expectations*. The candle was spluttering before I dropped my book and blew it out.

Little did I know how the rumors of war and the crisis that my father had mentioned would change not only our lives but irrevocably change the world.

"It is an economic axiom as old as the hills that goods and services can be paid for only with goods and services."

Albert Jay Nock
1873-1945
Memoirs of a Superfluous Man, iii, ch.3

DELIVERING THE GOODS AND MORE

It was a clearing blue sky, the marine layer seemed to be burning off, the sun was shining through and it looked like it would be a warm summer day. Alf Edwards climbed into his apple green delivery van with me to begin our rounds that day after we had loaded our packages and boxes at the dock of Pink & Sons, where I worked as delivery boy.

It was my first real job, paying ten shillings per week. I was eager to show Mr. Marsh, the Deliveries Manager and Alf, the driver, who had asked for me, that I was worth every penny!

I hopped onto the left side of the driver's seat and we chugged out of the yard onto Commercial Road to drive to Southsea, the area of Portsmouth that Marsh had assigned as our delivery route. I did not have any idea of the events being planned for delivery just across the channel for later that morning

In those days, the more affluent part of town was the district called Southsea, which considered itself separate from our little hovels dominating the skyline. It was rumored that the high flint-stoned and granite walls were built by convicts during the 17th century, to enclose the Royal Dockyard. The walls cordoned-off the dockyard with its miles of railway lines, sheds, workshops and ships lying alongside piers or propped-up above sea-level in the dry-docks.

Portsmouth was the dockyard. Portsmouth was also the home of the hundreds of working men and woman who streamed by on their bicycles like migrating grey and black birds through to the narrow streets outside the walls. They converged in ever growing numbers onto the main roads leading to the main gates flung open at 7am and again to receive them at 4pm.

Those were miserable stereotypical hovels: time and wear, war and priorities, depressions and poverty had made this minimal housing even more squalid and depressing. The working class lived mainly in drab narrow streets that clustered in shabby districts, relieved (if that is the word) by the ubiquitous pub, usually on a corner of a street or alleyway, and perhaps a small shop with meager stock, mostly sweets or tobacco and perhaps some cans of beans or fruit.

The signs and the colored tiles used by the brewers made them visibly standout amid the squalor. Names would be grandiose, such as "The Prince of Wales," or the "The Lord Nelson," or "the Victory," or "Wellington." Those pubs were a solace and a haven for the industrial slaves for a few pennies. It was a social center in the old days; each regular customer would be given a glass with his or her name on it hung above the counter! The pub would keep a book or ledger with each customer's name and portion for the Christmas fund. In the fifty one weeks to Christmas day, two or three pounds accumulated which were paid out by the publican! Of course, much of the Christmas money was poured into the thirsty revelers' glasses, so the pub would be in business!

Here and there an individual house would show the enterprise and spirit of its occupants by being cleaner, perhaps even freshly painted, or even have a window flower box containing a struggling geranium, but those were as rare as a full set of teeth. So ravaged by their circumstances and times were these people that there was no spare money for the kind of care and education that would have allowed them to even keep their teeth. But there were the pubs and the sailors who filled them, ashore for a few hours or a few days.

Pubs grew as a result of the need for a gathering place while drowning your misery in beer and jokes. It became a need for the men and a curse for the women.

Whatever time the sailors had, it was spent trying futilely to catch-up in those few hours with every birthday, every Christmas, every wedding or funeral they had irrevocably missed while away in the Med, in the Indies, or the China Seas. The release they obtained was illusory and the pleasure momentary. Often when slight differences fueled by their pent-up frustrations spilled over into bloody brawling and physical mayhem, the shore patrols would arrive and, rather than quell the fighting, would unleash their frustrations upon the combatants, adding to the bloodletting.

Then there were those who preyed on them: the street-walkers, the poor sods who were reduced to selling their minutes, their hours, their days in another "catch-up," the landlords squeezing up the rent while the "ships were in," as it was said, when a ship and crew returned after a long absence.

That was Portsmouth: the cramped, often rowdy seamans' and dockyard workers' part of town, where I lived and from which I devoutly wished to escape.

Southsea, on the other hand, was like the officers' quarters. In fact many officers had houses there. Many captains and admirals lived there, retired and active. The streets were wider, some were avenues with trees and semi-detached houses with red-bricked walls and neat gates with names like Burleigh House, Treadway, Longleat or Dovecote on plaques attached to walls and gates behind which neat gravel paths led to entrances with brass plaques that said, "Merchants & Deliveries at the back."

There were also small but pretentious hotels with formal restaurants and bars, mostly frequented by the officers and their families and, in the summer, by holiday makers "down for a spot of sunshine and sea air, don't you know?" These hotels would often advertise their snobbery by their preference for the quasi use of French: La Petit Maison, Le Escargot, La Beauforte or La Matelote. It was to this *upper market* part of town, as the snobs would call it, that we would be delivering today.

Often the larger detached houses had neatly trimmed lawns on each side of clean gravel paths leading up to and around the house. Sometimes as I approached the main entrances, a maid or some other domestic would appear to tell me sharply, as if they personally were offended by my appearing there at the front with a parcel, "Get round to the tradesmen's entrance!"

I thought they could have taken the parcel and saved their breath. But then I was only the delivery boy. *Just wait*, I would say under my breath. *Just wait.*

Occasionally, if the maid *was* really young I would get a smile and on occasion, if she was pretty, I felt like not only smiling back, but also prolonging the delivery! On one occasion I got a wink from an Irish girl, as if she understood or knew something that we could share. I wanted to talk to her but Alf tooted his horn, like he knew what was going on. *Well, maybe I'll get this route again*, I thought.

When I got back to the van, Alf grinned and winked at me! "She's a looker, that Caitlin," he said as he pulled away to return to Portsmouth. Somehow I was going to remember that, name. Caitlin, I said to myself.

"What?" Alf asked. "Oh, nothing," I said. "Just, nothing."

Alf grinned and punched my arm softly like Stan does. I was beginning to like being Alf's delivery van boy.

COOL SOUL'S SONG

It was a song of summer
Not a sad song, moon sung,
But a sun song of shining
That rose above the earth
As skylark un-meadowed:
Scintillating in sunshine.

This heart-bursting joy-song,
A paradise heaven-word
Sent to rainbow the light air
In Vivaldi tonic solfas
Scored for chance ears:
Time's divine arrangement.

It was a summer song
Not a sad song, fear sung,
A bright and golden thing,
That rose high above earth:
Cool soul's song of summer
Sung forever in His reason.

Kenneth Hugh Harrison

WAR OPENED WITH A SKYLARK

One bright sunny early morning, working for Pink's, I pedaled my delivery bike full of special packages of groceries ordered by the Marine Officers Mess out at Fort Cumberland, an old fortification built in the time of George the third in the late 18th century.

We were ever aware of the threats from our across the channel rival, the French and, with historical memories of Drake having to deal with the Spanish Armada in the sixteenth century in our home waters, it was, I thought, logical to have such strong fortifications like Cumberland guarding our most important naval base. After all, though Nelson had beaten the combined French and Spanish fleets at Trafalgar, we always had to be careful.

Now we were at war with Germany and it wasn't bloody armadas we were worried about! We had the largest, strongest navy in the world: the *Mighty Hood* and the *Nelson*, the *Rodney*, the *Repulse*, the *Renown*!

As I thought about such things, I began to feel a surge of energy and the sheer joy that fills my body when I'm free, running or cycling by myself, as the blood gets pumping and the adrenaline surges along with it.

I was glad to be out early, whizzing along to deliver an important secret package that probably contained a vital piece of enormously important equipment necessary for the successful defense of the harbor! Well, groceries, actually.

I turned off the far end of Eastney Road which took me to the beginning of the sandy gorse and fern covered spit that swept out from the corner of the island upon which Portsmouth was situated. This spit of land was little more than sand dunes, shelving down to the shallows, which swirled past the spit between Hayling Island into the Emsworth mudflats and so-called harbor, which over time had become little more than a channel through mudflats and sandy shoals.

At the very tip of this sandy spit was where Fort Cumberland was located. Along this spit a narrow, sandy, gravelly lane lead through the dunes, the ferns and the gorse bushes to the fort with its battery facing the sea and the approaches to Portsmouth Harbor. As I pedaled along this lane, having to really push down hard on the pedals since the small front wheel with its long wicker basket attached in front was not running too freely on the gravel road, I began to perspire in the now higher morning sun.

Above me, I began to hear the liquid song of a skylark. The reason that I knew it was a skylark is that it was hovering high in the sun, and though I could not see it, its beautiful continuous trilling fascinated me that morning.

I actually stopped the bike, not caring about the effort I'd been exerting, or that I'd have to re-double when I got going again! It was such a moment, such a really magical moment. With mouth open and eyes tearing from the brilliance of the sun, I stood astride that heavy bike listening, enveloped in a transcendental moment in my life, though I probably did not know it as such. Even now at eighty-nine, I can still feel the warmth, hear that "blithe spirit" as Shelley called it, and momentarily rejoin my youthful self in thrall and then coming to my senses and once again to the task.

Back in time and purpose, I pushed down on the pedals, got back into the saddle and heaved back towards the fort. While transfixed by the birdsong and sunlight, I had not noticed a faint wailing from the distant city behind me. It came from a local siren, a mournful yet urgent wailing sound, rising and falling, rising and falling, in what I suddenly recognized as an air-raid warning.

The first on Portsmouth, I thought, as I stopped the bike again, feeling momentary indecision, and not a little anxiety. I looked around, uncertain of what to do. *It is my first air raid*, I told myself. There was no warden in sight to blow his whistle and tell me what to do; no place to run into or shelter for protection. I propped the bike against a signpost indicating in black on white, "Keep Out! Government Property." Yeah, sure! How could I keep out and deliver the bloody groceries?

I laughed to myself, feeling in some control. As I looked back over my shoulder, I saw grayish-white puffs suddenly appearing way west over the naval harbor, dotting the sky! To the south, just visible in the bright blue sky, I saw what appeared to be a dark flock of birds. Then I recognized about fifty black Stukas, dive-bombers, with their gull-like wings flying in formation, flashing silver in the sun: an escort of M.E. l09s.

The barrage over Portsmouth harbor was intense. Those first few puffs of smoke had multiplied a hundred times so that the sharp cracks of anti-aircraft guns now merged into a continual series of sharp, explosive sounds, like huge firecrackers, and I actually began to enjoy the excitement! At that distance it seemed removed from me.

Then, as I stared in fascination, the Stuka formation began to break and a few fountains of white exploded water out in the Solent, spouting as some bombs were released prematurely. Suddenly, so unexpectedly, the whole flock of bombers began to change direction and now appear larger and immediately menacing overhead.

The roar of their engines and the now rat-tat-tat-tat of smaller caliber machine guns, along with the barking and banging of the echoing ack-ack guns, literally threw me to the ground, where I stopped my ears and pressed my face close into the sandy ridge of the shallow ditch alongside the road.

The ground began to heave, the noise deafening, the thumps and smells of acrid burned steel and the clatter of gravel and stone all around me, the acrid smell of burning wood filled my nostrils. The ground continued to heave and convulse, as if the world was in agony, and I could feel its tremors pulsing through the earth and up through my prostrate body, my hands cuddling my eardrums to muffle the crunching of the bombs in the earth and the crack-crack of the guns.

I had no sense of time or of how long I was face down on the ground, but almost miraculously I became clear-headed and, seemingly out of nowhere, I thought of Dad. Somehow I was no longer afraid; in fact, I became again myself, a young teenager, with more imagination than knowledge. *Ken, you never know,* I thought, *You might be asked for vital observations that might help the British government improve its defenses against the bloody Germans!*

I sat up, spat out little bits of sand and the taste of burning smoke which hung acrid in the air, licked my scratched, bleeding palms and stood up. I could feel bits of gravel still sticking onto my forehead and cheeks. As I brushed it off gingerly, I noticed my elbows and knees were scratched and bleeding a little, but I was otherwise unhurt.

My shirt and shorts were dusty and smudged, but I didn't notice as I ran my hand over my hair to rake the gravel out. Looking towards the fort as I picked up the bike and put back the torn parcel into the basket, I could see a huge brown and white cloud rising continuously into the bright summer sky. As it rose, I imagined I saw in its roiling an angry monstrous dragon recoiling away from its fire. I was myself again, alright! *"Your imagination will get you into trouble, young man!"* I could hear my stepmother's voice admonishing me even when she wasn't there. *Bugger her!* I thought, as I rolled the bike towards the smoke.

I got back onto the bike and it was hard getting it going again, as I felt sore all over. I was about a hundred yards from the fort when I saw the first craters.

They were pitted on the sea side of the road among the sand-blasted gorse and ferns. Tendrils of thin smoke clinging to some smoldering substance still rose up from inside the craters, like snakes writhing away from their holes.

As I pedaled a little closer to the fort, the stench of burning debris got stronger and smoke clouds hung heavy in the air. Now I could see bomb damage as I neared what would have been the main entrance and what should have been an imposing wrought iron arch, raised up on the huge six-foot blocks of concrete at its base, with the black and gold painted steel arch culminating in a shield with the King's Royal Coat of Arms embossed upon it, but was now a shattered shambles. Gone was the Royal coat of Arms. Gone was His bloody Majesty's gate.

It looked like the Fort was a goner, too! Craters now ringed the area, and I could see one corner of what appeared to have been a concrete block within one crater. I also saw what might have been black and gold metal, tortuously twisted and strewn among the rubble here and there.

The main shock was a huge gaping hole in what, I thought when I first set eyes on it was the thickest, strongest blockhouse I had ever seen or imagined. The marine and soldiers quarters had been built as part of the fortification itself. In fact, rooms were built into the enormously thick walls, which had six-foot deep casements, through which at one time guns had protruded to menace any passing ship in the channel.

So, to see this great breach revealing such personal and domestic belongings and furnishings as ripped and bloodied bedclothes, smashed crockery, splintered and shattered cupboards and hole-pocked lockers, odd shoes and the unidentifiable blobs of dark red which I did not linger on, was somehow not in my comprehension of war as yet and I turned quickly away, confused and stunned.

How many were killed? I didn't dwell on it.

The casualty list would be announced soon enough. Already, I had heard about them on the BBC radio at night as the summary of the day's retreats and losses was, with reserve, revealed. The official BBC voice was always so carefully modulated, as though they spoke "with marbles in their mouths," as some said, carefully enunciating each word, each syllable, in that clipped unfeeling un-emotive cadence that they called "Ox-Cam" because most had attended either Oxford or Cambridge where they talk like that. It was as though they had said it many, many times and of necessity made it objective and distanced. The old cliché "stiff upper lip" was never more displayed than on the BBC's "official" Home Service announcements of catastrophe and disaster. *But that was there and this is here*, I thought.

Brushing off his dust-covered be-medaled blues, a marine sergeant finally came up to me and inquired, "What the hell are you doing here, Son?"

"I've got a grocery parcel from Pink's for the Sergeant's Mess!" I shouted, unnecessarily, but I was still somewhat deaf. "Oh, it's you, young Ken, from Pink's! I didn't recognize you for the moment. Here, give it to me. I'll sign for it. The mess has been moved." He looked over his shoulder and sniffed and, feeling a pun somewhere in the offing, added in a Yorkshire accent, "A right bloody mess they've made an' all!"

He scribbled his name on the receipt book and handed it back with the admonition, "Get along, there's a good lad. Don't 'ang about!" I didn't intend to. The observer was relieved of duty. I was off. I couldn't wait to be back.

On my way back through the blasted gorse and ferns I thought of the skylark. Was it dead? Did it survive? Would it ever sing again?

I looked at my cheap watch and thought it had stopped. It showed 11:35am. I had entered the spit road at 11am. What had seemed a lifetime then had only been about thirty minutes! What I did not comprehend, perhaps fortuitously, was what had changed forever... my innocence. My naive War was no longer abstract. It had appeared close, violent, and indiscriminate as to who or what it might destroy. I came back through the town where people were discussing their own versions of the morning's raid while small kids raced along narrow streets picking up pieces of shrapnel and making up lies about where and how close it had fallen.

As I came down Fawcett Road and turned into Fratton Way, I could see the railway lines leading into Central Station, where apparently a stray bomb probably intended for a ship or the dockyard had fallen. As talk and obvious pride in military prowess revealed later, the bombers had been turned back by the ferocity of the defense barrage, but this bomb had landed on the tracks.

Workmen and machinery were already arriving at the scene to quickly fill in and replace segments of the tracks. I reluctantly pushed on and finally turned into Commercial Road and cycled up to Messrs. Pink & Sons and past it into the side street to the delivery dock, where I dismounted. Leaning my bike against the wall my legs felt like jelly for a moment as I realized how suddenly tired I was. But taking a deep breath I steadied-up and marched into the delivery room, a veteran now.

"What the 'ell' 'appened to you, young Ken?" Mr. Marsh, the traffic manager asked as I crossed to his desk to check in. He looked at me over his rimless steel glasses that were balanced halfway down his nose when he wasn't doing writing or reading. "I was bombed. I was bloody well bombed, Mr. Marsh," I said in a voice that didn't seem to be mine. As I said it, I remember feeling that I shouldn't show too much how I felt, but stiffen the old lip a bit. So I said what I said as I thought my dad would have said it. You know, like an old hand who's seen it all: been bombed, torpedoed, sunk a few times, and all that.

But Marshy (that's what us delivery boys called him) got up from his chair and looked kind of worried. "What's that you said... BOMBED?" He put his arm on my shoulder and led me to his chair. "Young Ken, you just sit 'ere," he said, "while I get some water and a towel." Suddenly all around me there were the rest of them, having the Mickey out of me. "Where did it get you, Ken?" "Was it a Junkers or a Dornier?" "Have you complained to the police?" "Did you save a piece for me? Ha! Ha!"

"Alright, you clowns! Back to work, that is if you want to be working 'ere next week!" ordered Marshy as he came back with a bowl of warm water and towel. I was never so glad to see Mr. Marsh as I was then. Later, after I'd washed up and had iodine put on the scratches, I was told to take off home early.

Boy was I ever glad of that, but I actually didn't go home. I wanted time to think about things and so I went where I always went to think or get away from voices, hurts, reprimands or just people: down to the Old Port near the sally port, where we used to wave off my father as his ship slid by out of Portsmouth Harbor entrance, with the harbor detail all standing to attention as the battle cruiser or ship moved silently out to begin another year or two of rumors, letters or occasional notations in the local paper that might reveal their whereabouts. The world was larger then, and letters sent mainly by fathers took weeks.

It was a small harbor yet coasters and small craft and occasionally a fishing boat or two took a quick opportunity to drop off a small catch for the local market. I liked to sit on an old bollard and watch the comings and goings and make up my own version of where they came from or where they were going. That little black and yellow coaster had come over from Amsterdam or Rotterdam, probably with cheese and stuff the customs might be interested in.

They say smuggling was still going on in small ways. French brandy and wines, they say. Boy, life seemed so much more exciting out there. You might say I had already begun to yearn for the far horizon and dream of a ship's engines throbbing beneath my feet as it took me to the far places I knew as names only: Gibraltar, Malta, Alexandria, Aden, Colombo, Bombay, Singapore, Hong Kong, Shanghai, The West Indies!

Oh, God! How these names were keys to open wonderment and fantasy in those long months and years when everybody and everything seemed remote and far away. I guess the Empire sure was spread all over. I remembered the pink on that map again in school, back of where I sat. We had one third of the world under our influence, Mr. Gardner had said.

But I didn't feel very influential. I couldn't even get my stepmother to let me go on to prep school. But, as I sat there on the bollard and the sun was getting well into the West, the early summer evening was coming in. I was hungry and I was tired now. All imaginary trips were stowed for the night, unless I got lucky and had one of my really good travel dreams.

I walked up the high street and, feeling a couple of coppers in my pocket, ran to catch the tram that was coming, hoping it would take me most of my way home. When I arrived home after walking the half-mile from where the tram dropped me at the junction of Commercial and Fratton Roads, I pulled out the latch key hanging inside of the letter box and let myself in.

A piece of brown bag was propped-up against the cold teapot. It said, "Ken, I've gone to the whist drive, back at 11 or so. There's a sandwich in the cupboard and milk in the kitchen. Gertrude." I made a pot of tea and ate the sandwich, after which I stumbled up the stairs and just stripped off my dirty dusty clothes and, having rinsed out my mouth downstairs in the scullery (it wasn't really a kitchen, she only called it that to put on airs), I tumbled into that creaky old bed with the thin blankets and told myself it was a good berth in a sound ship and I was a veteran. I didn't even dream, I don't think.

"Wisest men
Have erred, and by bad women been deceived;
And shall again, pretend they ne'er so wise."

Milton
Samson Agonistes, 1. 210

ILLUSIONS AND PRETENSIONS

The movies became a refuge from the grim, barren, unpromising existence that I viewed my life to be at that point. I now know that the cinema and Hollywood were not only my refuge from my rather dull, limited existence, but it was my reference, my substitute life whenever the real one was lacking in some way.

Of course, now from an older point-of-view, I realize I had been to the movies again in my head. I had already learned that in real life problems were not solved in 90 minutes, nor were they sometimes even resolved. Very seldom were there laughs or smiles or a kiss to soften the sadness that had been creeping into my awareness at that time. It wasn't that I was sorry for myself or even pessimistic, I just didn't feel like I belonged anywhere, certainly not at the same house as my stepmother.

I was determined to find a larger world and perhaps a place where I would, one day, belong. In the meantime, I had learned to find solace and comfort in my own mind. I began to enjoy my own *great expectations* of unknown places and as yet undiscovered possibilities and delights. Paradoxically, I already knew somehow that life was going to be better. I could not explain it, but I just knew something good was happening to me.

There were times when flashes from old well known scenes in movies would be remembered and acted out when circumstances permitted. Even gestures or phrases were memorized for assimilation, particularly in my early encounters with the opposite sex!

For instance, I did not like to smoke cigarettes, but everyone smoked in the movies! Young girls smoked in increasing numbers. So I began to carry some as a matter of course, since I had seen Humphrey Bogart, Robert Taylor, Clark Gable, David Niven and countless others opening silver or gold cigarette cases that slid easily and smoothly out of pockets to be proffered to their "dolls." The ladies leaned forward provocatively and, sliding one out of the case with their long manicured fingers, they'd drawl in a husky Lauren Bacall voice, "Light me up, why don't you?" The camera would linger on that moment.

My first attempt to be suave and what is called "cool" today began as practiced. I got some oval Turkish cigarettes supposed to be the most special and which I thought would make an impression. I took them out of the delicate, expensive, tissue paper lined box and packed the ovals in my new case. I had a date with a cute girl to go to the pictures. (In those days, we English called films, "pictures.") The case appeared like magic at the right time, the cigarette drawn out by her delicate manicured fingers, and as the case shut and slipped smoothly into my side pocket, I cupped a lit match in hands to immediately light both our cigarettes. As we both threw back our heads to exhale the exotic Turkish tobacco, our self-satisfaction was abruptly shattered by a raucous voice grating from the row behind, "Bloody Hell! Who's smoking that camel shit?" Thus ended that short lived experiment in savoir faire and being Bogart!

I eventually tossed the cigarettes away and turned to a new prop I saw in a movie: The handsome David Niven flashed a Pepsodent gleaming white smile, accentuated by a trimline toothbrush moustache, at Ginger Rogers. A he did so, he took the pipe out of his mouth and gestured with the stem, pointing with emphasis to accentuate his comment. I thought it was a most strikingly designed briar pipe with low-cut bowl and grooves carved around the bowl. The stem was glossy black and triangularly shaped.

It was considered by all to be "smashing!" "Where did you find such a great pipe?" was asked by all of my friends. Now, as for the pipe tobacco, I knew terms like "shag" and "rough-cut," and brands like, "Capstan" and

"Players Navy Rum Cured," but after my debacle with the Balkan Sobranie Turkish ovals, I was not going to risk the rum-cured stuff, so I settled for a less pungent shag that smelled sweet in the tin and mild in the pipe.

Although I practiced pressing the tobacco into the bowl while holding the pouch in my left hand and hooking the shag with my index-finger and my thumb while tamping it down into the bowl before rolling back the flap of the pouch with the left hand, placing it my jacket side pocket, placing the stem of the pipe in my mouth, teeth clenched, all in smooth succession, I could *not*, no matter how many times I brought lit matches to my bowl while sucking the stem, get the damn thing to stay lit.

It smoldered briefly, and then went out. I was left sucking air but no smoke. Not only that, but my mouth began to feel furry, and since I really didn't inhale the smoke anyway, I finally threw the whole lot over the side of the ferry one day while crossing over from Gosport to Portsmouth!

But back to my apprenticeship and on to my freedom and independence! I made a date with a pretty girl whose father was a navy officer, and we agreed to meet a at faux Italian coffee shop near the Guildhall square in Portsmouth. I put on my only sports coat, a little Brilliantine to slick my hair down and, after greeting her, "Hello, Beryl!" my breezy opening, she replied, rather stiff and awkward, "Hello, there," offering her gloved fingers fleetingly. I thought she must be shy or timid.

I watched her as she spooned sugar into her caffe latte with her little finger separated from the rest of her fingers as she stirred. She was a pretty little thing with her heart shaped face surrounded by that thick brown hair falling in soft waves. It had a little reddish tint to it, I noticed. Her smile was too perfect though, as if she had put it on as part of her make-up. I wondered where that idea came from?

She looked up from her stirring and arched her already arched eyebrows and, as she lifted the cup to her little cherry lips, asked me, with a voice that I had heard Betty Davis use in Jezebel a few days before, "What... did you say your name was?" I thought she must have forgotten my name. I guess I didn't make an impression when we met. I began to feel that she had an agenda.

I looked at her for a second, momentarily disconnected from my ogling, "Oh, um, what *name*, did you say?" I fumbled, taking a mouthful of coffee to gain time. "My name. What is *my family name?*" I'd never been asked in such a way before. It generally had been enough to know that I was Ken. *What's the game here?* I wondered.

"Harrison. Kenneth Hugh Victor Har... ri... son," I said quite deliberately and, I suppose, kind of pompously, responding to her attempt at putting on airs, which annoyed me.

But she had asked for it, the look she was giving me as she sort of examined me. "Harr...is... on" she stressed the last two syllables, "Oh, what a pity. I thought you said Harr...ing ton!" She paused, cup mid air with her little pinkie rigidly and unmistakably punctuating the difference. With an audible sniff she replaced the lipstick-stained cup back on its saucer and, rising from the little marbled table, stood there, markedly waiting for me to move her chair back, which I was going to do anyway.

But since she was so toffee-nosed and *putting it on*, I acted like I *definitely* was *not* brought up to be a... *gentleman*. I stood my ground, waiting for her move. She kneed the chair away enough to get out and I followed her, by now feeling decidedly that she was not that good looking, after all.

This was only one of the many ways that heritage and supposed status was attributed to family names in England when I was a young man. It carried over from earlier times when family names were perhaps currency for favor and privilege. In 1940 with the country involved in war and all of us "in the same boat," as it were, it seemed rather an anachronism and, in Beryl's case, ridiculous, since she was like me, a young nobody with some aspirations but hardly a basis for pretensions.

But, we English were all a little caught up in this awareness of history and of our lack, or otherwise, of privileged birthright. Even though the Norman invasion had taken place in 1066, in my young days in the twenties and thirties of the twentieth century, people who had bloodlines leading back to the Normans still sometimes would affect superior airs or expect some recognition of their invisible superiority merely on the strength of their surnames.

Even the difference between a Scott, an Irishman, or Welsh was generally noted, and some families for reasons just cited would change the original spelling to reflect some association or other.

A familiar example was the hyphenating of two Anglo Saxon names like Smith and Field resulting in a Margaret Smith being Margaret Field-Smith or by adding an "e," Margaret Smithe, and insisting in it being pronounced something grand or elevated as in their historical lineage! In my opinion it was a social phenomenon resulting from many centuries of Kings, Queens, Princes and Earls as our rulers with the attendant courts and their pecking order of privileged and lesser privileged and conferred or inherited titles, ad infinitum. All to suggest to the semi-literate something grand or elevated in their historical lineage!

As an American put it to me once, "We're all equal; but some folks are more equal!"

Little did I know then that my little brush with Beryl's peccadillo was an auger of my future, to travel far from that "Tight Little Island" (as I remember in a film from years ago) to a place where your name was as good as your reputation, and its spelling was of no consequence other than its spelling: America, the melting pot of the world.

However, that was a long way away and part of our dreams projected from our cinema university, where we learned of other ways of being and living. At least that was part of my weekly curriculum at the cinema!

INVICTUS

Out of the night that covers me
Black as the pit from pole to pole.
I thank whatever gods may be
For my unconquerable soul…

It matters not how strait the gate,
How charged with punishment the scroll,
I am the master of my fate:
I am the captain of my soul.

William Ernest Henley

THE FIRST STEP TO INDEPENDENCE

In August of 1940, when I had reached the age of 16 and a few months, I decided in my maturity to find employment that would take me out of the house and where I would no longer have to tolerate my stepmother and, perhaps in some way, bring myself closer to my ultimate goal of going to sea.

I had gone to the naval recruitment office and was told that I was too young to join-up, but I heard through various inquiries about an organization called The Navy Army and Air Force Institute (NAAFI) and that they took 16 year-olds as "apprentices." Where had I heard that misused term before? But I suppressed my doubts about that word and what it would portend.

I managed to find the NAAFI office down near the old docks, not far from my favorite quay at the old part of Portsea, where I knew Nelson used to be taken from there to his flagship, the Victory, anchored out in what was called Spithead. I used to frequent that area dreaming of sailing away whenever life was difficult or I wanted peace for my own thoughts.

The office was on the second floor of an old customs building and as I mounted those stairs I little realized how this visit and this inquiry would change my life and actually permit me to achieve those two goals: to get out of Gertrude's house and go to sea! After introducing myself to the middle-aged, tall, prematurely balding Mr. Williamson, whose name I had noticed on a small plaque on his desk, I got to my inquiry as to the possibility of being employed in the NAAFI apprentice program.

He asked, "How old are you?" I took a deep breath and said in as low a voice as I could muster, standing as tall as I could, "I was sixteen last May, and I have a letter from my father giving his permission for me to be employed anywhere you would wish to send me!" I gulped in one rush, as I fumbled the letter out of my pocket, feeling much a vulnerable sixteen year old at that moment.

"H'mm." Mister Williamson took the letter and as he glanced over it, he continued, "Your father is in the Navy in active duty?" he asked me. "Yes. Twenty-two years service. He was in before the war." "H'mm," was his only response.

But he took off his spectacles, stood up and, wiping his spectacles with his handkerchief that had been tucked in his top pocket of his jacket, said, "Well, we don't take underaged, but under these special circumstances, we might stretch the rule a little." Once again, an individual had made a decision that would take me in a new direction. I naively hoped that I would be considered "special" under the circumstances! Actually, I learned later it was the War that created the "special circumstances," not me.

However, the conclusion was that since a parent had sent a signed declaration of permission, I could, after signing an employment form or two, be sent to Lee on Solent, Fleet Air Arm Station, where there was a vacant slot for "an apprentice canteen worker" who would later, when trained, be posted as a canteen assistant. At the time I had no idea what the term "canteen assistant" implied, only that I had found a way to get out from under Gertrude's thumb, and I felt a flush of triumph. Though I was perhaps under-aged for the services, I was old enough to want to be involved in services, closer to the war itself in some way, however insignificant it might be. In retrospect, I see that I was eager to take my stance as a matter of self determination, a rite of passage, perhaps.

I returned to the house to pack the one case. There was little to pack, and after scribbling a note and leaving Dad's letter along with the note, I left the house, leaving Gertrude, I hoped, for the last time. She fortunately was away working at her job, and so there was no scene, no recrimination or bitterness or hysterics. I felt as though I had suddenly become free, to make my own choices for good or bad, to make my own life.

So began my humble job of peeling potatoes, washing dishes and learning rapidly to total up prices in my head as I served the Fleet Air Arm men and the young women in uniform that I learned were the W.A.A.F.s. I consoled myself as I did menial chores and labor with the thought that I would be 16 and a half in October which was only two months away. Who knew what this development would bring? All I knew was, I had taken a chance based on the need for freedom and some independence, though I had no idea of how long the path would be, and how many place it would take me, and how many people would be part of my life and contribute to progress and goals.

Lee on Solent was a Naval Air Station along the waterway called "the Solent" that led to Southampton. Nearby, closer to Southampton, was the Supermarine works where the Spitfire was being assembled. After a couple of days it was no surprise when the air raid sirens erupted and everyone rushed to their designated shelter. This particular raid was made by Junker's 87s dive-bombers, called Stukas, that swept up the Solent and straddled the air field with 250 kilo bombs, making a shambles of Navy fleet Arm planes that were either standing around or had just landed, or were being attended to by personnel.

I saw half a dozen Swordfish bi-planes mangled and on fire and several Grumman Martlets nose down with tails in the air, after trying to land as the raid went on. One particular Martlet dug itself into the soft clay soil half-way up the fuselage. These Martlets were the latest fighters from America. They were the ugly sisters to Spitfires! They had barrel-like stubby fuselages, with stubby, cut-off squared wings, much like the American racers I used to see in American comics before the war. However, they were a step up on the by-plane Swordfish, which were decimated later in the war by the Scharnhorst, then the mightiest warship, but that is another incident.

In the meantime, German dive-bombers arrived in a raid several days later and, when the smoke and noise abated, the air station was a bit of a mess, with bomb craters, smashed hangers and burning aircraft, including the wreckage of a couple of German Stukas (from the German *sturzkampffiugzeug*; sturtz, a fall+ kampf, a battle, + flugzeug, aircraft: literally "*a falling battle aircraft.*" Aren't words interesting?), shot down by the anti-aircraft guns around the perimeters of the field. The acrid smell of the scorched metal and burning wood and oil filled the air and yet, somehow, I felt calmer than I might have expected. Just being on a service camp probably helped stiffen my upper lip, so to speak!

In the event, I was trained to be a NAAFI employee on that base called *HMS Daedalus*, who you might remember from your Greek legends as the father of Icarus who made pairs of wings for his son and himself so they could escape imprisonment. I noticed the British tradition of using the names of Greek heroes and the heroic.

For the next transfer, after being certified as competent and fit for service in the NAAFI, I was to be sent to Belfast, where an old Blue Funnel Line about 8,000 tons was being fitted as a mother ship with workshops and fitters and very big holds that would be a floating warehouse, able to repair and replenish small ships doing escort duty or anti-submarine defense.

I was given a ticket to Stranraer by rail and a ticket for the ferry to Belfast, where I would be met by Ted Dawkins, NAAFI manager, my boss. A small step for one looking forward to his long waited independence. Onward to the future!

DAEDALUS

"Athenian inventor, son of Metion or Eupalamus and Alcippe or Merope, brother of Perdix and Sicyon, father of Icarus, a master craftsman. Daedalus and Icarus escaped from Minus by tying feathers joined with wax to their arms and flying away. Icarus was killed when he flew too close to the sun and melted his wax. Daedalus sought refuge in Sicily."

Daedalus was a flight arm airfield outside on the Solent near Southampton. The Germans bombed the airfield, but the Grumman fighters fought with their Stukas and Messerschmitts, and a couple were downed at the end.

KHH

DAEDALUS TO *PHILOCTETES*

After two months training at Lee on Solent, I was told I learned quickly and was ready to be sent to Belfast in Northern Ireland to join a submarine depot repair ship. I was given passes to trains from Portsmouth to London and from there eventually to Stranraer, where a ferry took me to Belfast.

There I was met by my manager-to-be, Mr. Ted Hawkins, who introduced me to three other young NAAFI apprentices: Keith, a small but smart looking chap from Lancashire; David and John, both from Scotland. David, the bigger of the two, was from Kirkcaldy and John from Dunfermline. My world was widening!

Neither of the two Scot's speech was clearly understood by me for several weeks, and although Keith's Lancashire accent and idioms were no less hard on my ear, I quickly learned to understand him and in fact, became friends very quickly. Not so with the two Scots. They were good-natured on the whole but in the manner of the day, exaggerated their differences between the "Laylanders and the Onglish," as they would put it!

So began my year and a half duty to West Africa where the submarine depot ship *HMS Philoctetes* was going to be based.

My interest in words and their origins and meanings continued. The name of the Fleet Air Arm Base was *HMS Daedalus* from the Greek Daidolos, the artful craftsman, who built the Labyrinth in Crete for King Minos and was then imprisoned in it until he escaped with his son Icarus with wings that Daedalus made.

Philoctetes, in Greek legend, was the warrior who killed Paris in the Trojan War with one of the poisoned arrows given him by Hercules. I had already been introduced to Greek legends and to their possible connection with my unknown future life. The importance of names and their impact on people was becoming more evident to me every day.

We boarded the single funnel, gray painted, ten thousand ton, refitted Blue Funnel Line merchantman, with workshops on several decks and a couple of 4 inch guns fore and aft, with some light antiaircraft Pom Poms either side. We were ready to set sail.

Our canteen and storeroom had been provisioned and I was looking forward to sailing out of the Harland Wolf yard in Belfast Docks to set sail for Freetown, Sierra Leone, West Africa, where we were to be based for eighteen months before going home again.

We settled down to the daily routine of life on board *HMS Philoctetes*. I was actually on a Naval ship! I had succeeded in, if not being in the Navy, at least being on one of His Majesty's Ships! I was quite pleased with myself!

Once again, however, I did not know how things would transpire to bring unforeseen changes. Leaving Belfast, we sailed by circuitous route to avoid U-boats active south of Ireland. We took approximately ten days to arrive at Freetown, Sierra Leon, West Africa. With the German defeat of the allied armies in France, and the subsequent occupation of France, the Mediterranean had become too hazardous for British convoys to sail through to supply forces stationed in Egypt or North Africa.

It had become necessary to go around the Cape of Good Hope and all the way up the east coast of Africa to enter the Red Sea and the Suez Canal in order to reinforce our Middle East forces and eventually, General Montgomery's build-up, which would allow him later to successfully defeat the General Rommel's German North African Army. Thus, Freetown would become a very strategic port along with Capetown, Mombasa and Aden, as convoys would be circumnavigating around one of the greater land masses in the world.

After ten days sailing we finally reached Freetown in Sierra Leone, West Africa. We would not return to England until June 1943, but much would ensue before then.

PHILOCTETES

I don't why the English admiralty name our many ships after Greek heroes and myths. This was a blue funnel originally used as a freighter, refitted as a depot ship for repairs to other ships.

Her new name was the *Philoctetes*, a Greek name for an Argonaut, the son of Poeas and Demonassa, who was bitten by a snake and, when the wound became malodorous, was abandoned to the island of Lemnos. Because of his arrows and his marksmanship, he was rescued from the island by Odysseus and Diomedes and was healed by Podalirius. He lit the pyre of Heracles and, it is said, killed Paris.

Such a famous name seemed rather ironic and a waste for a supply ship manacled by chains to another derelict called the Edinburgh Castle, which became another temporary quarters for seamen.

KHH

THE *PHILOCTETES* CHAINED IN FREETOWN HARBOR

After a week of steaming in convoy, the *Philoctetes*, with me aboard employed as a canteen assistant, arrived at Freetown harbor in Sierra Leone, West Africa.

It was November 1941 and, after a cold drizzle, the *Philoctetes* started from the Swan Hunter shipyard, where the old *Blue Funnel* merchantman had been refitted. In addition to workshops and repair machinery, it had copious holds and decks crammed with all kinds of goods including thousands of boxes of bananas!

She was to be stationed in the harbor just inside the boom at the entrance so that quick access by the submarines would be afforded. As it turned out, the *Philoctetes* ended up tethered by chains to another old and rather decrepit ship, the Edinburgh Castle, whose function, other than a floating rat-infested condominium and a holding base for naval personnel, I never fathomed.

In my immature view at the time, gone were the more exciting, glamorous expectations of seeing actual submariners popping up alongside and us repairing depth-charge damage or replacing parts damaged from enemy action or the wear and tear of continuous service in perilous sea duty. With such thoughts in the naive, romantically inclined mind, it was a let down and the reality was much more mundane.

As one monotonous day followed day, and another week passed into weeks and sweltering months, I longed for soccer: running on green grass again with the wind in my hair, feeling, as I always did when running, free and carefree. The confines of life on this sweltering, sultry, stale and smoke-reeking floating steel island began to get to me. I longed for the shore, which of course also became glamorized by my desire and its present distance.

One day when I came on deck after a particularly physically hard work session in the canteen storeroom several decks below, moving and storing boxes and crates as they were lowered down the cargo hold from the main deck, I was about to go to the head to relieve myself, when I came upon a half circle of seamen in sweat-stained t-shirts and miscellaneous other stains on their shorts, gathered around the entrances to the heads in the forecastle.

As I passed through the cordon one of them, Smitty, whom I had chatted with on several occasions, put up his hand to me and said, "I don't think you ought to go in there, Ken! Hogger is drunk and looking for blood!" I stared briefly, not quite comprehending the word, "Hogger" or its implications, since I really did have a blinding need to relieve my overextended bladder!

So nodding to Smitty and rushing into the head with its bank of urinals, I burst into one of them with a rush of sweet relief before noticing a bulky form lurking in the shadows of the entrance I had just rushed through. As I buttoned-up my fly and turned to wash my hands, Hogger, as I presumed him to be, lurched over in my direction mumbling something incoherently about "punching someone's fucking lights out," with glazed eyes and spittle-frothed lips as he loomed towards and over me.

I must tell you that in place of my almost painful desire to relieve my bladder was now an urgent rush of adrenaline that raised something primitive within my body. Not knowing the Flight or Fight syndrome, I eyed the rapidly diminishing light coming from the now blocked exit. I gathered a deep breath and lashed out with my right fist with all the force my 155lbs could muster at this slobbering orangutan of a beast, who was about to "blow my lights out." I felt bone meeting softer flesh, a sense of pain along with something warm and wet as the hog grunted and sagged long enough for me to slip quickly out of the exit and through the grinning group who were startled by my reasonably uninjured face but not noticing my bloody fist dangling by my right side.

Later that evening, when I opened the canteen for the 5 to 8 session, there was the usual line of eager, jostling *ratings* to get their candy, chocolate or cigarettes for the night. "Hey, Ken! You must have some kind of wallop to do that to Hogger!" That and grins and other more salty repartee followed from successive purchasers for the first 20 minutes before the wisecracks and commentary finally dwindled. Then a familiar bulk appeared in front of me, shoving his great ham of a fist across the counter. I instinctively flinched away from what I thought was an attempt to sucker punch "my lights out!"

But glory be! His hand was grabbing mine in a vigorous handshake! "Sorry about this afternoon," he grinned somewhat crookedly, squinting out of one blackened eye, "I hope I didn't hurt you," he mumbled," I was smashed, 'yer know?"

A blue cloud drifted between us as he puffed a few times on his "ciggy" before he released my squashed hand and, over his departing shoulder he almost choked in his cloud as he mumbled, "You din't hurt me none neither!"

The laughter that followed closed that incident and they never heard my sigh of relief as I promised myself to make sure in the future to relieve myself before starting a long spell of heavy duty!

After this incident I was more determined than before to get off this ship, particularly since it was now obvious she wasn't going anywhere, chained as she was to a buoy along with the Edinburgh Castle, which was even more decrepit than the *Philoctetes* was becoming: another rusting, clanking and groaning steel whale wallowing there in the tide swells, tethered under the relentless tropical sun, sweltering in its daily decrement under the humid, fetid and dank tropical air of the offshore anchorage.

So it was with some excitement that one morning I received the news from my manager that we all had to go up to the captain's quarters for an important change in our status. We five members of the NAAFI Canteen staff, the manager Jim Beecham, myself and three young Scots, Douglas, Jamie, and Willie, filed into the captain's quarters just below the navigation bridge. Little did we know what an historic moment it was going to be.

The captain picked up a document from his desk, turned to us in his captain's chair, cleared his throat and began reading from the document: "Received today, March 20th, from the Admiralty in Portsmouth this directive: Owing to enemy action following capture of civilian NAAFI personnel and subsequent treatment of said civilians serving on that ship, you are hereby authorized to swear said NAAFI civilians into His Majesty's Royal Navy, to be given rank according to responsibilities and duties currently performed at this time and place."

The captain placed the document back on his desk, and with a slight smile turned to his First Officer who had led us into the captain's quarters and said, "Well, Number One, I'll leave them in your hands, and you can make sailors out of 'em!"

Back in the canteen, I had little time to digest the implications of the captain's directive as we went right back to work, hauling up from the storeroom and opening cases of provisions, cigarettes, toothpaste, soap, biscuits, chocolate, etc., replenishing the canteen shelves before opening. Later, when Jim and I had time to talk, he filled me in with some details.

He had been given the rank of Petty officer, and the three assistants supply ratings, somewhat equivalent to "ordinary seaman," and I was given leading supply assistant with one hook, and one chevron.

What was important to us young neophytes was that we now were under direct command of the Navy. Which meant we had to learn quickly how to do things according to regulations! We had protected status when we were NAAFI personnel. We took no part in the formalities and routines that were part of naval procedure, other than to learn the basic Navy regulations. It might sound naive and even insincere, but I felt different about myself, and certainly had a change in attitude at this point in my life.

Another dull day followed another until I realized I had been in this sweating, repetitious routine for six months, since we had sailed from Belfast in convoy in November 1941.

It was now May 1942 and my eighteenth birthday would be on the 13th. I longed for a change and as though answering my prayer, I was told by Jim that a base was being constructed ashore not far from the anchorage, and a canteen would be included. "How would you like to take it over?" He grinned at me, knowing full well how I yearned to get ashore, especially since I had taken every liberty to do so, including being a member of the ship's soccer team. "You are ready to run the shore canteen, Ken." I was delighted. His comment was a surprise, but it cemented my confidence, and, in due course, I found myself at the base in its early conception.

It consisted of about ten acres of cleared jungle, stripped of all foliage and trees and leveled flat, surrounded by a chain-link fence with a small guard hut and main entrance. There were two or three block buildings with open sides to allow air-flow between the mosquito-netted wooden cots or bunks.

The canteen was a small Quonset with a large window hinged so it could be lifted up and form a shade over the small counter at which I did various transactions involving cigarette and candy supplies and sundry refreshments, including coffee or tea. Beer was rationed to two Canadian quarts, Dow or Frontenac, or four American cans, Budweiser or Pabst or whatever. The difference in volume was considered to be a fair exchange for the favored American beer, which was not always available.

There was also a so-called soccer field off to the side of the base, which, in fact, was merely a red dust plateau scraped level, marked crudely with once-white lines and goal posts at either end. This proved a favorite gathering place for the natives and it was a sight to behold to watch them racing with childish abandon up and down that pitch, kicking the leather ball hard with bare feet and talking continually or squealing delightedly!

Of course we soon formed a team at the base called The Navy Team! I played as outside right winger since I was a pretty fast runner, with a good right cross along with a fair shot. As you might imagine, I was very happy in my new circumstances. Another added activity on occasion was swimming from the palm fringed beach that lay over the jungle clad hills behind the base, about five miles away. However, the trail was primitive and wound over the hill to the coast.

The first time I went in a crowded lorry over those hills to the shore, I marveled at the way the driver negotiated the dusty single track that served as our road. When we finally arrived after an hour of a torturous spine jolting, bum-bouncing, kidney-jarring ride we were more than ready to flop into the azure-green waves.

One small incident has stayed in my memory all these years. One swimming trip found us on the beach during a sudden squall that blew up from the Southern Atlantic. The sky became ominously blue-gray as rolling, towering Nimbus clouds, riding the wind, roiled above the shoreline. Heavy rain cooling the higher atmosphere fell upon us. For a moment, we were startled by the pelting cold bullets of the tropical downpour but, en masse, we dashed into the now sullen-looking sea.

That's the moment I have locked into my memory. I was immersed in a warm soothing sea while being doused above by icy cold rain. In the distance on the horizon, lightning flashed in jagged bolts, illuminating the white-caps, followed by thunder-booming claps that were ear-shattering out there on the bay.

Realizing the danger, I hurriedly waded out of the surf and dried myself under a palm tree before getting into that lorry! Such a momentary thing, but by emotion or perhaps fear, etched large in my memory.

Time passed more swiftly now that I was in a more active situation on shore. Many soccer matches with the Army, which had garrisons scattered around, occasionally with teams from ships that came in from convoys and native teams from Freetown itself, which lay about two miles away from our base.

Another small but impressive incident occurred some months later. I was sent up to the military hospital on the hills above when the base doctor considered that I should get some small surgery on my adenoids! Lying there in the bed after the little surgical procedure, I noticed a sudden increase in the activity and bustle in the ward.

It appeared that a lorry filled with chaps going up the mountainous road to the beach had gone off the road and crashed. Among the casualties, of which there were many, would be the young telegraphist lying next to my bed. As soon as he had been bedded, screens were erected around him. In answer to my raised eyebrow, the nurse shook her head sadly and went away.

All afternoon and through most of the night, an unending stream of verbal data streamed from the dying telegraphist's lips: "One hundred, ninety-nine, nine-eight, ninety-seven..." (and, ten minutes later) "...eight, seven, six, four, three, two, one."

Then rambling fragments of his memory unraveled, recalling conversation, "No, mum, I don't want to... Why are you crying, Marge? Yes, sir, right away. Dit-dit dah-dah, dit-dit dah-dah-dit-dit... Watch out! Stupid bugger! you'll get me killed! Yes, I know, Jack told me... Oh, Dad! It won't be forever. I'll be back. Marge... Marge, Where are you? I love you. Bloody 'ell what's going on?"

This and much more poured from his cracked brain, for I learned that he had a badly fractured skull beyond repair. So, I was his witness to his fragmented dialogue, his dwindling life, like a tape unwinding, until in the early morning it ran out. The silence was poignant with whispered echoes in my head. Once again, I experienced, if not an epiphany, certainly an unforgettable lesson on the fragility of the mind and the uncertainty we call life.

One morning while visiting the *Philoctetes* and Jim Beecham, we were leaning on the rail chatting, when through the mist-shrouded boom opened to allow a large convoy of troop ships, including some famous liners and other large merchants refitted as troop carriers to enter Freetown harbor. As the last of the ten or more large ships came through the boom, there was a lapse of about five minutes before two sleek, gray, weathered destroyers, probably part of the escort, slipped through the boom.

With mounting excitement, I noticed that one of the old destroyers, a two funneled V&W post WW 1, D62, was the *Wild Swan*, my father's ship in which he had been serving ever since the war had first been declared, almost two years earlier! "Jim! That's my father's ship. I haven't seen him for two years, do you think I could get permission to visit her at the mooring?"

"Go ask Jimmy-the-One" (the First Officer), he said.

I returned five minutes later, a smile of my face. "I'm to go to the gang-way. They'll take me up to the mooring in the mail boat."

I duly found myself floating in more than one-way to see my father, whom I had last seen as he was recalled to duty after only one week of "retirement" after twenty three years continuous service in His Majesty's Navy. That was over two years ago, and I was just over fifteen years then! Now I was eighteen and in the same Navy! Remembering that I really had not known my father who had only appeared after long absences of sometimes eighteen months or more, I became more apprehensive as we neared his mooring up-river. There was so much to share, but so little time. What could we share? What would we say to each other?

DO NOT GENTLE INTO THAT GOOD NIGHT

Do not go gentle into that good night,
Old age should burn and rave at close of day;
Rage, rage against the dying of the light.

Though wise men at their end know dark is right,
Because their words had forked no lightning they
Do not go gentle into that good night.

Good men, the last wave by, crying how bright
Their frail deeds might have danced in a green bay,
Rage, rage against the dying of the light.

Wild men who caught and sang the sun in flight,
And learn, too late, they grieved it on its way,
Do not go gentle into that good night.

Grave men, near death, who see with blinding sight
Blind eyes could blaze like meteors and be gay,
Rage, rage against the dying of the light.

And you, my father, there on the sad height,
Curse, bless, me now with your fierce tears, I pray.
Do not go gentle into that good night.
Rage, rage against the dying of the light.

Dylan Thomas
1914–1953

THE WILD SWAN SONG

As I leaned over the rail I saw, coming out of the hazy mist that prevailed as a result of the monsoon weather we experienced, some huge grey shapes of one- and two-funneled troop transports coming through the harbor boom-nets.

They appeared almost like grey ghosts, followed for the next half an hour by a procession of assorted transports, infantry landing ships with landing craft hanging conspicuously from their davits, altogether with ten other large ships and the escorts following in procession. This made up the largest naval force I had seen in one fleet at that time.

It turned out to be part of force "H" from Gibraltar, which had escorted this very large and important convoy. The close escort included the battleship *Malaya*, cruiser *Hermione*, other ships including three destroyers, one of which, an old battered-looking V&W destroyer really caught my attention; but more of that later.

That large impressive force was on its way to take Madagascar off the east coast of Africa at the opening of the Indian Ocean. The Japanese were poised in Burma to threaten the Indian Ocean and Churchill decided it was necessary to create a base now by occupying Vichy-controlled Madagascar as a gateway to the east.

There was some concern at that time, since the convoy would be passing the Dakar area, where the French battleship *Richelieu* and three six inch gunned cruisers, *Georges Leygues*, *Gloire* and *Montcalm*, might sail out and meet with the battle-cruiser, *Strasbourg*, which the Admiralty knew was expected in the Dakar area on the fifth, to make a formidable intercept of this convoy.

The rest of "Force H," including the carrier *Illustrious* and the heavy cruiser *Devonshire*, with yet more escorts and ships, was over the horizon, acting as shadow protection in case of possible interference by the Vichy French fleet.

The assault ships had come to refuel and replenish supplies before resuming the long leg to Madagascar around the horn of South Africa and up the Indian Ocean to the island off Mozambique. I went up to the bridge to the signal station and asked the duty officer there if he could identify the last V&W for me, because I believed my father was aboard, and I hadn't seen him since August of 1939. "That's the *Wild Swan*," he said, and after a pause, "Why don't you go and see the First Office, and request permission to arrange for a boat to take you up to her anchorage, to see your father." "Thank you, Sir. I will!" I couldn't believe it.

First, the luck of being on deck just at that moment, when my father's ship should appear right out of the mist and out of the past, so to speak.

Second, to have a chance to go and see him miraculously being presented was fortuitous to say the least. I had almost given up hope that either of us would see each other until the war's end, *If he lasts that long*, I often thought.

You see, before the war, he knew where I was. And every so often, after receiving a letter or being told by Gertrude, I would have a general idea of where he was. Now, I had left what you might euphemistically call "home." Well, 68 Baker Street, where I came home from school and ate my meals and slept when I wasn't running errands or doing housework delegated by my stepmother. Dad would not know that I was now in the Navy and actually based here in the harbor at Freetown, Sierra Leone.

But back to that old battered, "war weary, worn destroyer," as someone later wrote in a book dedicated to her exploits. Once I had obtained permission to have a boat take me up the large crowded harbor to the mooring buoy assigned to the *Wild Swan*, I hurriedly changed into number ones (best uniform, pressed and tidy, which meant creases sharp and everything correct) and presented myself to the duty officer for permission to leave ship. I couldn't believe my luck when I found I was the only rating being taken in the boat that morning. How I rated such treatment I'll never understand, but I thanked God for arranging it.

As the boat drew alongside the chipped, rust-stained side of the destroyer, I grabbed the rope and wood ladder and, since the freeboard was so low, was on deck in two quick steps, saluting the quarterdeck and the duty officer. "Leading Supply Rating Harrison reporting on board to see his father, Leading Gunner H. Harrison, Sir!"

The young Lieutenant smiled, and turning to the boatswain's mate, ordered him to pipe-up, "Leading Gunner Harrison to the quarterdeck."

Almost immediately a tall gaunt figure in tropical whites appeared walking towards me, stooping slightly, as tall men often did from continuously passing through low bulkheads onboard ship. My first impression (which has stayed with me through the years) was how tired, weathered and old he appeared. His hair was gray, his face deep-lined and, I thought, just like the ship: weather-beaten and showing signs of extended service.

After all, he was called back to service two weeks after his retirement back in 1939, and had been at sea continuously since then. The last time I had seen him he was sun-tanned, healthy and happily planning his vegetable garden as part of his many intended retirement activities.

He had appeared to me, at the age of fifteen, to be a big strong man. But on this day, almost two and a half years later, as a young seventeen year-old boy-man, I thought he had suddenly grown old. I was shocked. He appeared somewhat surprised too. It took a second or two before I stuck out my hand, "Hi, Dad!" I managed to blurt out. He stared at me, strangely, "Son? Is that you?" He gripped my hand, "It is you! By God!" Then remembering where he was, he dropped my hand and addressed the officer requesting permission to leave ship with me.

We caught the boat that had brought me before she shoved off and managed to get taken ashore to the new jetty, where there was a canteen and available beer! Duly laden with our ration of two quart bottles of Canadian beer per man, we walked to a large banyan tree and sat down under its shade. Long absentee father, here with now "grown-up" son, about to share awkwardness with the aid of beer, and perhaps, with help, a thought or two that might bridge the space and time between them. But as for my part, I had no idea of how we could communicate, only a silent desire to do so.

When the first bottles were halfway empty and the restraints somewhat loosened, he began, "Well, How did you get here, Son? What ship are you on?" Safe enough questions that allowed me to fill in some time and detail, as we occasionally slurped through the second half of the bottles. He was smoking continuously as usual, I noticed. Chain-smoking, they called it: as one is smoked down to a stub, another is applied to the stub while still in the lips, and then as the new cigarette is lit and glowing, the stub is taken out and ground out or "stubbed" in an ash tray or the ground.

He seemed quite content at that moment, listening to my routine and dull explanations as if they were interesting revelations! Another period of silence and then, "Dad," I said, "your ship looks as if it's old and needs a refit. Is there any chance of one?" He immediately seemed relieved to switch conversation to more familiar ground. "Well, Son, she's already twenty two or three years old. We've steamed continuously and been in action quite a bit during the two years I've been on her. Dunkirk runs, Atlantic and Western approaches, Gibraltar runs from here to there. It never stops. But we are scheduled finally for refit in Portsmouth when we return from this lot!"

That was quite a lengthy statement for my normally taciturn father. So I waited for whatever more information or commentary he might add, while gulping the last of the first bottle of Canadian beer, feeling as if I was handling the situation quite well. "How long have you been here in Freetown?" he asked as he opened the second quart, and, holding it in his left hand, put a new cigarette up to the butt in his lips and drew red into it and spit out the butt.

In 1942, smoking was widely accepted as a social habit considered at best, by those who did not smoke, as "a nuisance." By those who were like my Dad, well and truly addicted to the nicotine, it was a need and as natural as breathing. Little was publicized or perhaps not known of the time-bomb effect to lungs and heart, so the chain smoking habit that I had now noticed was just that: noticed but not dwelled upon. Though, even then my eyes would begin to sting if I was in close company with his smoke. I did not connect his smoking with my earlier attacks of asthma, nor was I even vaguely familiar with the term "psychosomatic" or any possible psychological reactions to the presence of my father and the anxiety that arose from that combination of toxic haze and the threat of his anger, fueled by Gertrude's criticism of my "lack of respect," as she put it, and its consequences to me.

That afternoon under the banyan tree with my father now, as I felt it, man-to-man, I had not thought of my mother-in-law or of past misery. I was a sailor drinking beer with another older sailor who happened to be my father. In fact, as I looked at him then, I remember, as I looked intently into his lined, seamed, weathered face, I felt, unexpectedly, a surge of compassion I had never felt before. Perhaps I had never been this close, had never been able to disregard his authority, his intimidating physical domination of everything around, or so it seemed.

For instance, I remember clearly, that one day when he was home from his eighteen-month Far East service on the Nelson, he tied me to the clothes pole in the garden that I had helped him to erect at the bottom of our narrow back garden.

He was threading the line through the pulley that was fastened to the narrow end of the fourteen foot pole, prior to pulling the thick end of it into the two foot hole he had dug in order to anchor it securely, creating a clothes line capable of withstanding the pull and force of flapping sheets and clothing in the wind.

After we had managed to get the pole upright, and after I had shoveled the clay and wet topsoil into the hole, he tamped down the earth around the base of the pole and after pulling the line up, he looped the end expertly around the cleat, finishing with a clove hitch.

I was duly impressed with his expertise when it came to rope knots and hitches. "Dad," I said, "Can you show me how you tie some of those hitches?" "Sure, Son. Just put your two hands around that pole just above the hitch, and I'll show you a real good hitch that would keep the *Hood* tight alongside!"

Eager to learn this super-hitch that would be strong enough to hold a forty-two-thousand-ton battle cruiser to the dock, I said, "Ok, Dad, show me that hitch!" I did not give a second's thought to the disparity between a piece of cord and the heavy, four-inch needed for mooring such a heavy ship. His manipulation was so swift that, before I could even follow the manipulation of the cord he produced out of nowhere, he secured both wrists and double lashed them tight to the mast, which was what the pole had become to me.

"Oh, Dad! That's not fair! You didn't really show me how you did it!" But I was addressing his disappearing back, as he slipped swiftly through the back door of our house. I laughed, as I thought he'd come right back out. But after minutes went by, I was still roped up to that clothes pole and it was no longer fun. Nor was it a joke. It was getting cool, and a slight drizzle was blowing in from the Channel.

"Hey! Dad! Come on! OK! It's a strong hitch all right. I can't loosen it. Dad!" Deep down resentment, perhaps built up during what I had considered unfair and spiteful, even demeaning treatment by my stepmother, Gertrude, and long suppressed, began to well up. I began to feel anger. As my wrists chafed in the tight cords, my eyes began to tear as my thoughts dwelt on not only this perceived present humiliation, but on others long past now, unfortunately resurfacing.

By the time my father did come out with a cigarette glowing between his lips, and stood for a minute smiling at my obvious futility, I had nothing to say. I waited for my release at his pleasure. "So, now you know what a clove hitch is. Do you think you could tie one?" I didn't answer. When he loosed the hitch, rather easily, I thought, I walked, cheeks burning, past him straight into the house. I felt I had been shown up, ridiculed, and my self-esteem bruised again.

Brief encounters with my father often ended either in frustration or confusion or worse, some deep unrequited need that ended in hurt feelings. Dad, though, would not have known of my deep rooted resentments and confusion, since he lacked schooling after the age of thirteen and whatever he knew about life and human beings was gathered as a hard and bitter harvest from the barren decks of ships from hardened men of war, or from occasional brief warmth or affection either given as gestures or desperately bought from girls or women, perhaps whores, with whatever charm or money he could find at the time.

His classroom was the world that British seamen discovered as they sailed it. From Plymouth to Portsmouth or Chatham to Gibraltar, Malta, Alexandria, Aden, Bombay, and Trincomalee, Singapore, Hong Kong, Shanghai to Yokohama and down to the Pacific via the Philippine Sea and past New Guinea to Sidney, Australia, Auckland, New Zealand and across the southern Pacific to, isolated and lonely in those days, Far Pitcairn, then around the Horn through Drake's Passage into the South Atlantic and up to the Falkland Islands, that lonely outpost 450 miles from Argentina, but almost 10,000 miles from England. Not to mention the Virgin Islands, known to us then as the "British West Indies."

Yes, my father spent the greater part of his life enrolled in the Royal Navy's theater of learning: the seven seas and the great ports that ringed the pink world on Mr. Gardner's Map on the wall in Flying Bull Lane's Senior Boys School in Portsmouth. But, my father did not understand his son's needs or his own, really. He was, after all, trained like a meat and bone animal to obey orders, to be quick-about-it, and to get small allowances and compensation, if his reports were favorable. The slightest protest or questioning of authority, albeit sometimes in the wrong, was to be marked in your report as a malcontent or troublemaker.

I began to understand why those old sailors suffered quietly and took their pleasures where and when they could. They had come to understand only too well what being born on the "wrong side of the sheets" meant. When I read Joseph Heller's *Catch 22* years later, I immediately thought of my father's choices as being catch-twenty-twos. But that was yet to be and I was yet to know, but I was learning. However painful, I was learning.

So, the surge of compassion I felt as I sat with my dad under the banyan tree that fateful day in Freetown, Sierra Leone in West Africa, I now see as a sign of my impending maturity and, perhaps the beginning of a new self. I no longer harbored resentment or even regret for whatever my circumstances had been, for what my stepmother did or did not do, or for my father's many and long absences during my childhood and growing up. I saw now a worn, harsh taskmaster doing the best he could under the burden of a large navy spread all over the world, and a man who had little formal education and even less opportunity. As if reading my thoughts, he suddenly blurted out as if the words were choking him, "I'm so sorry, Son, that I've fucked-up your life. It's been on my mind." His cigarette-end glowed as he drew a big breath, maybe a sigh, and as he exhaled he took a last swig of the remaining beer and dropped the empty bottle to the rusty damp earth where it rolled up against my foot. I stood up and compulsively reached out as almost simultaneously, he lurched also to his feet.

We stood there for a moment, before I could find the words to reassure him. I surprised myself by hearing my lower deck gruffness: "It's OK, Dad. It's OK. You didn't fuck-up my life. Look at me! I'm not fucked-up."

I felt it and I meant it. I felt his leathery cheek, his beard stubble, and his tobacco-fumed breath against my own and then we released each other, separating, once again father and son. But this time it was *different*. We had communicated, however briefly, however gruffly, we had bridged the not-so-grand canyon of loneliness and need keeping us apart, out of touch.

Little did I know then that this would be the last time we would see each other. What transpired six weeks later would give even greater importance and meaning to this chance meeting with its shared healing and exchange.

We walked, maybe somewhat slower and less sure-footed, down to the jetty to return to our respective ships: he to the *Wild Swan*, and I back to the *Philoctetes*.

We parted at the jetty and I returned to the hot tedious routine on board, the *Philoctetes* anchored, as we were, permanently as a submarine depot ship there in the tropical, stiflingly humid heat of Freetown harbor. The war was just a few miles into the Atlantic and reports were continually of ships being sunk, U-boats attacking and being attacked and survivors being picked up before the sharks found them.

Freetown was an increasingly important base, for the Mediterranean was closed to us at that time and therefore, supply convoys needed this refueling and refurbishing base for the long journey around the Cape, up to the Red Sea and into the Suez and our army in North Africa. But the war seemed remote to us on an anchored depot ship inside the great harbor.

My remove from action and my feeling of remoteness was shattered one day in June a few weeks after my chance meeting with my father. I was listening to the BBC overseas evening news on the Tannoy system, being relayed by the radio office: "One of His Majesty's ships, a destroyer escorting and defending an inbound convoy off the Bay of Biscay, was attacked by continual flights of *Junkers 88*s and after shooting down six of the attacking planes, was finally sunk. The next-of-kin are being notified." The cryptic, controlled voice was not going to reveal the identity of that ship but in my heart and in my mind, an arrow had struck. I somehow knew that it was my father's ship.

You see, Dad had revealed on the afternoon we met by chance that the *Wild Swan* was finally going home to Portsmouth for that long delayed refit. He also mentioned that twice before she had been on her way to the refit when she was suddenly recalled to active duty to help convoys in distress. I remember his feeling that the return home was a cruel carrot being offered by Fate, withdrawn just when the forward motion to achieve the carrot was gained. He had become, if not truly apathetic, then stoically accepting of his ongoing rigors and somewhat pessimistic of the *Wild Swan* ever getting that needed refit.

Nevertheless, when I asked if I could send a couple of letters over to him to take back to England, since that was where the *Wild Swan* was scheduled to go in a few days, he agreed to post them for me at the first opportunity. One of those letters was to my grandmother, his mother in Southampton. It wasn't the letters that I was thinking of that night when I slipped into my hammock and finally got to sleep.

About two weeks later I was handed a telegram, obviously an admiralty mail call opened by the censor, in the original official envelope. It read cryptically on little strips pasted onto the form: *We regret to inform you as next-of-kin that your father, Leading Gunner H.V.D. Harrison, was lost at sea following action with the enemy.*

I have no recollection of surprise. It was as if I was only getting confirmation of something I'd already known. Of course, I had not known my father's death was fact until the telegram arrived, but one cannot account for premonition or foreboding.

It had docked in safety in Plymouth with a promised refit in Portsmouth, but a recall was issued in Plymouth, and most of the crew were recalled and the *Wild Swan* was summoned to its demise. Such is Fate's roll of the dice. The convoy was being attacked by flights of *Junkers 88s* flying out of St. Nazaire airfield in relays. In attempting to aid the convoy in the Bay of Biscay, the *Wild Swan* was bombed repeatedly. After a hit, she split in two and my father apparently succumbed to his wounds and exposure. He was united with some of his shipmates, to ever ebb and flow on the eternally sea where his life was, and his death.

"He now being lifted into high society
And having pic'd up several odds and ends
Of free thoughts in his travels, for variety,
He deem'd being in a lone isle, among friends
That without any danger of a riot, he
Might for long lying make himself amends;
And singing as he sung in his warm youth,
Agree to a short armistice with truth."

George Gordon, Lord Byron
LXXXIII
From Canto III, *Don Juan*

MY NAME WAS POSTED ON A LIST

I awoke one morning in my mosquito net and sat up with a quivery shiver. I was sweaty and had a headache. I tried to get up and stand by the bed, I tried to dress, but with difficulty.

One of my mates looked at my sweaty, shivery self and noticed I was pallid and weak. He came with another mate with a list and called, "Ken you're on the list to go home today!"

I said, "I can't pack my ditty bag. I haven't any energy to carry my bags." But my mates stuffed my kit and within ten minutes I was dressed and shuffled off the ship and one of my mates carried the ditty bag on his shoulder, and a green suitcase in his other hand.

We were checked off the list at the key and got into the dingy, with my mates on each side of me and when we went aside, one mate was on the ladder before me, and the other mate shouldered me on each wrung.

As we scramble on to the deck, names were shouted and directed to the deck as number were shouted out for each name. I stumbled on to the hatch as my number was mumbled, and I actually fell and tumbled down to the bottom of the deck.

As I became conscious, I found myself in the sick bay: it was three days since I had fallen unconscious down the hatch! As I gradually regained consciousness, I found that I had malaria, bronchial asthma and diarrhea! I was quite weak.

Ten days after I had fallen down the hatchway we arrived in Scotland, and we were in high spirits and ready to get off the boat, to get upon the solid earth!

Well, I was transferred to a medical tug, with dozens of other medical patients. We made into Clyde after several miles and came to a hospital-key, were we entered into a ward, were un-dressed and given a bed.

As I looked out of the windows, the fields of wheat were miles in the distance. I slept in peaceful consciousness.

I was in the hospital at a month where I regained my health and was ready to get on ship.

I got a train to Glasgow, and was soon on my way to London, to Surrey to Esther, where NAFFI head quarters were located. I arrived the next morning by 10am.

I found a Petty Chief Officer to whom I gave my name and rank. He smiled and said, "Ah, your name came up yesterday. You had a nice stay at the Scotland hospital and now we have a ship, where you can find a nice berth!"

Well, it seemed that I had a berth on a new destroyer as a canteen assistant. A train ticket and a meal ticket were issued and I was on my way to Newcastle, and along the Tyne to Wall's End, was my new ship, a destroyer.

As I was musing as I wended my way to London, I began to dwell on the month in the hospital. After this peaceful mend, I became a new man. I went through some of circumstances: meeting my father after two years. Did we meet by fate? For just in a moment I asked the officer, "is that *Wild Swan*?

That day, was a moment, that was fate to meet my father. We had only met four or five times in our lives, yet we communicated in a few words that bridged our souls, bridged that not-so-grand canyon of loneliness and need, keeping us apart... We met, and our soul touching, met.

We arrive at Euston and the Newcastle express was to to depart at 2:30pm, and I went to the 3rd section, put my suitcase on the wrack, and sat in the corner. As it was an express, I expected the train to get in 6:45pm, and I would get a room in the Railway Hotel in the Newcastle station. So I spread my map and tracked along the Nottingham, Leeds, York, Teesside and Newcastle main tracks as I would get a dinner at the Railway Hotel, get a 10am, local along the river and would get to Wall's End and walk to the H.M.S. *Vigilant* which I would see in the morning.

As the train gained more speed, I got more sleepy as the train clicked over the rails and I nodded off. As I woke up and had a sip from my bottle, I was more aware of my companions who had been seated before me. We began to converse and socialize and be friendly. As the time went by, I gazed through the windows and the station Durham glided by and we could see the Cathedral along the river. As we viewed the scene and the Cathedral, we all chatted and commented on getting to the end of the journey.

"Newcastle! Newcastle!" The attendant called "Newcastle! Last stop!" As I let every passenger in our compartment go before me, I gave a greeting and hand clasp.

I hastened to the Railway Hotel, and said to the clerk at the counter, "I am on my way to London and need a room for the night." I was taken in the lift to the second floor and to room 223, and I tipped the attendant and close the door.

After I washed my face and hands I slipped to the lift and went down to the dining room. After a light supper I went to my room got into my pajamas, clicked the light and went to sleep.

MURMANSK MEMORY: REVISITED

Sometimes, even now, in flickering light,
I almost see the glints of sea-foam caught
In still negative pictures of that night:

And, old eyes closed, feel stinging whipped salt
See pale moon floating in the dark, faces
Stark masks, past complaint or care or need,
Eyes squeezing the grey light, scanning fears shapes,
Looming, peaking, falling in white tumult,
A hissing monstrous chaos off the capes;

While somewhere out there, the doomed and the not,
Like us, plunge forward to our rendezvous,
Cold feet, damp socked, dog deep within sheepskins,
Awaiting their masters call to the bones,
Crouched, listening to heartbeats, rhythmic now
In the thin vibrating steel shell beneath them.

Abrupt, violent sent up from the deep,
Hell exploded, ripping steel, erasing men,
Ear-bursting fireballs blast the brittle night.
Enflamed in full, doomed decks begin their slide,
Eyeless fingers lose their last touching clutch,
While those afloat still haul luck away.

We who were left to recollect and cry,
Witnessed some random captain's choice,
And, for my time, having no voice to change
The pre-disposition of both stars or man,
Felt no guilt, but in calm, safe retrospect
Come now to a simile: like my Titanic faith.

KHH

HMS VIGILANT

As the shipyard came into view at the river's edge at the bottom of the drab short street filled with the head-ringing sounds of riveting, hammering, and clanging of metal against metal that signaled ship construction, a feeling of excitement was lifting my feet I was actually going to see her! For a week now, I'd heard talk of her, had general descriptions of her, and even been told how she was the latest type of anti-submarine escort destroyer with the latest detecting equipment.

Showing the dock pass and my ship's assignment at the gate, I was directed by the Geordie gatekeeper past the several slips where raw-metal shapes of ships in varying stages of completion loomed above me as I picked my way across rail lines, cables, ropes and debris to the designated finishing quay. I stood for a moment to take it all in: the hustle and bustle of it, the kind of chaos out of which a ship is shaped.

I was deafened by the machine-gun clatter of the riveters, voices shouting above the noise, and dazzled by arcs of bright blue sparkle from the welders. I stood totally enthralled, reflecting on the process, and I took it all in for an unforgettable totally Zen moment of being and knowing and whole.

I was told it would be a few more weeks before she would be ready to move out under her own steam to join the fleet up at Scapa Flow or wherever she was destined to go. After the hull is completed, the engines installed, and the hull is closed-up, with the main deck and super structure built-up, the decked-over hull is launched down the slips and towed to the finishing quays or docks. There the final touches to the miles of electrical wiring and guts of her communication and control connecting bridge to engine room to gun turrets to platforms are eventually completed.

The ship then has to be fitted and provisioned before she can proceed to trials, a week of daily testing of engines, guns, communications, detection devices, depth charge throwers, ammunition supply, internal communication system, everything that goes into making a destroyer, or corvette, a cruiser or battleship, into the efficient war weapon these ships were designed to be.

And I was where I had imagined myself and had wanted to be for such a long time. Soon I would be preparing to join "my ship." I finally came to the directed pier, delayed somewhat by the bustling activity around the yard and the chaos and cacophony and newness of it.

There she was! The *Vigilant*. The crane high overhead was lowering a piece of equipment onto the afterdeck and the sound of riveters and the blue sparks of welders continued to fill the eye and ear. By the look of it, we wouldn't be leaving for a while yet. Glancing up at the flare of the bow as we stepped gingerly over the many thick power lines and cables leading to and from the ship, I could see she would cut waves down to size as she sped through them. I couldn't wait to see her when she was completed ready for action!

This was what I had dreamed of since I was a boy waving-my union jack as Dad came home onboard the deck forward of the throwers. Now I was going to sea. *Let someone wave me in*, I thought. Dad was gone now, never did get to enjoy his retirement, or his runner beans and his little flower patch. Just two weeks, and just like that, Recall! Shortage of expert seamen, they said. *Christ, hadn't he served enough?* I thought then. *Twenty-two years of service that included the First World War. Now he's gone.* His body slipped over the side of the crowded Carley to float out somewhere in the Bay of Biscay, to forever be part of the ebb and flow of the sea he had spent most of his life on and in and now under.

"Watch it, Mate!" The warning came just in time to snap me out of my memory trip as I ducked a swinging sling being returned to the dockside by the crane above. "Thanks, mate. Sorry," I mumbled, embarrassed, since I was in uniform now and felt a sailor should be more aware.

I finally stepped onto the main deck of what was going to be my home for the foreseeable future. Two Oerlikon anti-aircraft guns up on the superstructure, abaft the stack, completed the original armaments. A couple of light machine guns were later installed one each side of the bridge.

To me she was the re-incarnation of my father's old World War One V&W destroyer, the *Wild Swan*, sunk in the Bay of Biscay last year, but with more powerful engines, faster at 28-30 knots at full speed and more deadly main armament and more efficient equipment all round. She was one of the new V&Ws being built in haste and in numbers to combat and defeat the German U-boat offensive which had reached crescendo in May and June 1941, 119 ships with a total tonnage of 635 tons were sunk in the North Atlantic area off Freetown, West-Africa, where I ran into my father after not seeing him in two years.

Well, that was then and this was now! How much clearer everything is in retrospect, after time has added distance.

That night back in the shore quarters in Walls End On Tyne, which was room and board at a local boarding house we were assigned to while the ship was being completed, I sat down to write a letter to a girl I met while on leave, after leaving the hospital near Glasgow, when I had returned from West Africa with Malaria, Bronchitis, and Dysentery (a combination of misery, believe me!) after eighteen months in the Naval Facilities in Freetown. It began on *HMS Philoctetes*, a submarine depot ship to which I had been assigned as a young, raw, barely seventeen-year-old rating, and concluded eighteen months later while serving ashore in the naval base there. The day my relief arrived I came down with Malaria. But that was history, and I was on a new adventure.

Two weeks later, when the ship had been fully fitted and commissioned and we had already arrived off Greenock at the mouth of the Clyde, at an anchorage waiting for the day's trials before getting clearance for duty, her answer arrived in the ship's mail. It was brief and, like the one it was responding to, trite and vacuous, devoid of substance:

Dear Ken,

Thank you for the letter. It was nice of you to remember me. I enjoyed meeting you too. How interesting that you are going to be on a new ship. I hope you will like it and will be alright.

Yours truly, Cynthia Greene

But I had received a letter! Adrift as I was then, without anchor or direction, and since I had broken any contact with my stepmother, Gertrude, and the house in Portsmouth, in my mind I was now an independent person. Perhaps I was temporarily sublimating my need for inclusion through letters: *any link back to the outside world of teen-aged fantasy and sweet smelling hair, lipstick, soft embraces and, if you're lucky, an invitation to visit a home*, that was something all young sailors valued more than perhaps their daily tot of rum and supply of cigarettes, by which all else was measured in those days of doubtful survival.

We lived not for the King or Country, but for shore-time, leave, and the next girl. There was no thought to the long term. A letter was fuel for dreams, ink promises for the imagination, and, however fanciful, a fragile link with the other wished-for world which in imagination was visualized in fantasy more like the movies we all attended as our alma maters of romance and an unreal wished-for world of beautiful girls and us handsome boys.

You could see young men around you after mail call, holding their letters to their noses, inhaling deeply to pick up any trace of perfume left with the red lip impressions that amorous wives or girl-friends kissed onto the backs of the envelopes as they sealed them. But mine was pristinely free of advertising of any sort.

"Duty watch, prepare to leave harbor stations!" came over the Tannoy speakers, announcing our departure from Greenock and the end of trials. We were officially one small, 1,800-ton addition to the British Navy. *HMS Vigilant* was only one of dozens of destroyers, sloops and frigates that had been and were still being rushed into the war at sea and particularly into the anti-U-boat campaign swiftly reaching a climax in 1943.

We were beginning to match the flow of U-boats with our own flow of corvettes, sloops and destroyers, all designed to hunt and destroy U-boats before they could destroy ships in convoy. (All that is knowledge gathered partially from Admiral Raeder's account of his planning and execution of Germany's U-Boat Campaign, just prior to beginning this biographical recollection at the age of eighty-five in 2009. Because of interruptions in writing this biography, you might understand that certain time fragmentations might occur!)

I found myself then, at long last, on the *Vigilant*, on my way to Loch Ewe on the western coast of Scotland, to join our first convoy to Russia, in sharp contrast to my recent West African experiences. Not the least was the weather, which was artic, icy and stormy, with huge waves, as well as the U-boats and torpedoes and sudden explosions as some ships were sunk.

At this time of the war, the escort forces were far stronger and better equipped to deal with U-boat packs, which by now had also multiplied. It was quite common for packs of six or eight U-boats to have some contact along the way, and torpedoes known as T5s were fired at destroyers as well as merchant ships. Lookouts were put on both sides of the bridge and the Asdic (anti-submarine detection device) was switched on and manned continuously when in passage or convoy, but more often than not, detection of the enemy subs was only made after an initial explosion of a torpedo hitting a merchant ship announced its presence.

Our problems were made even more difficult by the weather and mountainous seas and, as we went further north, closer to and deeper into the Arctic Circle, the below-freezing temperatures. After several days of arctic storms with visibility down to almost zero, the guns would be covered with sheets of ice, the decks awash and life-lines frozen. The ice would have to be broken off with hammers as it froze-up the guns and depth-charge throwers. All this was complicated by the ship's violent rolls, lurches or shuddering as she plunged on, in and through the steel-gray wind-whipped violence of those artic storms.

There were times when just to make your way from aft to forward would be to literally take your life in your hands, since all that was between you and the arctic sea and a quick slip on the icy deck was your holding onto the frozen lifeline. At such times, the food would be reduced to cold sandwiches, since the galley would become a shambles and it would be virtually impossible to keep pots on the stove, even with restraints. Also, scalding hot liquids would slop all over the place, adding a further hazard for the cook.

The pitch and yaw along with the roll, while the ship made headway in rough seas and howling gales, made walking a struggle, involving both hands on the lifeline and often, no feet!

I was in such an incident, when a sudden huge wave came over the bow and tons of water rushed aft and took my feet out. I was slammed against a stanchion with one leg over the side and the other hooked around the stanchion! Thank God! A big shipmate hanging on the lifeline was behind me and grabbed me by the hand and hauled me onboard. I was wet but thankful for my rescuer and God's mercy.

When a ship was torpedoed and sunk the estimated time for survival in that water was two minutes. The temperature was freezing and drifts of ice accumulated as the sea drenched everything. Quite often the guns became ice-locked. A hammer was used to free the breech. So, it was understood that rescue of anyone in that water was fruitless. Eyes were often averted from faint red lights dimly seen moving away and down in the faintly illuminated sea and our ears closed to even fainter cries in the night.

We might see a sudden eruption and fire before a ship would slide suddenly beneath the dark waves, the sea gradually extinguishing the flames and squeezing the glow to a glimmer and, like a sputtering candle, the glimmer would be doused as stygian darkness prevailed again to blanket the sight.

A wave's wash, perhaps pearling in the moonlight as the pale moon broke from the clouds, might be seen as a periscope wash, which sometimes it was! The constant unremitting vigilance not only created eyestrain but, eventually in the biting arctic wind and stinging sleet, bone weary tiredness that took many a seaman to his hammock fully clothed. He knew that he should take off his wet, frozen, duffel coat and stiff heavy sea-boots; but, when such lead heavy tiredness drained not only the body but also the brain, the body did not respond to fleeting "oughts" or "shoulds."

The anti-submarine action had in 1944 begun to be sporadic and broken because of greater numbers of escorts and more efficient equipment such as radar, Asdic and RDF, to name the three most important electronic devices, which made a U-boats presence no longer secret or hidden. But the tension on board an escort and conditions on those Arctic convoys to Murmansk were unremitting.

Murmansk, our destination, was a port in the western part of the Russian Kola Peninsula. An incident took place on one of the *Vigilant's* first convoys: by then we were getting many more escorts.

The convoy steamed out of Loch Ewe with twenty merchant ships escorted not only by us but by ten others as well: *Hardy*, the flotilla leader, *Savage, Venus, Offa, Obdurate, Inconstant, Virago and Stord*, a Free Norwegian destroyer that sailed several times with our group, and two corvettes, much smaller escorts with only one 4 inch gun forward and depth charge throwers aft with which to do the job.

You cannot imagine how they made their way sometimes in the menacing, huge, wind-whipped waves of an Arctic storm. I would marvel at how we would slide down, down a huge trough of white frothing deep steely blue-gray ocean, almost disappearing from the sight of our larger wallowing merchant charges, only to rise up, up on the crest once again, shedding cascading tons of water from the bow and foredeck like an emerging gray Sperm whale, as we plunged back into that awesome maelstrom.

To this day, I have not only retained that awe of Nature on the rampage, but also the excitement of being involved in and vulnerable to nature. I am fascinated by the sea and its power, sweeping in from the Pacific, where I live on the California coast.

But, back to the convoys. A minesweeper completed the escort force. We had a ratio of nearly one-to-two; that is, eleven escorts to twenty merchant ships, which would seem like plenty of "protection."

But string that convoy of merchant ships in four rows of five ships, with appropriate space between each ship both ahead and astern, with maneuvering space between the columns. Then, distribute your nine escorting destroyers and two corvettes plus your minesweeper, and you will begin to comprehend the problems and the area over which we would have to spread to protect the convoy from U-boat attacks.

These attacks often came from several different directions, when groups or "Wolf-packs," as they were called, rendezvoused with the convoy, having received direction and speed estimates, radioed information from planes or other U-boats which might have spotted us on the horizon.

For instance, the flotilla leader would most likely be free-moving because it would want to speed to whatever section or ship that needed, for example, some prodding or guidance in the event of a slow response to signals to change course. Three destroyers, using the Asdic to search both the front and sides of the convoy, would be assigned to each side, with the first two a little ahead of the lines sweeping, in theory, for possible U-boats.

At the rear, the seventh destroyer accompanied by the two corvettes would be trailing and keeping watch for possible surface U-boats attempting to close in, alerted by their "wolf-pack" possibly strung-out ahead, guided by coded radio transmissions relayed from either the Norwegian HQ at Trondheim, Narvik, or Tromso, or even from Admiral Raeder back in Saint Nazaire or Lorient in Brittany.

Added to all these considerations was the average speed of the convoy, which was based on the slower ship. As a rule most convoys with older ships might be steaming at seven to ten knots! A "fast" convoy could attain and sustain twelve to fifteen knots. Contrast this with the top speed of the destroyers, especially newer ones like the *Vigilant, Verelum, Stord, Venus,* and *Hardy* and others in our group, which could hit close to thirty if necessary for short periods.

The corvettes were slower and could do fifteen to eighteen knots. It was more than just "escorting" the lines of ships, but attempting to sweep a large area as big as a two or three miles square. The more ships, of course, the larger the area that it needs to spread the columns of ships safely and subsequently, the greater area of ocean that has to be searched and covered as the convoy proceeds.

But back to that particular night that I remember well: We had been alerted that a wolf pack was being directed to the convoy and radio traffic between several individual U-boats was picked up by our radio operator and relayed by the captain to the crew. Though no Asdic pings had revealed the actual presence of a U Boat yet, "Action Stations" was sounded on the Tannoy speakers, the gun crews closed up, the depth charge crews assembled aft, and bridge lookouts doubled.

The whole ship's crew, even down in the engine rooms, was tense with expectancy of "the unknown," for many were young raw sailors; stories of what had happened to others they often assumed to be their lot, too. This state of readiness follows when "action stations" went into effect prevailed for several hours before the pale light of an overcast December day dwindled just before dark.

And then, without warning, a brilliant flash lit up part of the convoy over on our port bow. We were the third ship in the starboard line of three destroyers defending the right flank of the convoy. Almost simultaneously our Asdic operator reported to the bridge, "Strong contact at 90 degrees starboard quarter. Range 1750." The information relayed immediately to the leader, *Hardy* with an order "to attack contact."

The *Vigilant* picked up speed and the depth-charge throwers on the starboard side aft were readied. In the meantime, another flash, somewhere closer, possibly a merchant ship on one of the inside lanes has been hit. All I could see from my position on the port wing of the lower bridge were flickering flames glowing against the darkening sky. In the meantime we closed up on the contact quickly at twenty-five knots, while orders were given for "Both Port and Starboard depth-charge throwers to be loaded and ready!"

As we passed over the area indicated by Asdic contact, and the "pinging" resulting from the sound wave generated from and to the Asdic apparatus picking up an echo from the steel U-boat's hull, the captain ordered, "Port fire one and two, Starboard fire one and two!"

There was a series of dull thumps as the four heavy canisters were propelled in arcs on each side of the white wake astern as we ploughed through the sea over the spot where the officer on the plot had calculated where the U-boat might be, given his guessed speed of the underwater submarine and our speed and time to reach the last known echo positive.

If everyone has done his job, the depth charges, set for the estimated depth that the submarine could reach given all the coordinates, will explode each side of that submarine at the precise depth and position. But all that is in the perfect world of theory and mathematics and physics. In actual practice, given the variables of weather, human fatigue, wrong guessing and errors in communication, the success rate was less than theory and perfect execution would expect.

There have been occasions where we spotted a U-boat on the surface approximately a mile away and, even racing at thirty knots with forward guns firing away, have arrived at the spot only to find empty sea and another frustratingly long search with the underwater Asdic pinging. In our case, there were four enormous eruptions following the muffled booms below the surface, but no success. The throwers were loaded again immediately; then we all waited, alert to the threat now. Another explosion in the rear of the convoy resulted in two destroyers appearing astern of us, coming from around the end of the convoy with spume flying from their bows. Behind them, great eruptions suddenly broke the surface, with huge upheavals of water, followed by a series of dull booms that were felt reverberating down inside the hull, inside the steel compartments.

As the Asdic operator put back on his hydra-phones and continued to listen for echoes from the sub, the captain steered a course already calculated on his guess of the U-boat's evasive actions assuming, unless we receive proof of oil, clothing, or wreckage of some particular nature, that we didn't get her.

Then the whole thing is repeated if contact is established and the sub is thought to still be there and, therefore, the convoy still vulnerable. That particular night we lost three merchant ships and two more the next night. One destroyer, the *Obdurate*, was also hit, but was able to return to port.

But one particular incident remains clearly etched in my memory from that night. It was the first ship to be hit by torpedoes on the first night of the attack. We had been steaming steadily since we had left the Western Approaches of Scotland three days since, and approached the Faeroe Icelandic Ridge, on our way to the port Murmansk on the northern coast of the Kola Peninsula, still some fifteen hundred miles to the northeast of where we were that night.

The short day was turning into night and our silhouettes were stark against the fading light. An abrupt exploding flash illuminated ships on our port side, followed by a larger explosion of yellow red flame that shone eerily on black rolling nimbus clouds of oily smoke, rising quickly into the darker night. It was a large tanker in the center of the second row of the convoy.

As we quickly turned to port and raced between ships plowing ahead in the first column, the Asdic operator was already listening for the tell tale echo from his searching ping. Racing over to the stricken ship, we received an order from the flotilla captain to "maintain station and do not - repeat - do not attempt rescue. Keep assigned station and follow Asdic search red on your flank of convoy."

To turn about and leave what we knew from experience were burning, drowning men, some already aware of their impending death as they found themselves in a burning sea, chilling their bones even as the flames crept closer, was a worse experience than being physically wounded. I know that on that cold, merciless night, I learned how deeply I felt and that I had somehow personally participated in the inhumanity.

I have been one acquainted with the night.
I have walked out in rain—and back in rain.
I have outwalked the furthest city light.

I have looked down the saddest city lane.
I have passed by the watchman on his beat
And dropped my eyes, unwilling to explain.

I have stood still and stopped the sound of feet
When far away an interrupted cry
Came over houses from another street,

But not to call me back or say good-bye;
And further still at an unearthly height,
One luminary clock against the sky

Proclaimed the time was neither wrong nor right.
I have been one acquainted with the night.

Robert Frost
Acquainted with the Night

HMS BERWICK AND THE GOLDEN FLEECE

The pride of the Royal Navy, *HMS Hood*, thought by many handsome but thin-skinned, by false pride had more armaments, more ammunition lockers on her decks than others. She was a false idol and when she engaged the most modern battleship then floating, the mighty *Bismarck*, in a running battle off Iceland in the Denmark Straits on May 24th, 1941, the *Hood* was enveloped in a salvo which pierced some shells into her magazines and in two minutes, in a gigantic explosion, she was blown in two and disappeared.

How was that stark reality, that instantaneous catastrophe, revealing the flaws in the once thought impregnable pride of the British Navy, and the idolized symbol of British superiority, to young sailor's sons playing at war in countless empty lots all over England?

But I was conscious of somehow being linked to my always-absent father who by then was permanently gone, having been slid off a raft following his death from wounds and exposure in the Bay of Biscay. In life, his whole being was tied to the sea; in death he was united forever with his mistress.

Funny, how retrospective thinking brings one to new insights about relationships that no longer exist. The mind seems to have a life within a life. Thoughts come without permission and connect you to that which has long been disconnected.

I see my father, on the one hand, as a simple English sailor caught up in His Majesty's Service, serving a king with whom he had no human contact or personal knowledge, and yet to whom he was tied as closely as the shoes on His Majesty's feet, though he did serve a few months as part of the crew of the Royal Yacht back in the thirties.

He was a victim of "lower" birth, destined to play out his role as a hand on the royal gun, a body in the line-of-fire, so to speak, a nobody the King (or the Queen, for that matter) was unaware of, yet, one of the many hundreds of thousands whose existence throughout their life was orchestrated by the needs of an archaic authority attempting to hold sway and dominion over a third of the world.

I suppose thoughts like that are rather naive and such as the officers might think, just "bolshy-talk!" "Just what might be expected of lower-deck mentalities!" "Bloody communists!"

But I also see my father, like myself, as a young English boy caught up in circumstances beyond his ability to affect or change, frustrated in his desires to improve his lot and the life of his family in spite of his lack of education and the occasion of two world wars in his forty-four year life. He was one of millions caught up in the futility of war and the preparation for war and subsequently, one of its endless casualties.

His greatest desire was a garden to tend, to grow flowers and vegetables after he retired. Sadly, one week after being retired in 1939, after

22 years service, after having tilled his "little garden" (really only a patch of ground) and planted two rows of runner beans with stakes and string lines all neatly installed, he was recalled into service, to never realize his dream.

Well, thoughts and questions that would not have arisen in my father's Navy time have certainly come to be aired in mine. The world is changing, and democracy and free speech have allowed the son to think and say what the father dared or could not. I would have liked to be able to comfort and help my father in his old age and to have shared his story, his life and perhaps discover more about my mother and the circumstances that led me to the orphanage at the age of three.

But war takes many lives and leaves many wounded hearts as well as bodies. Regret is a constant companion of desire, I suppose.

But, back to the *Berwick*; with the change from a four-inch gunned, 1,800 ton destroyer to an 8,000 ton ten-inch gunned cruiser, I was now older, with a larger battery of memories, needs, and discontents. It was not as if I was bitter or turned into a malcontent; it was rather that I had, at the age of twenty, become more introspective and analytical. I was certainly becoming aware of the world as I was being introduced and, in a way, seduced into.

The events of 1944 indicated that the war was now a temporary state of affairs, and I was becoming aware of future needs, and of the need to take charge of myself.

But thoughts turned still to the day and the task or the opportunity free time might offer. It was just such a time when I was told I could take five days leave and asked where the railway pass should be directed? At that time I had no connections emotionally or actually with my hometown or anyone there. But, as I searched for a likely destination, I found a scrap of paper scribbled with a name of a girl I'd met when visiting Stan Thomas down in Poole on my last leave.

We were in a queue at a bus station in Bournemouth down on the south coast of England, waiting for a bus to Poole, a small town then, nearby where Stan lived and worked as a shipwright, building motor torpedo boats (MTBs).

Stan, incidentally, was envious of my comings and goings as a sailor and, as is often the case, exaggerated in his mind the benefits and embroidered the adventurous aspects of being a sailor. Ironically, I envied his skills of carpentry and his ability to build boats. In fact, ever since childhood I envied his family and the many encouragements they gave him, including piano lessons and his apprenticeship arranged by his father, himself a senior shipwright in the Royal Navy Dockyard at Portsmouth. Working skillfully with his hands had always been Stan's talent. His early grasp of Jazz improvisation on the keyboard was another envied aspect he showed me on frequent visits to his nearby house when we were kids.

So, there we were, waiting at the bus station when he nudged my arm and in a low voice urged me to, "Take a look at the two girls in that queue over there!" And added, "They're looking at us." I took a look and replied, "Yeah, so what?" "Well, why don't you go and speak to them," he nudged again. "Stan, for God's sake! If you like what you see, why don't you speak to them?" "Aw, you know I'm no good with that stuff! You go and give 'em the old charm, Ken!" His excitement was obvious and he added, "Boy, I really like the redhead!"

Leaving the queue and the amused eyes of onlookers behind, I strolled over to two giggling young girls who obviously had understood our attentions. "Hi, girls!" I said without palaver. Then addressing the redhead, "My friend over there is too shy to tell you that he is gaga over you. So, I thought I'd better come over and ask if you'd like to take a later bus so we could all calm him down," I said with a smile meant to charm away all anxieties or doubts. They looked at each other, burst into laughter and Redhead said, "Oh, well, yes! We were wondering if we should catch a later bus, anyway!"

By this time, Stan had gotten the picture and had sidled shyly over and stood like a schoolboy awaiting invitation. "Stan, this is Joan and this is Pauline," I said, smiling directly at Joan and taking her arm, I walked off with her, leaving Stan and Pauline paired.

We spent a carefree couple of hours in Poole, even renting a small skiff and sailing on the inland waterway for several hours. Stan got on well with the blonde and I was having fun kidding the redhead, who turned out to be a little foxy. We four spent a couple of happy hours that afternoon and again the next day before the two girls had to return from their holiday to their homes in Chesterfield in Derbyshire. In those days it didn't take a whole lot to have fun, given the times and uncertainty of tomorrow.

But that was eleven months previous in the early summer. It was now May of the following year, 1945, and I was looking at Joan's address on a small piece of paper I kept folded in my wallet all these months: "3 Coronation Terrace, Calow, near Chesterfield" was written in her small neat hand.

That's where I was headed according to the railway pass for my five-day leave! I had been invited to visit Joan in Derbyshire should the opportunity ever occur. I was now taking her at her word! As I settled in the train compartment at Edinburgh's Waverly Station, I was anticipating not so much the overnight journey, since I would be arriving at 5am, but rather in the arrival at a place not familiar, a part of northern central England completely foreign to me. I settled down in the smoke-reeking compartment with other soldiers and sailors all intent on getting some kip (sleep) while on the long journey to their destinations.

In 1944 crowded, smoke-filled train compartments, huddled servicemen attempting sleep while squeezed in minimal space was a common sight, with heads lolling in every which way as the train swayed and jerked and puffed and belched its smoke and steam hour after hour through the cold wet night. I awoke with a start as the train shuddered to a halt, breaks screeching, and a voice vaguely distant shouting: "Chesterfield… all out for Chesterfield!"

I stumbled out into the damp, chilly darkness of a five o'clock morning onto Chesterfield's station platform, shivering as the train huffed and puffed its steamy smoking way out of the station, its red lights disappearing down the track. The stationmaster was opening a door to his warm office as I reached him, "Can you tell me how I get to Calow?" I asked. He put down the lamp inside the office door, before turning around in the yellow light streaming from the single bulb hanging from the ceiling.

"Kai low," he said. "Thee wants t' get to Kai low?"

"Yes, Is there a taxi? Or a bus I can take?"

"Thee'll nah be gettin' a taxi or a bus this early," he said.

"Well, could you direct me how to get there?" I asked. "How far is it walking?"

"It'll be a fair walk or more. Ye' go own 'ill from station, turn riy'at an' go a past a mile past yon' graveyard an' turn left onta Chesterfield Rood, an' keep going 'bout eight mile 'til you coom t' row o' miners' cottages 'jus' past crossroads. That'll be Kai low. An' good morning t'ya."

He moved inside the doorway and, closing both the door and our conversation, left me to face the early morning drizzle and his "far walk to Kai low."

As I walked down the hill from the station turning up my raincoat collar, with the cold drizzle hitting my face, it struck me as being rather like an Alec Guinness movie where the main character (me) has found himself in a strange environment due to his own inept choices, ill-equipped to deal with it. At the same time I had a sense of adventure, the unknown ahead, with possibly new experiences and new consequences.

I began to whistle and found myself walking past the wet, musty, glistening dampness of the local cemetery with its gray concrete and marble headstones, crypts, and winged statuary, dimly throwing less-obvious shadows and shapes from the yellow light of the street lamps along the way. I quite involuntarily quickened my pace, the whistling perceptibly louder.

As I turned onto the Chesterfield Road, I felt my spirits rising. I've always had good feelings when on a journey. Wanderlust, they used to call it: the journey, not the destination. But, in this case, I looked forward to the destination, especially since I was now cold, damp, and hungry. But, again, like the movie character, naive, trusting and perhaps full of illusions.

Mile upon mile I trudged, wondering what the hell I was doing tramping in the middle of Derbyshire? But, the unknown was exhilarating! I arrived eventually at about seven in the morning, at "row o' miners' cottages," as the stationmaster had cryptically described them. The red-bricked cottages were set back from the road on one side, with small front-gated gardens. Across from the cottages was a small shop-fronted building and further along on the same side was larger building with a signpost in front indicating it was the White Hart, a pub.

I was surprised to see a pub opposite the isolated miners' cottages, but then I realized there were numerous farms and scattered villages around that contributed to the pub's income! I learned later in my random readings that there were considered to be 75,000 pubs in England! So, Calow was as good a place as any for a pub. Little did I know that a pub, though not this one, would prove to shorten my stay at Calow!

I found a row of four cottages called "Coronation Terrace," which was part of the address I'd been given by Joan at the end of her holiday with Pauline in Bournemouth those months ago. *Number 3, my lucky number,* I thought. *Good!* I looked at my watch, ten after seven, *I wonder if they're up yet?* I raised the knocker and rapped on the door which was almost immediately opened by an anxious looking, middle-aged woman wiping her hands on her apron. "Are you Ken?" she smiled shyly. "Yes! I am. Hope I'm not too early?" *A stupid question,* I thought. The bloody train arrived when it had. Not much I could do about it! "No, of course not. Come in."

She was warm and hospitable, I discovered, as were most all the people I came into contact with during that time and in that part of England. Her husband, Mr. Barlow, a miner, was a different matter. He came in from the back of the house where he had removed his boots at the back door and washed the coal-dust off his hands and face before coming into the living room, where he now stood facing the fire, rubbing his cold hands as he looked me up and down.

"So, you're the young man my daughter's been talking aba'at these months?" His face was inscrutable; his voice, however, suggested that he was unimpressed. He reinforced my impression, "I suppose you Navy types find it easy t' charm young innocent girls?" I wasn't sure how to reply without being flippant, sensing that I'd better tread easily here. "Speaking for myself, sir (I thought, *deference might be wise here*) I don't get much chance to be charming since I'm on active duty on convoys much of the time."

"Oh, so 'yer a real sailor. Not one o' them 'as never been on bloody ferry, never mind ship!" he said with an attempt at irony, though he had an edge that boded resentment.

After a brief hug by Joan when her father's back was turned, I was finally shown to my room upstairs by Joan's mother. About eleven o'clock I was sitting at the kitchen table drinking a second cup of tea, Mr. Barlow having retired to take a nap since he had worked the night shift and was now off for twenty-four hours, when the sound of a motorcycle revving at the front caught Joan and her mother's attention. They rushed to the door and greeted someone with delight.

"What are you doing here, Bruce?" I heard Joan say. The answer was muffled by laughter and excited mixed voices. Into the kitchen they came, Joan and her Mom, followed by a young smiling red-haired guy in Air Force blue who was introduced as, "My brother, Bruce, who's got twenty four hour's leave from his base! Isn't that great?" "This is Ken, that I've told you about." We shook hands and I, for one, wished I had a beer in front of me and that we were in a pub, maybe where we could talk more man-to-man, as it were. As if to read my thoughts, Bruce asked, "Where's Dad?" and, on being told of his father's nap, proposed, "Why don't Ken and I go for a beer and get to know one another?"

We were soon mounted on the bike, a BSA, and roared off in the direction of Chesterfield, adventure and future consequences! We parked the motorcycle outside a pub that seemed rather noisy and boisterous for noontime. We were greeted with such loud cheers and jollity that for a moment I was quite puzzled, until Bruce shouted in my ear, "The war in Europe is over! Everyone's gone crazy!"

My excitement surged, and everyone had such smiles, glows of relief, and sheer joy! It's over! Of course being in uniform at that time we were the objects of jubilation and pride. Pushing our way past slaps on the back, hugs from some, singing from some, and smiling, laughing happiness radiating from every face, we were already feeling the beer when we squeezed into a space on a back bench between two good looking girls who moved to make room.

Keep in mind that I was a sailor in Derbyshire, smack in the middle of England, landlocked you might say! My reception in that bar was way beyond my wildest dreams and certainly not deserved or merited. But I, along with Bruce, was by happenstance a symbol of our victorious servicemen, those who could not be there. So, there we were being feted as the heroes we were not, but getting more and more into the spirit of it!

It was May 8th, and news had reached Chesterfield that Eisenhower received Germany's unconditional surrender from Doenitz who, prior to Hitler's suicide, had been appointed President for the last week leading to the surrender.

The sheer joy and release of emotions that took place cannot be really captured in words. The consequences of peace were not any more considered than those of yesterday's war. All that mattered was surrendering to the joy of having survived and of temporarily being the "victors." Perhaps, in some way we were aware how death had suddenly had been replaced with "life." How hollow that "victory" might be was for us to find out later.

The party was on! What a wild day it became. Bruce and I were plied with an endless supply of beer and the pub, which would have ordinarily closed at 2pm, stayed open, as the owner declared, "Bugger the law! We'll not be closin' on this bloody day, I'll tell thee! Drink 'oop, lads! There'll allus' be an England! I'll tell 'ee! By goom!" So we did drink-up, and sing-up, and laugh-up. Time had no clock.

It was past 1am on the following morning when Bruce and I somehow found our way to the bike and managed to climb on and wobble down the road. We were in no state to think of possible consequences of one war ending and another beginning! Clinging onto that back seat was a full-time job! And I don't remember anything about the ride home except Bruce mumbling, "The old man'll be doing his nut about this." I was past caring about anything but hanging on for dear life!

Calow was not particularly attractive at seven in the morning, and it was even less so at 2am on a bitterly cold night. May it might have been but it felt like November! We pushed open the gate and staggered to the door where Bruce announced in a hoarse whisper, "The bloody door's locked!" I gazed at him uncomprehendingly.

Suddenly, a latticed window above squealed open and a harsh voice asked, "Is that you, Bruce? "Yes, Dad. The door's locked. We can't get in." "Is that bloody Ken with you? You can tell 'im 'ees bloody-well out a' house in t' mornin'! That's a fact!" With that solemn pronouncement the window closed, followed by the door bolts being withdrawn after a few moments, and footsteps retreating upstairs again.

"Christ. I'm sorry, Ken!" mumbled Bruce, as we stumbled in. "Tha's alright, Bruce, old mate! Not your fault! It was bloody good fun, though, ol' mate!" I mumbled with effort, "Goo' night!" We shook hands grinning and finally stumbled up to sleep and temporary oblivion.

The next morning, after a surprisingly good sleep and minimal hangover, at least considering the longevity of the "celebrations," after shaving, brushing up, and packing my one small suitcase, I came downstairs into a morgue-quiet living room and a cool reception. Bruce had gone already, back to base I supposed, and his father had gone thankfully to his shift at the mine. Joan had come briefly into my room upstairs to tell me that she understood. "I knew when you went off with Bruce there'd be trouble. But I'm sorry about Dad. There's nothing I can do." After thanking her and apologizing for my thoughtlessness, we hugged and she went with tears in her eyes to her room.

Joan's mom came out of the kitchen, her eyes were damp and she wiped them with a corner of her apron. "I'm so sorry things turned out this way, Ken." I reached for her hand, but then, impulsively, hugged her. "I'm sorry if I caused you or Joan trouble. Thanks for inviting me." I turned and picked up my case and as the door shut behind me I felt a brief sense of remorse. But as I walked to the bus stop, I began to feel a sense of escape, a feeling of lightness and freedom as if I had freed some restraints of some kind! I actually began to whistle as I made for the bus stop I'd noticed at the end of the terrace.

The small almost empty green bus had only a couple of passengers other than myself as I swung onto the step, "Do you go to Chesterfield?" I asked the driver. "Oh, aye," he said, as I fumbled for change. Sitting there in that little bus I began to wonder what I was going to do with the three days I had left of my five-day leave. I'd no idea that things could change so abruptly, I thought, as I sat there while the bus made its way through that still-damp countryside I'd only recently walked on my way to Calow.

I had no clear idea of what to do next. Feeling in my jacket pocket for my return railway pass, I felt a crushed cigarette box, and wondered how did this get there? I don't smoke! Pulling it out, a faint recollection came back! Last night! Margaret! A faint whiff of perfume reinforced my memory as I pushed the empty tray out of its sleeve, turned it over and there it was! Scrawled in lipstick pencil an address in Worksop, another village a few miles outside Chesterfield!

I got up and walked to a seat nearer the driver just as we were swinging into the bus station. "Can I get a bus to Worksop?" "Oh, aye. I'll give ye a transfer! It's number 3 over there," he added, "You'd 'ave 'eard bloody war's over fer us then?" "Yes, I heard it yesterday," remembering the party! "But there's still the Japs!" I reminded him, but getting his drift, I reassured him, "No more bombing, at least." I waved to him over my shoulder as I stepped down off the bus, thinking, this will change things!

I didn't have time to contemplate further as I sat in number 3, having given the driver the transfer and told him to let me know when he was coming to Elmwood Hill stop near Worksop. Talk about fast acts and quick changes! What was I going to say when I unexpectedly appeared on the doorstep of Margaret's house after I only just met her and spent an evening in her company at the V Day celebrations at the Golden Fleece in Chesterfield?

Well, the War was just over, and this was an "emergency" of sorts and sailors, particularly in landlocked Derbyshire, were not only a rare sight, but fondly thought of as "our Navy boys fighting not only the raging seas but those blasted Germans and their U-boats!" So, mindful of these circumstances, along with a certain sense of being in a Hollywood-style plot as my compass, I headed once again for the unknown.

I dropped off bus number 3 and stood about halfway up Elmwood hill and looked over at a cluster of houses lining a semi-circle on the opposite side. Elmwood Circle, I surmised. How neat and logical! Checking the lucky lipstick address, I looked for number 36. Wow! Threes again! Twelve of 'em. An omen? I took a deep breath and breezed up to the front door as if I owned the place and pressed the bell button and stepped back.

The door was opened by a plump, pleasant, pink-cheeked middle-aged woman, wiping her hands on her flour-dusted blue apron. "Is Margaret in?" I asked, smiling to reassure her. She paused for a moment, and then called over her shoulder, "Margaret! There's a young ma... sailor asking for you!" I realized the intrusion and mumbled a half apology, "Sorry, I couldn't call to tell you I was coming!" (That old ruse!)

She stepped aside, and out of the doorway came Margaret, flushed and excited, as though she was expecting me! I found myself willingly embraced as we came mutually together, her perfume remembered. "I've been thrown-out!" I whispered in her ear quickly. "Need to stay here!" It did seem right out of a Hollywood movie now, as I look back on it.

Which, given the times, the emotional impact of war, the meetings, the partings, disruptions, uncertainties and the destruction and violence and losses, the impact of those movies on our juvenile naiveté, perceptions and psyches, was probably greater than it might or should have been. For me personally, the names, *Bogart, Stewart, Taylor, Niven, Mills, Rooney, Garland, Grable, Hayward, Hayworth, Hepburn, Vivienne Leigh and Elizabeth Taylor et al*, were of people that I "knew:" real people whose screen lives I had absorbed as part of my own, as I'm sure in those days many did as an escape from the bleak and unpromising lives we were living.

So, in those fleeting moments of "make-believe" (*scene 2, take one!*) when Margaret and I embraced after having met each other only hours before in a wild party atmosphere during the "V-Day" celebrations at the Golden Fleece, it followed according to the "script," that "anything" could happen, especially if we two young actors could make it happen! In the event, it all unfolded according to script!

I was taken in and embraced happily as a welcomed guest, and one real live brave sailor, to boot! There was no spare bedroom in Margaret's home so I was cheerfully bustled down the garden path to a gate that opened onto a neighbor's garden. "Our good friend, Sally Green, has a spare bedroom that you can use!"

The ease and simplicity with which these arrangements were made could only be understood by one who lived in those times and in those wartime circumstances among such warm openhearted people. Even now I can recall the warm feeling of not only acceptance but also of goodwill.

Especially now, from the rather more cynical, harsher, more jaded views of 2016 with its Terrorist Alerts, and families far-flung across America; where the emergence of a car from a garage is perhaps the only sign that people actually live next-door, and where "Thanksgiving" is a frenzy of going and coming as families unite to commemorate the death of a turkey!

But, back to the set, Scene 3: the new arrival meets the father.

"Would you like a cup of tea?" Mrs. Mason asked me. Before I could reply, Mr. Mason, a short, stocky genial man with a seamed and weathered face, waved his hand in a gesture of objection as he insisted that, "Now, Mother, young Ken and I are going t' club, t' meet brothers and likely 'ave a pint to celebrate!" He continued, "We men will be back fer Sunday dinner..." he pulled his vest-pocket watch out and, flipping the lid, peered at the numerals and, snapping the lid shut, concluded, "at two pee-em!"

I could not believe my good fortune! Not an hour or so ago, I'd been thrown out of one house by an irate father who was the very epitome of Scrooge himself and here I was being fully embraced not only by a warm, loving daughter, but also by her mother and her father, who at that moment was all a father could be to a poor thirsty sailor seeking a safe berth for a short voyage! I said to myself, *Thank you, God! And the Golden Fleece!* Not then knowing of Jason or the Myths but sensing something good was in the stars for me at that time.

As we came along the road from the Worksop Labor and Social Workingmen's Club, we were singing, arm-in-arm... "We'll keep the red flag flying high!" I suppose in those days singing a Communist rallying song was not out of mode but quite natural since "we were all brothers" as the members at the club called each other, and me, too! Phrases like, "Working men of all countries, unite!" and "United we stand, Divided we fall!" were uttered sporadically after gulping back a beer or two.

But on the whole, most of what was uttered by these hard-working, long-suffering but friendly men was not hardline communism but half-hearted socialism born out of a need to have some power over their lives and the conditions in the mines. Perhaps they sensed power in unity, and in fellowship they found a compensatory comfort in knowing the equality of hardship, labor and need for all, a better tomorrow.

The recent fact that Russia had been an Ally whose losses and suffering by far exceeded those of England and America was also a contributing factor of influence among these coal miners in England.

The recent Great Depression and its consequential unemployment and near starvation loomed as a shadow on these men's minds. All this I now know. But then, my younger, more naive mind was existentially in the now. I was enjoying this latest experience of good fortune and camaraderie among these tough, rough and hardworking Derbyshire miners who welcomed a young sailor as their own.

Sitting at the table that Sunday afternoon, sharing roast beef in brown Bisto gravy and Yorkshire pudding, with succulent brown roast potatoes and fresh green Brussels sprouts followed by some apple pie and hot custard, I could be forgiven for having no sense of guilt or regret over recent happenings. How the Masons managed to get such a generous joint of beef in a time of scarcity and food rationing was beyond my understanding.

I compared that meal with the spam sandwich and tepid cocoa that I made do with on those Russian convoys, when the fresh meat and vegetables ran out and the weather made the galley virtually untenable owing to the violence of the seas. At that moment, I truly appreciated that the War was over. I understood my good fortune and how life could be good once again. I was rejuvenated, and shared my gratitude later with Margaret.

I found myself going on my last journey to Norway in World War II, but not on aircraft carriers with planes fully armed and bomb loads to destroy airfields or installations as we had in the past.

This journey was to take the surrender of Trondheim's submarine pens and its submarines that contained them and the military installations and armaments.

During that week, I undertook a trip of unofficial English diplomacy by taking food (such as it was) to a family I had been introduced by chance. It was a symbolic gesture made impulsively when I saw their plight.

Strangely, inside myself, I had a deep empathy to the Harrelsons, possibly because of my own name, Harrison, and our common heritage. However, there was a bond between us that was beyond words.

KHH

A NORWEGIAN FAMILY FAREWELL

Three days later when I returned to the ship which was docked in Rosyth, on the Firth of Forth, where I had five days before begun my journey by way of Edinburgh to Derbyshire, I knew in my heart everything was going to change now. When I had started my five-day-leave, the war was still on: month after month of often dreary and sometimes dangerous moments up in the Norwegian and Arctic seas, escorting convoys, attacking U-boats, or accompanying carriers and battleships off the Norwegian coast to attack German airfields, ships, installations.

Finally, the biggest most powerful battleship, the *Tirpitz*, the one remaining, most powerful German battleship hiding in a fjord near Tromso, was sunk by Royal Air Force bombers, dropping a huge "tall boy" bomb on her, after the Navy had spent countless sorties from aircraft carriers over two years in efforts to sink her hiding in the Norwegian fiords.

I had every expectation of more of the same when I returned from that brief fling. But as it happened, I returned knowing the war in Europe had been declared over. The Germans had surrendered, Hitler was dead, and the future lay ahead, filled with new opportunities and anticipation. Little of this was occupying my twenty-one-year-old head. At this time, there wasn't much in it. Day-to-day survival without much independent choice had been the order of things for the last five years. Until I would be demobilized sometime in the future, routines would not change drastically. But they did!

One last assignment was given us in the complicated process of showing the flag, so to speak, in all the various ports of now liberated Europe, but especially in the previously German fortified U-boat ports along the Norwegian coast. *HMS Berwick* duly found her way on May 6th across the North Sea to Trondheim to accept the turnover of the port and all the submarines stationed there. Other ships were designated to do the same at the ports at Tromso and Bergen, in fact all the major ports of Norway and the rest of the northern European coast.

As we sailed up the fjord leading to the Trondheim harbor, the sheer height of the steep sides of the fjord dwarfed our ten thousand ton cruiser, and awed me, too! I noticed the huge concrete shelters for the U-boats that had been cut into the side of the fjord near the docks and I now understood how difficult it had been for our carrier planes to successfully bomb or sink U-boats berthed in them! I had been on several operations on the *Berwick* escorting carrier aircraft designed to do just that. Now I was there, I could see those raids were largely futile.

Now however, I was more interested in Anglo-Norwegian relations. I went ashore as often as was granted during the six days, sometimes merely to walk and "gawk" in Derbyshire! During our stay there I did have a brief but unforgettable encounter with a Norwegian family, the Harrelsons, which, as you will read, remained impressed in my memory these long years.

I was wandering around the town bent on finding the local Post Office to get a stamp souvenir, so I asked a young teenaged girl if she spoke English. In English with, of course, the slight accent that one might expect, "Ya' I speak Anglish!" "Could you direct me to a post-office?" I asked her. "I vill tak yo to it, yes?" I smiled and nodded, "Would you?

Thanks." And off we went, up the cobbled streets, around a corner, and there it was, and in Ingrid and I went.

After visiting the post office and obtaining a couple of souvenir stamps, we stood outside and, for the first time, I noticed how thin Ingrid appeared. We had exchanged names and noticed how similar our surnames sounded, at least that was the feeble attempt to extend our conversation!

"Harrison and Harrelson!" I exclaimed, "You know my ancestors could have been Norse or perhaps Vikings, since 'Harri' and' Harrel' are possibly from the same or similar origin!"

Of course it was glib, and merely a stab at extending her stay by continuing the conversation. Well, five minutes later I was invited to walk further up the mountain to meet her family who, she assured me, "Vould be most interested to meet an Anglish sailor from the cruiser which everyone vas excited about. Ve most admire your Navy all through the war." What could I do but respond to such praise and acceptance by our Norwegian admirers? Echoes of the Golden Fleece and Chesterfield? Who knew? Follow the flow.

We walked and, in my case with considerable effort, up the considerable slope of the mountain upon which much of Trondheim sprawled up from the fjord. Ten minutes later we arrived at a white, wooden-framed, two-storied house set back just off the winding road with several other houses clustered here and there among the pine trees. As I looked back and down at the harbor below the city, I could quite clearly see the ship, though it appeared dwarfed and puny from this height. Rather like a toy, I thought. Not any longer what she really was. I hadn't realized how high up we'd come. I was introduced to Ingrid's parents who, surprisingly, also spoke English, and in an animated conversation I learned much about their feelings toward the recently departed German occupancy, the relief at seeing the British cruiser arrive so quickly after hearing of the German surrender, and of their joy at realizing that a renewed life ahead now was a reality when so short a time before they were in despair that they would ever be free again.

I also learned of the hunger for food and how the Germans rationed the civilians so severely that ulcers developed in the mouth and on the tongue. The food produced by Norwegian farmers and fishermen was co-opted for German troops and thus little was distributed to the civilian populace. I resolved to do what I could to lift their spirits and bring some food, even though I didn't yet know what or how.

In spite of all the hardships and scarcity, the Harrelsons insisted on making a pot of tea and offering some black bread, which upon my assurance that I was not hungry, was placed carefully back in its tin.

Our conversation was surprisingly warm and good humored. They even ribbed me about being only an English "lately," as they put it, and went on to say that if I pursued my genealogy I'd probably find a Viking in my family tree! Once again, in company of strangers I felt a kindred warmth beyond logic or reality. On leaving, with urgings to "please come again before you leave!" I resolved to do so if it was at all possible.

Back at the ship I realized that we, too, were rationed and food was scarce, in fact, it was very difficult to obtain even a piece of extra bread between mess issue for each meal. During sea-going duty, about all that could be expected on a cold, wet night on watch was a cup of cocoa.

Our "meals" were commonly stews of unknown origin: steamed dishes of odd pieces of lamb or beef with dehydrated vegetables under a thick cover of soggy pudding-like-pastry which often had puddles of hot water on the grease paper "covering" the contents, as the dishes were taken out of the huge steamers used to cook (steam) our food. These meals were collected by the rating designated as mess "cook" for that day, and carried to his particular mess-deck for serving onto plates. If your mess was at some considerable distance from the galley, which often it was, the amorphous conglomeration that arrived on our plates was without recognizable shape or definable flavor!

However, when compared to the Norwegians and others under German occupation, we were better fed and in better condition. So, I scrounged around the canteen where I was the "assistant manager" and was able to put together some chocolate bars, cigarettes, and cookies, to which was added a couple of items donated by the mess cook!

When I left the ship the next day to revisit the Harrelsons, I had sundry items distributed all over my person so as to avoid an unusual bulge in my uniform or to be seen carrying a package, which would not pass muster at the routine pre-going-ashore inspection before leaving the ship. One item in particular, a pound or so of cheese, began to exude an odor not commonly associated with aftershave or deodorant, and I got several critical looks from those closest to me in the inspection line!

I retraced my way to the post office, and from there remembered the general direction up the road to the cluster of houses that included the two-storied white house of the Harrelsons. The door was opened almost immediately: they had been waiting eagerly for my return visit, though I had not specified a time. I stood at the table in the somewhat barely furnished room and began, like a conjuror, I thought, plucking objects of wonder and delight seemingly from thin air but actually from various pockets in my jacket and blue raincoat: two tins of sardines, two half-pound bars of Cadbury's fruit and nut chocolate, two one pound packets of tea, and a half-pound packet of McVitie's Digestive biscuits. In the retrieval of the carton of Players cigarettes and the block of cheese which I had tied on opposite sides of a length of cord and hung around my neck so they fitted roughly under my arm-pits (thus, covered by my raincoat, though lumpy, they were hardly discernable to the casual eye), I felt like a clumsy horse, being un-harnessed!

Throughout my "magic production," the Harrelsons were alternately giggling, clapping their hands like delighted children discovering gifts at Christmas, and sobbing as they held first each other and then, when I had divested myself of overcoat and contents, encircling their arms around me in a silent but emotional embrace.

An epiphany, beyond words. I recall that moment when, sixty-eight years ago, I stood embraced by three virtual strangers, experiencing a shared moment of childlike joy and humbling gratitude. It was a moment that one might have experienced in a church, when hearing words beyond utterance and the holy silence. I sensed an acceptance of myself. I was no longer a "Catholic," but a quiet wet-cheeked joy released now from communal hugs.

The family bustled around, helping with laying cups and saucers, plates, dishes and cutlery on the scarred wooden table which had now been transformed into a feast, or a communion, by their best white lace table-cloth, "We only use it for Easter and Christmas!" they explained with smiles and, in the case of Ingrid, a giggle, as if sharing some little joke.

"Sit you down, Ken." Mr. Harrelson gestured towards one of the chairs at the end of the table. "Yo' are the guest 'ov 'onor." God, I'd never been called that, certainly not at the Barlow's house, or even at the Mason's, though I did feel welcomed there.

The sardine can was opened and one sardine placed singly on small wedges of dark rye bread, sliced from a part loaf produced by Ingrid's mother, and thin small slices from the cheese block, placed on crackers which I had provided. The preparation of each item was done with reverence as if laying out the bread and wine for the Eucharist.

We sat for a long minute holding hands around the table, no one venturing to say a word. At that moment I certainly could not have produced appropriate words. I'd been too long absent as a refugee from the Catholic Church to have grace come easily from my mouth, and the absence of such spiritual influences from the daily routines of seeking, finding, and then destroying German U-Boats and their crews; surviving consequences were such that silence was most appropriate at that moment and place. But the unstated blessing was as palpable as the food we ate that day. And from the looks and appreciative sounds being made, you'd have thought it was Christmas!

The fact that I had reached my twenty-first birth-date only a week or so before this incident added relevance to my personal enjoyment of the occasion! My only previous celebration or acknowledgement of becoming twenty-one was being offered a sip of rum from the tot issued to several of my fellow petty officers in the mess, which was the traditional way of "celebrating" such an occasion, but hardly "a party!"

The time came to leave. Saying goodbye to that family so recently met, still emerging from the hardship and suffering under German occupation, and yet so warm and accepting of me, was difficult to do. Of course, I was quite vulnerable since I had no family of my own. Everyone embraced me, and the smiles lit up their thin faces, and as we bid our farewells, Mrs. Harrelson embraced me and said, "We will wave a sheet from the bedroom, when yor ship leaves!"

The next morning as I stood in line up on the foredeck as preparation for leaving harbor, I managed to be in position to look left and up high on the mountain to the vicinity where I supposed the Harrelson's house would be, up on the side of the fjord and, low and behold, two very white "flags" (that I knew were sheets from their beds!) could be seen waving from the upper windows. I nudged the arm next to me and out of the side of my mouth urged him to, "Look up there! See the white "flags" waving us out!"

That scene, an epiphany of sorts, has stayed with me for all my years of accumulated memories: a sign that German occupation and subsequent hardships had not erased the spirit of Norwegian kindness and sense of connectedness with those who for so long fought to free them and ourselves from the boot of the oppressor.

I hardly noticed the huge concrete bomb-proof U-Boat pens, or the many submarines now lying silent, harmless, and secured at moorings waiting their final disposal or destination, as we slid out of the harbor and down the fjord, on our way out to the sea and home to England.

There was both the sense of an end to what had been and a stirring of hope for what might be now possible. My communion with the Harrelsons by chance was another reminder of God's grace.

A HASTY DECISION, QUICKLY REGRETTED

I must confess it was a case of physical attraction at the onset. My libido was running strong, but my budding intelligence had not mastered it. Looking back now, I can see that the decision was not only hasty, but also not a good one. As time passed, the combination of my naiveté coupled with the later circumstances of my employment, and her willful selfishness and lack of integrity was not a firm foundation upon which to build trust, and certainly not a marriage as it turned out.

KHH.

A HASTY DECISION, QUICKLY REGRETTED

I met my first wife, Dorothy, in Portsmouth in February, 1946, while stationed on the old *Queen Elizabeth*, a 1920s battleship tied up to the dock at HMS Vernon, a shore base where submariners generally billeted and assembled as crews before being sent over to the submarine base on the Gosport side of Portsmouth harbor.

I was temporarily stationed there, waiting to be demobilized from the Navy, after being in active service since November of 1941.

I was introduced to Dorothy Hands by a friend in Portsmouth in November 1945. I was a 21 year old Petty Officer recently transferred from the heavy cruiser, *HMS Berwick*, to *HMS Queen Elizabeth* (an irony since I was fated to be a steward on the famous liner, *RMS Queen Elizabeth* on her post-war maiden voyage!), waiting for my demobilization papers from the Navy while running the canteen on board that old battlewagon, firmly secured to the dockside.

I was free to go ashore after 4pm each day and thus began my brief courtship of Dorothy, who lived with her younger sister and their mother, a widow, originally from Birmingham. I was quickly attracted to her as she was an exotic, beautiful girl with a lithe, shapely figure that caught my eye immediately!

I must confess it probably was a case of physical attraction at the onset. My libido was running strong, but my budding intelligence had not yet mastered it! It didn't take long for us to get serious and marriage quickly followed in a simple civil ceremony with Pat and Don Pink as witness and best man. I've often wondered if that quick, impetuous pairing would have taken place had I a family to give me a second opinion! In the event, I had acted hastily, and my decision would be regretted not long in the future.

Looking back now, I can see that the decision was not only hasty, but also not a good one. As time passed the combination of my naiveté, coupled with the later circumstances of my employment, and her willful selfishness and lack of integrity, was not a firm foundation upon which to build trust, and certainly not a marriage, as it turned out.

It seemed fine while we were together but later when I got a very lucrative job (particularly so in those early post-war days) as a first-class steward on board the *RMS Queen Elizabeth*, with my enforced absences, things came apart.

She found that being married to a husband who was away for ten days at a time with only one overnight visit every nine or ten days was not for her. One time when I was in Southampton on a one-day turn-around, I came home to find no Dorothy and no note or message. She did not arrive by the time I went to bed. Next morning I had to report to the ship at 8am, since we scheduled to leave for New York at 12 noon. I was obviously dwelling on Dorothy's absence as I went down to my cabin in my uniform with my suitcase, when I actually left the QE on the spur of the moment. Since I had received no word from or about her, I let my emotions get the better of me and, after cramming my clothes into the suitcase, I pushed my way down the gangway as the last of the stragglers were pushing their way up! This decision, though well intentioned, was motivated by panic, not calm reason, and it would remain as an indelible question mark on my record in the future.

She arrived on the Monday and after a confrontation, admitted she had been with her mother in Portsmouth, and "forgot" my arrival. I promised to get a job so that we could be a normal couple together. However, I was not satisfied with her lame memory loss. Later, *it all hit the fan* when facts were revealed.

In the event, I found a new construction of a big store, the first to be rebuilt after the bombing and fire raids, detailed in the Southampton news.

I actually did get a job in the May Company's new three-level department store, just being finished on the Southampton High Street. The building erected on the badly scarred, bombed-out high street was the first sign of post-war re-building of the ravaged, burned-out center of the city.

How I got the job was another lesson in self-confidence. I went to the site of the temporary personnel office, which was next to the almost-finished store. I walked up the steps of a mobile building used as the office and, as in the pre-war search for a job, did not give a second's thought to résumé or experience. As I came in the door and introduced myself to a receptionist at a nearby desk, I told her I'd come in answer to the advertisement in the local paper for experienced applicants.

Of course, I knew I was not "experienced," but she didn't, so I figured I could face the inevitable request for "experience?" when it came later, probably from her boss, I hoped. Youth, I found, was a spur to action before thinking!

Sure enough, five minutes later I was in the inner office, standing in front of a smartly dressed, tall, dignified woman in a tailored suit and the swept-up hair fashionable in those days. "Yes, Mr. Harrison," she noted on a piece of paper in front of her, slipped in front of her by the receptionist. "What can I do for you?" "I hope you can find a position in your new store for me," I said rather assertively, hoping that might spark interest in me. She raised an eyebrow, "Oh, are you experienced in retail?" she asked. *Well, here goes*, I thought. And what followed was a balancing act of the experience in the NAAFI: stock-keeping, pricing, display and service, balancing books and inventory and customer service, with avoidance of particulars, because it had only some relevance to her concern for experience in a high quality department store!

She cut to the issue by saying, do you know anything about "soft furnishings?" "Well," I hedged, "not actually," adding quickly, "but I am a quick learner and," I rushed on, "I can assure you that with my experience dealing with customers on a daily basis in all manner of situations and my quick learning capabilities, I know whatever job you give me, I will do it well." I equated verbosity with assurance in those days.

Even now, as I reflect on my temerity and the attempt to sell myself, rather than worry about the unknown problems, I can see that my experience with the American public on those trans-Atlantic runs had stood me well. I was not really Ken Harrison from Portsmouth; I was a brash young man from Hollywood!

She rose from her desk, patted her upswept coiffeur and smiled as she said, "You sure have the gift of the gab, and if you use that charm on my customers along with the quick learning I no doubt you *have*," she paused for a moment before finishing, "I'm sure that you will be an excellent salesperson! You have the job selling soft furnishings, and Mr. Skinner will be your supervisor. Report to him with your employment card on the second floor of the store Monday morning at 8:30 sharp." With that, she offered her hand, which I enthusiastically shook as I thanked her.

Leaving that office, I went for a quick half-pint of beer at the nearest pub, and toasted smart, well-coiffured personnel managers with a sense of humor! And, I might add also, to my good luck! At least in one respect, for my move ashore did not work out, and my having left the *Queen Elizabeth* hurriedly, just before sailing, would come to haunt me later.

Soft-furnishings were bolts of many materials such as silk, lace, damask, brocade, chintz and so on, sold by the yard, and, as I discovered, boring as hell compared to the hectic life on a cross Atlantic luxury liner. But as Fate would have it, or my luck changing for the better again, I was not long for May & Company and selling soft-furnishings!

One dull morning, while straightening up the shelves and tidying up the bolts, the sound of animated voices came floating up the broad staircase from the ground floor and into view came three young tanned smartly dressed men. I instantly recognized two as old shipmates and stewards from the *Queen Elizabeth* and as they saw me, smiles broke on their faces and the two, Fred Izod and John Chalmers, seeing me in my rather formal attire of dark blue suit with white shirt and wine colored tie, just about to trim the end of a bolt of chintz that was left slightly askew, broke into satirical mimicry of what they thought was someone they knew otherwise being "la-de-dah!" Fred, with his hand on his hip, minced over and, in a falsetto, said, "Young man, can you match the material in my slip?" as he pretended to pull up his skirt!" Frank dropped to his knees with his chin level with the counter, and in a little boys voice asked, "Can my mum 'ave a 'alf-a yard of lace fer the loo', please!"

I was looking over their shoulders for Mr. Skinner, expecting him to appear any minute. I was grinning, but inside I was uneasy. "Look you guys, do me a favor and calm it down! You'll get me sacked!" They grinned at each other at my obvious discomfort but lowered their voices as I walked them around the corner to the elevators.

"What are you up to, anyway?" In brief, they told me they were in Southampton for interviews for positions as stewards on a new cruising ship that had been built especially to cruise in the Caribbean out of New York.

She was called the *Ocean Monarch*, a small, one funneled, 13,000 ton beauty that today—with 80,000 to 100,000 ton monsters afloat, and the *Queen Mary 2* a gigantic 150,000 tons—would be considered a losing proposition by any steamship company in the business since she only carried 350 passengers! But that is now, and this was then, 1949, just four years since the war in Europe ended, and things only just beginning to get back to "normal," whatever that was. So Furness Lines were in a hurry to get back into the cruise business, and this small ship was a start!

My urge to join them began as a faint wish, but by the time they had finished, with happy faces and excited gestures, extolling the expected benefits of getting a job on that cruise ship, and all the fun they were already imagining and conjecturing as they reminded me that, "She's going to be based in New York as home port!" that wishful feeling had grown into a full-blown desire to be back on a ship, moving, traveling anywhere, the destination didn't matter, just to be at sea again! That pent-up desire had probably been suppressed all those months, since I had pushed my way down the gangplank to get ashore at Southampton with my suitcase under my arm, and still in uniform, even as my mates were all pushing to get on, five minutes from leaving harbor!

"I'll see you down at the Union office!" I told them over my shoulder, as I raced away to find Skinner and ask for an early lunch, which, since we obviously were not busy, he gave readily. Little did I know how long my "lunch" would last!

On the way to the Union office, down by the docks where the interviews were to be held, I had a few minutes to reflect on the situation and my impulsive actions. For one, I had not succeeded in really cementing my marriage relationship with Dorothy, my wife. Though we were on the surface amicable, something was lost. She seemed distant and still had taken every opportunity to go to Portsmouth, which was 21 miles away, to "see Mum," as she put it. I found later she was dance crazy, and it didn't take long for 2 and 2 to come up with 4! Fidelity was not in her character.

Another factor to be considered was my lack of financial reserves and the inability to save enough money to get our own place. We were renting, and the salary I received at May & Company was very much less than the money I was used to as a steward in First Class on the *Queen Elizabeth*. Although I was motivated to dash out to an early lunch, caught up in the talk about a new beautiful ship based in New York, I had no letter for Furness Lines and no appointment for an interview! Such was the lure of travel and adventure! It was like a fever!

As I got off the tram down by the docks and crossed the road to the side street where the Union office was, I noticed a crowd gathered down in the direction of the Union building. Several familiar faces were among them and some shouted out, "Hi, Ken, how's it go?" and similar remarks as

I shouldered my way through a milling mob pressing towards the Union steps! "What's going on?" I asked one of the familiar faces. "We're all having interviews for the *Ocean Monarch*," he said, breathing beer fumes all over me, though it was only just 12 noon. I could not believe my eyes! "There must be several hundred here! I thought there were only forty stewards being hired from Southampton?" "Yeah, but they'll be turning down a few of this lot!" He thumbed at a couple sitting on the steps with ale bottles in their hands.

As the minutes ticked away I glanced at my watch and realized my "lunch" hour was going fast and I was going nowhere slowly. I was in one of those rare moments in one's life when somehow events were unfolding almost without me. The great doors of the Union building were pressed open and a voice called, "Jenkins, Green and Hopkins!" I recognized the Union guy as Frank McCauley and at that precise moment, made two decisions that would change my life in ways I could not then imagine.

One was that I was going to follow my impetuous decision to its end, whatever the consequence, and two, I was determined to press on until I could be close enough to get Frank's attention. Not that he was a friend of mine, but he had always been friendly whenever we had crossed paths, and as I fingered my last one pound note in my pocket, I resolved to use any means to get Frank's ear, just for a moment. I was that sure without any reason to be so! But first, I had to buy more time.

I pushed my way to a public phone-box outside a pub nearby, and called Skinner. "I'm unavoidably detained, Mister Skinner. Could you please cover for me and I'll explain when I return as soon as I can? Thank you, sir!" A risky, irrevocable decision had been made.

But, surprisingly, I was now quite calm and content to let things work out. This kind of calm resolution has come upon me three or four times in my life and, perhaps if not real epiphanies, important junctures in my life, as they turned out.

As the crowd dwindled to perhaps sixty or seventy, I was in the front ready to make my move the next time Frank came to call out the names. "Taylor, Williams,"... and as he caught my eye... "Harrison!" I shook his hand, leaving my last pound note in it. "Hi, Frank, how's it with you?"

"Cor' Blimey, mate, it's a zoo!" he grinned, as he motioned to Taylor and Williams, "in there," pointing to a door.

He pulled me inside the great door of opportunity. Turning to me, he said, "You've got the letter?" "Frank, I couldn't find it (fibbed)! But please let me go in, anyway." He looked at me for a brief second, "Wait here," and disappeared behind another other door. I looked at my watch, which was barely discernable in that hallway, it being autumn in Southern England. My God, it was four o'clock! (I gave no thought to Mister Skinner or soft furnishings!)

Frank appeared, "Listen, Ken, I'm letting you go in, but I know nothing about the letter, OK?" He ushered me to a second door along the corridor, opened it and whispered in my ear, "Good Luck, mate!" I walked into the room, strode towards a figure in shirt-sleeves sitting silhouetted against dim winter light coming from a bay window behind the desk which had several stacks of letters and papers on it. The gray-haired figure continued to write and without looking up, he reached out his left hand and uttered one word. "Letter?" At that moment, I was in the hands of God.

"I never received one," I said. He looked up at me for the first time. He peered at me for a long second. "Seaman's Book?" He again reached out his left hand. I gave it to him with mixed feelings, glad that I had it on me (although when I think on it, why did I have it on me?), but apprehensive about that missing sign-off stamp reflecting my abrupt leaving of the *Queen Elizabeth* when Dorothy went missing. (The past is indelible.)

He flipped the pages over, "*Queen Elizabeth*, Good! Cabin Class, First Class, *Queen Mary*, First Class, good! Ah, *The Mauritania*! Cruising in the Caribbean. Very good!" He frowned suddenly, peering closely at an entry, and with his right finger pointing accusingly at the space, where the missing "sign-off" would have been stamped had I completed that particular *Queen Elizabeth* round trip, "What happened here?" (At that point I had my fingers crossed and a prayer whispering in my ear). Deep breath. I told him about my marital problem ending with, "So, I felt worried about my missing wife and was unable to sail without finding her. I was in a dilemma. Going out of my mind, so to speak. I suppose, with my worry about my wife, I lost my normal composure. I'm pretty controlled, normally." He lit a cigarette and inhaling deeply, he pursed his lips, blowing a stream of smoke up into the air. "How do I know you won't do it again?" "Because I am getting a divorce," I blurted out, as if pent-up and just waiting to be said. As I said it, I felt unburdened as though a weight had been taken away.

It wasn't pre-meditated but was said without hesitation. A *self-fulfilling prophecy*, as it turned out. He stared at me, once again letting out a blue-gray cloud that drifted up into the gloom, then suddenly he penned his signature onto a form in front of him and handed it to me, stood up smiling, and said, "Well, Good Luck! I know what you're going through, and I hope this will be an opportunity for you. You have a good name anyway!" I thanked him, and as we shook hands I was in a daze, not quite realizing my incredibly good fortune until I glanced at the signature on my employment form. It was "William Harrison!"

Another serendipity, another example of one of those special occasions of fate where you stumble into fortuitous circumstances that you could not have imagined and which allow what seemed very unlikely to become realized. I had several of these charmed incidents that proved to be important turning points in my life and its direction. I might not be rich, but I have been blessed quite a few times in my life. Individuals have appeared as "guides," or "angels" who gave me direction, and more.

NOTATION

At the end of the war, the *Queen Elizabeth* was six-years old and finally sailed from Southampton on 16th of October 1946, thus establishing a joint commercial service for the time. The thirties saw the advent of super-liners, but the most glamorous and commercially successful period was the decade that stretched from 1945 into the mid-fifties.

Of all the passenger liners operating the North Atlantic service, the *Queens* were not only impressive but from the beginning, they were popular and showed immense profits.

KHH

THE *QUEEN ELIZABETH*

After my attempt to join a rescue tug (that was supposed to be one of the strongest tugs at the time) I got to Swansea, after a short but tempestuous voyage from Glasgow in a rough sea that threw this small ship around like a cork.

Having experienced storms on the way to Russia and Murmansk just recently on a destroyer, I thought rough weather was old hat. But this small ex-Navy tugboat was, as I said, like a cork in the mountainous swells in the Irish Sea, bobbing up and down and sideways, even laying on her side in the huge waves, to where I feared we would ship the waves down the funnel! Even the ship's cat, even the skipper (a neophyte, by the way) were both sea-sick, as was every crewman during that trip!

When we limped into Swansea my idea of making a ton of money from salvage from this tin can melted away, and within a few hours I could not get quicker off this vessel and back to Southampton where I had left three days ago.

I found myself in a pub just a block from the Cunard White Star Line. I was looking out of one of the pub's windows and saw two tall towers in red with black bands around the tops. I realized I was looking at two funnels! I asked the bartender, "What ship is that?" pointing to the red and black funnels. "You're not from here, are you? That's the QE, the sister ship of the *Queen Mary*. She's getting ready to make her maiden voyage with passengers since she's been carrying troops through the war!"

I finished my pint, and thanked him. "Where are the Cunard offices?" He thumbed out the door and said, "Across the street at the end of this road, on the other side. You can't miss it. It's the biggest building on that street! Good luck, mate!"

My excitement was beginning to rise as I walked to the corner and crossed the other side and came to the imposing building. A sign above the main door informed me that I had indeed found the Cunard building. I entered and found another door with a clear glass view of a long counter and many desks behind it.

I went in and stood for a minute or two and no one asked me what I wanted. "Excuse me, could you direct me to the employment desk?" A bald man with a cigarette dangling from his lower lip came to the counter. "Do you have your union card?" he asked me. "No," I said, and added, "How do I get one?" He took his cigarette out of his mouth, looked at me with a smile and said, "You have to get a seamen's book before you can get a union card. Where are you from, Son?" I was puzzled for a moment.

"I'm from Portsmouth and I was demobbed from the Navy a couple of months ago," thinking that this information might be relevant. He smiled in a condescending way that a parent might, "So, you're a Navy boy? Look Son, I'm writing a name on this piece of paper, and you go to the Union Office down the road and give this note to the Union Officer and maybe he might give you a card. If you have a pound in your pocket and come back and if you're lucky, I might have a job for you." I thanked him and noticed his name on his desk, and ran out to the Union Office.

I arrived breathless at the Union Office and stood at a smaller counter with only two desks behind it. A small man with a moustache and in his shirtsleeves sat at one of the desks, with his coat draped on the back of his chair.

"What do you want, son?" "I want to join the union, sir. Mr. Williams at the Cunard office sent me here." He got up from his desk, and came to the counter. I offered him the note from Mr. Williams. He scanned the note and asked, "Do you have the fee for the union card?"

I fumbled in my pocket for my last pound note and offered it, but he said, "Not now! It's irregular, but as soon as you get the job, come back, with your quid, and join the union. OK?"

I raced back to the Cunard office, breathless, and Mr. Williams, just lighting a new fag, looked up and, with a smile, said, "You're back! You're in luck, son." He got up from his desk, puffing from his fag. "This is the last job left on the QE! Here, sign here," pointing to a line on a form. Before I could ask about the job, I scrawled my signature and he said, "You are the radio officers' steward, son!" He beamed, shook my hand and reminded me, "Go back to the Union office and get your Union card. Good luck, son!"

Well, I got the Union card, and I had a job on the QE, but when I reported on board to the Chief Steward, I realized I was the low man in the dining room. It took me half a trip to understand that the radio officers were not passengers with the money or the tips. Before I finished that trip I visited the Maître d' and told him my background and he was impressed enough to take my name and said if there was an opening in the dining room he would let me know. On the day we arrived in Southampton I was sent for by the Maître d': apparently one steward was leaving and he offered me a position in the First Class dining room. He said, "I'll keep an eye on you, and see how you perform." I thanked him for his confidence. What luck!

Everything was as I expected, and from then on I was in clover, as they say. The *Queen Elizabeth* was a beautiful ship. For five years during the world war she was stripped of her glamour and donned the dullness of camouflage to disguise her lines.

She was sailed away from England to New York but eventually finished in a dry dock in Singapore and sailed to Australia, where she was joined by the *Queen Mary*. Initially both ships carried Australian troops to Suez for the Middle East. Being the fastest ships with big capacity, the two *Queens* were picked as the obvious modes of transportation and took American troops quickly and efficiently to Australia.

As the demands rose for more and more troops as the war dragged on, both ships would eventually transport entire divisions, roughly 15,000 men. Special canvas bunk beds hung in tiers six at a time were erected wherever space permitted. A two bed-roomed stateroom could accommodate as many as forty soldiers at a time, and there were at least two shifts a night. Feeding the troops was a continual process throughout the day and involved consecutive shifts in the dining rooms.

It was quite remarkable that no one who traveled on the *Queens* during the war lost their lives. There was one tragic accident that serves to mar their otherwise impeccable war service record, which occurred off the coast of Ireland on a westbound crossing in October 1942. Travelling at top speed (28 knots plus) and fully laden, the *Queen Mary* rammed and split an escort cruiser in two, *HMS Curacao*. The warship was sunk in minutes and three hundred and fifty dead. A tragic occurrence made worse because of war and circumstances.

On another occasion later that year, the Germans claimed they had scored a direct hit on the *Queen Elizabeth*. It is true that several torpedoes were fired but fortunately none found its mark. So both huge ships survived the perils of war and were sent to John Brown's Shipyard for refurbishment.

Churchill acknowledged their valuable contribution when he said:

> *The world owes a debt to these great*
> *ships that will not be easy to measure.*
> *Vital decisions depended upon their*
> *ability to continuously elude the*
> *enemy, and without their aid the*
> *final day of victory must unquestionably*
> *have been postponed.*

For the *Queen Elizabeth*, this meant now, 1946, she was back to her dazzling self. The decor on the *Queen Elizabeth* varied greatly from her companion ship, the *Queen Mary*. Although a large quantity of wood was put to decorative use, the overall effect was much lighter and brighter. The most striking difference was the addition of two garden lounges situated on the promenade deck.

These beautiful new areas provided passengers with an "open air" effect while being protected from the unpredictable elements of the Atlantic. They were filled with an exotic array of foliage in addition to all the fresh flowers, which kept a full-time gardener busy. A large quantity of leather in the paneled walls and many brass and copper engravings and glass sculptures graced her public rooms.

The most striking individual decoration on the *Queen Elizabeth* was a huge marquetry panel depicting Chaucer's Canterbury pilgrims. The design incorporated seventy types of wood, many from England including a veneer taken from a Virginia creeper grown at Hampton Court Palace that was said to be 120 years old.

A great Trans-Atlantic map was situated in the First Class smoking room, showing the relative daily position. By the way, the first commercial trip from Southampton to New York was in October the 16th, 1946.

The two great liners passed for the fist time on the evening of 25th July 1947. Their paths crossing on the Atlantic within sight of each other was planned as a marketing ploy.

What could I say about my trips as a steward in the First Class dining room? I had many famous notables at my tables. One particularly humorous incident was concerning Oliver Hardy, normally accompanied by Laurel, but on his own one morning having breakfast at one of my tables. He glanced at the menu and asked for Honeydew melon, two sausages, bacon, and two fried eggs, with white toast and coffee.

When I got to the kitchen I was not aware that the sausages on the menu that morning were chipolatas and when I served his breakfast he poked the chipolatas with his index fingers and said, "Wot's them things there?" "The Italian sausages, Mr. Hardy." He poked them again and said, "Them are not bangers. I ordered bangers!" I assured him that I would get his bangers right away, "Sir!" I told the chef that, "Mr. Hardy would like English bangers. He doesn't want the little chipolatas."

The chef put four pork sausages on a silver dish with a sprig of parsley, "I hope his majesty likes them," he said. When I presented the four sausages on the silver dish, he grunted as he nodded his head and said, "Now, them's bangers!" I served him two with his bacon and his two fried eggs, and he pointed to the other bangers on the silver platter and said, "You can put them with them others, steward, thank you."

When he finished his breakfast, he hooked his pinky to call me to the table. "Now, steward, them's bangers. Thank you for a nice breakfast." He left a ten-spot under his butter plate! I had a good laugh about it all.

I saw many film stars and notaries in politics and other internationally famous people. But those years that began so humbly as the radio officers' steward gave me many memories and personalities and warm generous friends that filled my life with interest and travel.

THE EPILOGUE

In 1972 following a 6 million dollar overhaul, The *Queen Elizabeth* caught fire lying in Hong Kong Harbor. The fire raged for two days and finally she capsized. She lay in the harbor until she was scraped for scrap. What an ignominious end to a glamorous lady.

What a time I had trying to get on her! I got the last job left on the ship! But, in the end, while I have my memory, I will still hear the throb of the engines as she cut through the waves, a regal *Queen* that reigned over the seas. I hear her as she surges at thirty-one knots across the Atlantic from Southampton to New York. There are bigger boats now, but not so graceful. Some of them are 150,000 tons that resemble skyscrapers on their sides! We will not see such elegant beautiful proportions as the *Queens*! God Bless them.

You will be what you will be;
   Let failure find its false content
   In that poor word, "environment,"
But spirit scorns it, and is free.

It masters time, it conquers space;
   It cows that boastful trickster, Chance
   And bids the tyrant Circumstance
Uncrown, and fill a servant's place.

The human Will, that force unseen,
   The offspring of a deathless soul,
   Can hew a way to any goal,
Though walls of granite intervene.

Be not impatient in delay,
   But wait as one who understands;
   When spirit rises and commands,
The gods are ready to obey.

Henry Drummond

THE MAURETANIA

By today's standards, the Cunard *Mauretania* was not a large ship, being only 40,000 odd tons displacement. But she was a beautifully proportioned ship, painted in the traditional Cunard style: white super structure, red funnels, black hull with a red waterline band. She had two funnels, a reasonable rake to her bow and a clean flow to her super structures above deck.

    Her seaworthiness was often evidenced in the Atlantic winter storms of the late 1940s, when the two "*Queens*" often lowered their speed because of the severity of the wind and waves battering their great 82-84,000 ton bulks, causing them to roll and plunge in those days of no-stabilizers. The

Mauretania, for reasons beyond my particular understanding other than her beautifully proportioned lines and her ability to be "well behaved in rough seas," as mariners might say, could steam on at reasonably fast rates and get in on time, while the *Queen*s were experiencing rough conditions due to the heavy weather.

Not that the *Mauretania* didn't experience the same conditions, but we all agreed she was a very well-built and proportioned ship that steamed her way through weather which might slow other liners.

I joined her from the *Queen Elizabeth* especially to go cruising in the Caribbean in the winter of 1948, when she was first to provide post-war cruising for Americans, scheduling her cruises round trip from New York to New York.

We laughingly referred to the passengers then as "the Fur Trade," since in our view they evidenced much wealth in mink and sable coats, in those days the symbol of American affluence among the ladies, whom I'm sure were oblivious to the plight or welfare of the weasel, stoat, mink or fox and were openly delighted in their pleasures and possessions as the natural result of being Americans, riding on a crest of post-war exhilaration and celebrating the natural enjoyment of survivors and victors.

That exuberance of spirit, that optimism, that *outflowing* of optimism on the whole and the generosity so impressed me that I'm sure it was then the seeds of desire were sown in me to become *like them*, to be happy in the sheer pursuit of life itself, the action, the interaction between people and events, to become more involved, to become American! I know this may sound trite and perhaps naive, but I began to feel it as I associated more and more with Americans during those heady days of exciting cruising and conversations in the dining room and as we met in bars and restaurants when we went ashore. My inner yearning became a desire to start a new life! Anything was possible! It was as if new life and new blood had entered my body. I was literally renewed in mind and spirit.

As perhaps an indication of my new-found sense of freedom, I found myself ashore on one trip rendezvousing with a beautiful dark haired, sensuous lady from the medical officer's table to which I had been assigned that trip. I noticed her immediately as I entered the doctor's cabin to serve cocktails prior to dinner on that first night.

She smiled repeatedly as she conversed and her dazzling white teeth and that black glossy hair were like a siren's beacon to a sailor! As I passed among the guests crowded into the confined space of the suite, really a large cabin with a dividing door between lounge and bedroom with a couple of small brass framed windows affording the outside light rather than portholes since it was high on the boat deck, I found myself beguiled not only by her aura but her perfume, which I later discovered was *Bellogia*.

It was not your light flowery *Lily of the Valley*, or *Fleur de Roccale* variety. It was musky, perhaps even redolent of tropical exotica, which clung to one's olfactory memory long after its introduction. Years later, after experiencing *Frangipani* and *White Ginger* and *Gardenia* in the Hawaiian Islands, I still was able to recall *Bellogia* and its beguilements!

Later, I became quite interested in different perfumes and their wearers, and in the process, learned rapidly about the other subtle nuances of females and the not so subtle aspects of their personalities, particularly their moods.

But back to the *Bella Donna*: I managed to get a brief conversation as I had taken care of the rest of the guests and she wandered into the corridor, which seemed planned for my benefit. In a few seconds, I made my pitch to escort her on shore if she would like a guide, since I knew Nassau, and she perhaps would appreciate company? Her eyes and smile were my acceptance, and she replied, "How kind of you! I would love to join you, Ken. Shall we meet at the dock gate, say, at 2pm?"

It was as though I was in a movie again, another role that I had fanaticized. My college had long been the Hollywood curriculum: studying the social habits and behavior of the beautiful women and handsome men and their moves. Those were my mentors and models, since my normal environment was somewhat dull and limited in those days of post war emergence. I was a *Walter Mitty*, living partly in and out of the reality and dreams or fantasy that was a heritage from the war years. God knows the reality was not likely to give hope or create a glamorous future. Yet, the future was to emerge from my naive, optimistic attitude built from my secondhand Hollywood curriculum!

Let me develop how I was becoming more aware of the wider world and the opportunities that Fate can place in your way. Every change in circumstances is generally the result of chance or opportunity afforded by what I may call fateful encounters with "angels," or if you like, *catalysts* appearing just when it seems that you are ready to change.

One such meeting was when I was acquainted with a family, the Battaglias from Philadelphia, who became not only such warm friends but led me to feel a regard for America and its people, which indirectly led me to desire to immigrate, though the cause that took me eventually to America was in the future, where my life changed and where my boyhood dream became a reality.

I first knew the Battaglia family in 1947, when I was a steward on *RMS Mauretania* in the first class dining room. I was also the assistant of the Maître d'Hotel, who picked me for some reason, for which I was delighted, since that was a lift and excused me from other menial task that every steward had to do (such as polishing the silver or cutting the grapefruits, etc.). As his assistant, I was exempt from those boring necessities. We would be in port placing passengers at their respective tables.

Part of my new duties was helping the Maître d' in port, handling the mail requests for favors or choice of tables, or if there were more than one sitting (though when cruising there was only one sitting). As you can imagine, some of the requests were from prominent people or well known notables who were listed on the VIP list. Another might be from a brash nobody but accompanied with a $50 bill, asking to be put on the Captain's table, which must be handled with kid-gloves, so to speak, perhaps guided smoothly on to the Doctor's table, or perhaps the Engineer. After all, a $50 dollar bill cannot be returned!

If they were regular passengers or well known by the company or the captains or celebrities, we would try to place them on one of the senior officer's tables. For instance, the Captain's table was, of course, the most important; next was the Chief Engineer's table, next the Doctor's table. In the event, this particular trip was crammed with important people, so we had a time placing appropriate guests, not only by importance to the company, but also by mixing groups or interesting personalities by compatibility to the table.

When Doctor Battaglia and his family came up, the Maître d'Hotel said, "I don't know where I could seat him in the dining room, because he is very intellectual and loves conversation. He is from Philadelphia, and this cruise is to celebrate his anniversary with his family. I want to find a good table with a competent steward to make sure he's happy." I knew the Maître d' had received a letter from Doctor Battaglia, because I opened letters in order to list requests, but I also knew he had also received a $50 dollar bill from Doctor Battaglia.

So, I said to him, "Maître d', why not put him on my table? You know I'll take good care of him and his family." I figured if he had more of those $50 bills, why not take care of him? The Maître d' stared at me for a second and he smiled. "You're learning, Ken! OK. You can have him at your round table for six. And take care of him!"

In the event, I got the Battaglias on one of the First 1949 Caribbean cruises that were resumed after the war. It was a ten-day cruise that included Bermuda, Cuba and Nassau. In those days, those three islands were much favored as destinations, but it was not long before Castro's communist revolution in Cuba would isolate Cuba from American cruises and American trade and dollars!

Hamilton, on Bermuda, was a delightful port with many beautiful locations and beaches within those few small linked islands, including Saint George at one end and Hamilton Harbor at the other. One large resort was the Elbow Beach Hotel, with its lovely pink sandy beach and its glamorous bar on the hill with sweeping views of the green lawns and the azure Caribbean. It was one of my favorite places and, much later became the site where I got to know my second wife, Louise Everett from Wilmington. But that was later, on a different ship.

Back to the Battaglias. They were a gregarious group. Dr. Battaglia was a tall, grey haired chiropractor whose practice was in Walnut Street (I learned later) in downtown Philadelphia. Apparently, he was well known and respected. His wife was full of smiles, cheerful, plump and talkative.

She had three daughters, two smiling thirteen-year-old twins, and one sixteen year old: a doe-eyed, voluptuous, beautiful girl with long black lustrous tresses. The guests that made up the round six were two uncles from nearby New Jersey.

At that time, I was seeing to the family in my care, as the Maître d' asked me to. But as time went by, I had many conversations with the doctor, who seemed more interested in me than my partner and went out of his way to broach conversations with me that went beyond chit-chat into conversations quite philosophical and deep.

When the ship arrived at Nassau in the Bahamas, he gave me his card and invited me to come to visit him in Philadelphia where he would treat me of my sinusitis, which he had noticed without my telling him. I had a continuing problem with my deviated septum and often contacted sinusitis!

In the meantime I noticed that Gloria, his sixteen-year-old daughter, stayed after the mother and the other two girls left, whenever he began our conversations after the meal was over and all passengers at my tables had gone.

She came into the conversations with her father and myself, being intelligent and more mature than one would expect of a sixteen-year-old girl. I found her to be very interesting and we three got to know each other beyond what you normally would with passengers, friendly and warm though they might be. And I must admit, she intrigued me. Her mezzo throaty voice was distinctive, even though I was aware of her youth.

When we got to back to New York, his handshake and sincere repeat of his invite, the most generous gratuity in the envelope, and the hugs and kisses from the girls, told me that we had made a bond beyond the normal warmth that most passengers in those days showed to us British stewards. After all, it was only a couple of years since we, the Brits and the Yanks, were embraced in a common struggle. I still feel the warmth and acceptance of the common bond we had in those days.

The Maître d', at the passenger table-plot for the next cruise said, "I heard the Battaglias thought you were the best steward they'd ever had.

What the heck did you do?" "I followed your orders, Maître d'! I took care of 'em! And they took pretty good care of me!" The Maître d' smiled. "Let's see what we have this trip," gesturing to the mail piled on the saloon table. Those were the days!

We returned to Southampton in April to resume our normal turn on the Atlantic service, with basically ten or eleven complete days from Southampton to New York and return. After about a year I was transferred to the *Queen Elizabeth* again, since I did not want to do the next Caribbean cruise. A Few months later, on one of the New York dockings with an overnight stay, after the passengers had debarked, I received a message that a "smashing" young girl in a white Cadillac convertible was at the dock gate asking for me. *Who would that be?* I asked myself. I finished my dressing for ashore, I came to the dock gate and there and behold was Gloria, sitting in the Cadillac!

As soon she saw me approaching she tooted the horn and waved an arm. Her big smile and her throaty, "Hi, Ken!" let me know that she was in charge! Well, she drove me to Philadelphia, which was her father's plan. She went by way of New Jersey, going from one small town to another, waving occasionally, tooting her horn to various family members, uncle this and uncle that, with such remarks as, "That's Uncle Vince, who runs the numbers!" "That's Georgia! He runs a book!" Finally, the last toot as we passed a flashy restaurant and bar outside a town, where a large rotund Italian individual smoked a fat cigar while standing outside the restaurant, waved as she came by and she said, "Marco, who owns that nightclub. He likes the track." "The track" was the big track outside of Atlantic City, called Atlantic City Race Course. Once again, my fate was on a journey so that I was at that track years later as a guest of Caesar Innocenti.

Finally, we arrived in a part of Philadelphia with broad avenues lined with mature trees, substantial and handsome well-kept graystone houses fronted with neat lawns and handsome doors. We parked in front of one of the graystone houses and Gloria tooted her horn (which I had heard before!) and before we could reach the door, it was opened by a florid, portly man in his fifties with a smoking cigar clenched in one side of his mouth.

"Uncle Florio! Meet my English friend!" He stuck out a fat hand with a solitaire on his pinky, "Y'use from England?" he asked, "Really a genuine Limey!" He smiled, his gold filling glinting through the smoke.

The house was filled with many people and much conversation. Gloria introduced me to at least five aunts and uncles, and finally, a hug from Gloria's mom and her two sisters, who were taller than I remembered, since we had not seen each other since they had left the *RMS Mauretania*.

Doctor Battaglia came up and gave me an embrace, smiling, "Hi, Ken, I see Gloria got hold of you! She took a chance to find you! You know her, once she gets an idea in her head!" He put his arm around her, "I'm glad you are here."

The table seated twelve, and the meal served was enough to feed an army. The first course was an Antipasto, enough to be a meal by itself, accompanied on the table by toasted garlic bread, followed by Minestrone soup with Parmesan cheese sprinkled on toasted rounds of thin melba. Then, the great round bowls of spaghetti, doused with Marinara sauce and heaps of meatballs, to which everyone helped each other. To complete the banquet, we had my favorite spumoni ice cream with chocolate biscuits.

By then I could hardly get the spumoni down after so much food, delicious as it was! As I looked around the table, I could see why this family had a common appearance: they shared well-stocked bellies and satisfied round happy faces! I looked at Gloria and wondered how soon she would resemble her plump mother! But the whole family seemed close and warm with happy dispositions.

Fate was to be the architect of new beginnings and, in the following year I was to meet and fall in love with a beautiful, gentle, intelligent and talented girl from Wilmington, put in my path on a new ship called "The *Ocean Monarch*."

But that was in the future in 1950, and this Philadelphia episode was in 1948. Much would ensue before I would meet Louise M. Everett, who two years later would be my wife, and eventually mother of my two beautiful, intelligent, talented daughters.

I continued as a steward, but was transferred back to the *Queen Elizabeth*, and more of the Bella Donna Gloria Battaglia.

> "I cannot rest from travel: I will drink
> Life to the lees. All times I have enjoy'd
> Greatly, have suffer'd greatly, both with those
> That loved me, and alone, on shore…"
>
> Alfred, Lord Tennyson
> *Ulysses*

A SCOTCH OR TWO, WITH HOSPITALITY

When I first boarded the *Ocean Monarch* in October of 1950, she was in the Gravesend docks on the south side of the Thames, opposite Tilbury. She was one of the first post-war passenger ships to be built in Britain, and was by today's standards of huge mega-liners of 80,000 to 150,000 tons, a diminutive 15,000 tons or less! I believe she accommodated only 300 passengers and was specifically designed and built to cruise from New York down to the Caribbean.

At that time, only five years after the end of the Second World War, there was a huge demand in America for such cruises and New York was to be our homeport, which meant that we signed on at Gravesend for a two-year period of service in which we would essentially be calling New York "home!" The ramifications were not to be known at that time, but as I had learned in Southampton that day I took an "early lunch," one decision leads to another and irrevocably life takes another turn!

Before we could go to New York, there were test runs to check all engines, equipment, machinery and electrical functions, as well as the performance and behavior of the ship under way. This meant going up to Greenock at the mouth of the Clyde for a week of trials for a certificate of sea worthiness. I had been on such tests during the war when I joined a new destroyer, *HMS Vigilant*, built in Swan and Hunter's yards at Walls End on Tyne.

We steamed up to Scotland by turning south, rounding the North Foreland and turning southwest through the Dover Strait, into the English Channel and around Land's End, north into the Irish Sea, and up to the Firth of Clyde, where we anchored off Greenock.

The ship was a beautifully proportioned vessel. She was a single funneled, gracefully raked, clean-lined beauty. With her black hull and gleaming white-painted super structure and red funnel with two black bands, she was a sight to see. After the years of sailing on the huge *Queen Mary* and the equally mammoth *Queen Elizabeth*, it was especially nice to be on a much smaller, intimate ship, where one could feel much more relaxed in a less formal environment. I began almost immediately to enjoy my return to life aboard.

Because of her relatively small size, she could be more easily accommodated alongside docks and piers, which meant she would be perfectly suited for the Caribbean, and particularly, Island facilities such as Bermuda and Nassau in the Bahamas where we would be going.

Also, because of her size, 15,000 tons, one could get around her quicker, thus seeing more of the outside decks and more fully experiencing "cruising" in the sparkling turquoise waters under a blazing sun, rather than being interred deep inside the bowels of an 83,000 ton floating hotel which at times the *Queens Elizabeth* and *Mary* resembled. After days of not actually being outside of the dining room or the lounges or your cabin, located deep down below the main deck often situated close to the huge shafts that supported the massive main screws thumping unceasingly as they propelled the huge hull through the grey-green mass of the Atlantic Ocean, you would yearn to be upside breathing the sea air and seeing the green or azure sea.

Often on the Atlantic it was quite stormy and overcast, cold and sullenly gloomy, with the cloud ceiling so low it appeared you were steaming through the actual sky itself rather than an ocean. The regularity with which both these *Queens* rolled and sometimes wallowed in winter gales, before stabilizers were designed, reminded both passengers and crew that they indeed were seaborne.

Often during the Atlantic winter, despite the size of the massive ships, an even greater mass of wind-whipped ocean and voluminous waves would force the captain to moderate his speed, while the violence of the ship's movements as she rolled, dipping and bucking and crashing through mountainous seas, created chaos inside the dining rooms. It often made it impossible to keep crockery, glasses or silver in place, even on wet table cloths, "damped down" after table flaps were raised so plates, cups and saucers etc., might be relatively stabilized!

Considering the size of these two ships and the power of their turbines moving through the ocean at maximum speed, 30 plus knots, it can be understood why the collision in February, 1942, between the *Queen Mary* and the light cruiser, *HMS Curacao* about 20 miles Northwest of Bloody Foreland, Ireland, was so tragic. The cruiser cut across the *Queen Mary's* bow during a U-boat alarm and was cut in two, with a loss of 338 men and only 26 rescued!

Over the years, well-traveled passengers learned to live as best they could, coming down for their meals regardless of conditions and cheerfully putting up with the hardly elegant service, but the less experienced might not be seen for days outside their cabin! The production, service and consumption of the normally lavish cuisine would dwindle to as low as 30% in those times. In huge stormy seas, the first class dining room, which normally seated 700 plus in those mammoth liners, looked deserted with only a couple of hundred sprinkled around!

You can imagine then, my sheer delight in being on board this new, small, intimate ship with such delightful prospects of warm tropical cruising and all that it might suggest.

When we arrived off Greenock and anchored offshore, it was raining and as some wag put it, "This is Scotland. What did you expect, sunshine?" I had, of course, been many times to Scotland during the war when on both *HMS Vigilant* and *HMS Berwick*, but mostly up on the Firth of Forth and further north based in Scapa Flow in the Orkneys. Though when on the destroyer *Vigilant*, and on the cruiser *Berwick*, I sailed with convoys from the Western Approaches and operations against the Germans along the Norwegian ports, the Minch, Firth of Clyde and several times to the Firth of Forth and the base at Rosyth, near Dunfermline.

But this time it was different. I was five years out of Navy restrictions and with more freedom as a civilian to take advantage of my free time to go where I wished whenever the opportunity arose. The tender came alongside at 4pm in driving rain, and when it left to return to the shore I found I was the only one going ashore that afternoon!

In fact, as I looked up at the main deck of the *Ocean Monarch* as we pulled away, a couple of the lads were leaning over the rail shouting, "Hey, Ken! Save your money for New York! There's nothing but sheep and bagpipes here!" Other witticisms were no doubt hurled into the wind and rain with much laughter, but by then I was out of earshot and could care less.

Looking back on this, I could understand their personal ignorance of the warmth and acceptance of the Scots that I had found whenever I had occasion to meet them on their home ground and in their homes. Particularly was this true in Edinburgh where I had fond memories of Scots hospitality extended to me when on leave from Rosyth, on the north shore of the Forth. I also remember their kindness shown to me when I was in a Naval hospital in the country outside of Glasgow in June of 1943.

As the tender ploughed through the wind and rain towards the shore, I admit a momentary doubt as to why I was bothering to go ashore in such weather. I had no plan, no goal and no reason other than my curiosity and an unremitting thirst for travel and discovery! Perhaps, a sort of compensation for my earlier feelings of rules and restrictions?

I got off the tender at the pier and was lucky to find a bus waiting at the stop at the end of the key and hopped on just before it moved away. I gave the conductor sixpence and asked if he could "take me to the town center." He grinned at me and with his Scot's brogue asked me, "Do ye mean the main street shops?" "Oh, aye! Yes, I mean, I do!" I grinned back. He punched a ticket and gave it to me. "I'll let ye knew!"

And so he did, and so I was in the center of town and by then the rain had stopped, though it was damp and cold. I walked along the street among the shoppers until I came to a corner of a side street. I spotted a green tiled pub front on the other side and crossed over to it.

To a sailor, a public house is a temporary home from home. It is a place where food and refreshment can be had without palaver or formality. It is a place where a stranger can find himself an instant fraternity if he be of good will.

I entered the first door I came to which turned out to be the entrance to the public bar, as the main room is generally called, there being sometimes a smaller, quieter, often carpeted room called "the saloon," in which mixed couples or families could feel more comfortable and of course, pay a penny or two more for such accommodation! An even smaller room called "the bottle and jug" with a "privacy" window over the bar end of the room allowed privacy for the customer who required only a bottle or jug of ale, porter, stout or bitter to be carried off the premises, traditionally known as "the pub." The "public bar" was traditionally a men's bar and so the talk and behavior was, to put it mildly, "rough and ready."

I unobtrusively took my stand at the end of the bar and was approached immediately by the friendly female bartender, who said, "Hello! Stranger. What can I get you?" "A nut-brown ale," I asked. "Would you settle for a McEwen's?" she smiled. "That'll be fine," I grinned, glad that my warm regards for the Scots was reciprocated. The second McEwen's was poured by a younger version of the first bartender. She had the same auburn hair as her mother, but her smile seemed even more friendly.

As the evening progressed, I managed to equally juggle my wit and conversation between both the mother and the daughter and in fact, managed to give enough information about myself and circumstances at that particular time and place that I was surprised when I heard her Mother call, "Time! Gentlemen, please!"

But in post war Greenock, Scotland the home of thrift and Presbyterianism, where the closing hour in 1950 was 9pm, as compared to the 10pm closing of English pubs, even 10:30 in parts of London, the talk and behavior in this particular bar was civil and restrained. Jean, the daughter, came to collect the glasses left on the counter as I was finishing up my third or fourth glass of McEwen's. The mother, Meg, leaning over to me said quietly, "*Not* you, Ken. Stay," as she walked around the bar to usher out the last of the reluctant locals, "Yes, goodnight Fred. Goodnight to you, Tom! Goodnight, Jamie."

She closed the door and locked it. As she entered back behind the bar, she tossed me a clean white bar towel, saying, "Jean will wash and you can wipe, Ken," and added, "if you like." I liked it a lot, and we all laughed a lot.

It was time to go, Meg had cashed up and all was neat and tidy for the next day. Meg called to me, "Ken, take a bottle of whatever you like. We're going up to the house. I've got guests!"

I looked at Jean. She grinned and shrugged, waving towards the array of various bottles. I chose a fine bottle, a single malt, Dalwhinnie, really conscious of my good fortune. Meg waved her cigarette at the bottle of Scotch I had chosen, "Well, well, the sailor likes a little malt with his Scotch with his rum!" she quipped. We all left the premises and she locked the door. I admit, I had taken her at her word and didn't think she meant beer when she had said, "a bottle of whatever you like!" In the event, we three climbed into her Rover and off we went to her house at the top of the hill overlooking the harbor and into the bay.

The house was a three-storied grey granite front with bay windows on the ground floor and steps up to the front door opening into a foyer with mirrored hat and coat stand and a crammed-full umbrella stand. I could hear the muffled voices of animated conversation and a sudden eruption of laughter that sounded promising, since I was looking forward to "a party" ever since Meg had mentioned it!

She opened the door and immediately greetings were showered on Meg and Jean. "Ha! She's here at last!" and," Meg my gal, we've been waiting for you!" and "Hi, Meg, darling! It's good to see you!" and some less coherent addresses from upheld glasses in front of flushed faces.

Then it was my turn to be introduced by Meg's cigarette-hand making an elegant spiral as she waved vaguely first at me and then at the room, "This is Ken, Jean's nice sailor friend from that lovely ship in the harbor." The chorus of greetings left no doubt that I was welcome to the party. "Ooh, I like sailors!" and, "Come here! Sit next to me and tell me a sea story!" "Keep your talons off that young man!" (This by Meg.)

I squeezed onto a corner of the sofa which was rather difficult because several other rather extensive thighs and bottoms were already berthed comfortably! The conversation was fast, witty and somewhat risqué. I learned that Meg had been in "show business" and these people were from the ensemble playing at the local theatre and that it had become custom to "drop in at Meg's place" on the closing night for a party. Well, fine by me!

I had a great evening and, three Scotches and hours later, after much good natured repartee, laughing and finally intoxicated singing by those capable in the ensemble, farewells given and returned, umbrellas retrieved and shaken out and the front door finally closed and locked, I was guided by Meg to my room for the night. I tried to thank her but she cut my rather strangled attempt, "Thank you, so much, for, for… "She shushed me with her eloquent hand making spiraled plumes, "I'll wake you at six with a cup of tea. Goodnight, dear Ken." The cigarette spiraled its way out of the room. Strangely, I had not seen Jean to say goodnight and I was somewhat deflated to say the least.

When I had washed my hands and face, cleaned my teeth and prepared for bed, I peered out of that window on the upper floor and there in the now bright moonlight, I could see the *Ocean Monarch*, a little toy boat in a make-believe harbor where the lights twinkled upon the painted water.

I was caught in a real life play where nothing was as it seemed. I have never forgotten that moment and that feeling, Thank you, God, another serendipity! I got into bed and was drifting slowly into that pre-sleep state where all senses seem to gradually withdraw as the mind releases its control, when I was alerted to the bedclothes being lifted on one side as a scented young body slipped alongside me.

I turned, raising myself on one elbow, and Jean's face appeared on my pillow. Her arms reached for me and without words, we became lovers. A couple of hours later, she kissed me for the last time, smiling and called out, "Goodnight, Ken dear!"

When she had slipped quietly back to her room in the pre-dawn light, I slept briefly but soundly. The knock on the door and Meg's voice, "Six o'clock, Ken!" and her presence with a cup of tea came as naturally as the last scene in a play.

It was as if she had written the play. It was a short run but it was a good plot, with an even better ending! When I returned to the ship by tender from the pier and stepped back aboard the *Ocean Monarch*, I felt as privileged as a king. I did not confuse the cynics by telling them the truth and my good fortune.

"Yes, it was raining." "Yes, it was cold." "You were right!" "There was nothing really there. It was *unbelievable*."

TWO QUEENS

The *Ocean Monarch* proved to be not only a happy ship but a fortuitous one for me, for while on our third trip out of New York to Bermuda on a seven day turn-around trip, I met Louise Everett who almost two years later would become my second wife and the mother of my two daughters, Heather and Colleen. But I am getting ahead of things. There was much to take place and nearly eighteen months to pass before we would become man and wife.

It began one day as the ship was leaving New York for Bermuda in April 1950. As the passengers came into the dining room for their first meal, having embarked at the pier in New York between 2pm and 5pm on this particular day, my station partner, John Futscher, a good-looking guy with a dazzling smile that came easy, came sidling up to me as I was checking the round six and said, nudging me excitedly, "Check the two lovelies on deuce 24!"

I gave a glance and, laughing, said "Johnny, take it easy. Calm down." Noting the "lovelies" were a willowy blonde and a slender brunette, both in their late twenties, I was particularly struck by the brunette's radiant smile and eyes. There was an elegant air about her.

Nothing more was said as the dinner progressed that night, though I was attentive and strangely aware of her all through the meal. Johnny's smile was, of course, focused on the girls every time he passed the table, which was frequently! As the next day's meal times came and went, both Johnny and I did what we were trained to do, and we were good at it. We made ourselves available and affable at all times while gradually drawing out the two girls in brief conversations between our services to the rest of the passengers on our station. We found out that the two girls were friends: one, Louise, from Wilmington, Delaware and the other Joyce, from Philadelphia.

By the end of one complete day and three meals we were on a first name basis with everyone on our station, and seemingly quite indispensable for their pleasure and comforts. Johnny was showing signs of preference for Louise, the raven haired one, I noted. As we drew near Bermuda and an arrival expected by 9am the next morning, Johnny asked, as he set the tray down loaded with six entrees for the round table, "Aren't you going to ask about Elbow Beach tomorrow?" In other words he was hot to trot on a date, and I was to make the play. It wasn't that Johnny was shy but that he had learned there was some smooth subtlety and savoir fare needed when dealing with sophisticated ladies and for all his appeal, Johnny was not long on subtlety. If he were a dog, he'd be salivating!

During dessert, with Johnny fully occupied with the six-table, I smiled down at Louise and Jean as they finished their Bomb Jubilees, and as I filled their demitasses, I said, "There is a first-class resort hotel called Elbow Beach with an unbelievable view, the best dance floor and orchestra that has not only the best cocktail bar with..." and before I could complete my scenario, Louise broke into one of her dazzlers and burst out with, "That's where we are staying!" I could hardly believe my luck. "You are? Why that's wonderful! Perhaps Johnny and I could buy you cocktails before your dinner tomorrow night?" The girls looked at each other for a second before Jean looked eagerly at Louise, "Why, that would be fine, wouldn't it, Louise?" "Yes! That would be nice, Ken," Louise said softly, seemingly in control, "What time had you in mind?" "Would five-thirty be OK?" "Oh! Sure! That'll be perfect."

I smiled. *Boy! How lucky can I get?* I said to myself. I was immediately filled with a strange bliss that belied my normal outgoing gregarious self without knowing why.

After the ship docked and the passengers gone ashore, the ship had to be prepared for the return to New York in 24 hours, but by 1pm we were free to go ashore. We rented two scooters equipped with little two cylinder engines that sped up to twenty-five miles an hour through the little hedge-rowed lanes festooned with wild hibiscus, morning-glory, and purple bougainvillea, past azure blue-green glimpses of the sea, sparkling between the pastel colored cottages and guest houses that sprawled over this handful of tiny islands linked by little bridges.

That was Bermuda, 800 miles out in the Atlantic and surprisingly warm, since fortuitously the Gulf Stream flows past and creates a subtropical paradise. It was in this idyllic setting that I took another turn in the long road of my life. It was in this most intoxicating environment that I fell in love, though I would not know it until later.

Bermuda is a collection of a few little islands, actually over 140, but the main ones were linked with little bridges. Each part of the main islands was a Parish: Sandy's Parish is situated at the western tip of Bermuda and comprises Ireland Island North, Ireland Island South, Boaz Island, Waterford Island and a small section of Bermuda.

The northern section of the parish is occupied by the Royal Naval Dockyard, a former military dockyard and fort made into cruise ship docks, Kings Wharf, Heritage Wharf and other facilities. Somerset Parish includes two golf courses.

Warwick Parish lies at the center of Bermuda Island and includes its best beaches. Warwick Long Bay is the longest beach and the most crowded other than Horse Bay. Other places include Jobson Cove, Astwood Cove and Stonehole Bay.

Pembroke Parish encompasses the island's capital, Hamilton, with many attractions near or in the capital. Paget Parish is a popular destination and its biggest draw is the area called Elbow Beach, including the Elbow Beach Hotel, where we were headed to meet the girls.

Devonshire Parish lies in the center of the island. Smith's Parish is the smallest and residential. Hamilton Parish wraps around the Harrington Sound, which is the only public beach, with LF Wade International Airport.

George's Parish is the most easterly district. St. David's Island, formerly a US Air Force base, now occupied by LF Wade International Airport was, in World War 2, part of an arrangement between Great Britain and the USA. This group of islands is roughly 500 sea miles off the Carolina coast and part of an archipelago. 21 miles in area, Bermuda is beautiful handful of islands that have been very strategic in times.

These islands have been pivotal in my life and are part of my history and etched in my memory. From Hamilton through Pembroke Parish we rode our little motorized bicycles at a tidy clip as we sped by mile upon mile of picturesque views, whooping with joy and anticipation of our journey.

We entered Pembroke Parish along the shore and could see the azure sea on our right as we neared the entrance to Elbow Beach Resort. We wheeled up the hill to the magnificence semi-circular cocktail lounge and parked our bikes in the car stripes.

We stood for a moment looking at the sweep of the ocean flecked with gently breaking surf upon the silver sand below the hill. After making a visit to the toilet and washing our hands and grooming our hair, we emerged into the bar refreshed and anticipating the two girls. I had a vodka and tonic and Johnny went for a Mai Tai, and we chit-chatted at the bar as we relaxed.

The Elbow Beach bar was the epitome of glamour, with sparkling chrome, glass and black marble tables, black terrazzo floor, and one step down inside a brass rail were tables and chairs on several levels. From the stools at the bar, through the wide tall windows, we could see down the green hill and in the distance, the sparkling ocean and sweeping vista. The bar was a crescent, full of tanned faces from the day at the beach, happy faces, reflected in the floor to ceiling mirrors.

Added to all this was the mystique of the jeweled liquor bottles of every size and shape lining the glass shelves of the back-bar. These images reflected in the mirrors were, perhaps, of the illusory nature of reality.

In front of those bottles with their various colors and shapes were three bronzed bartenders, immaculate in black ties and starched white cut-away jackets. They looked and were skilled and smooth with ready smiles. In the hands of each expert, a Martini, Manhattan, Daiquiri, Mai Tai or Frappe de Menthe would be placed in front of each customer as an original creation, accompanied with a smile that could melt the ice in the glass! I guess we ordered another and, as time went by, more guests came through the big glass doors and the bar began to buzz with conversation.

We had been there about forty minutes when suddenly I saw through the glass doors a face I had anticipated during those sixty minutes.

I only saw Louise, who was in a black crepe dress with a big bow on her left hip. The neckline was squared and around her elegant neck was a roseate string of pearls that gleamed opaquely against her peachy-skin. Her hair was swept and piled into a swirl of black curls and waves that made her coiffure a crowning glory.

As she approached us with her blonde friend, I stepped between them and gestured to the vacant stool to my left, as rehearsed in my mind an hour ago!

"Why don't you sit here, Louise," I suggested, which successfully put Johnny next to me with Jean next to him. It was so natural and so smoothly done that Johnny, who was into his third Mai Tai by then, didn't realize that I had chosen and he got Jean! He was his smiling-self and in a few minutes, he was pouring on the charm and off the races!

I was in an absolutely heavenly space in which I was mesmerized by Louise. It was a surreal time where our conversation flowed and whatever we talked about, it became interesting and I, in thrall. It was a mystical force enveloping me that guided me from wit to humor!

I suggested we go to the dining room and take the girls to dinner. Arriving there, I couldn't believe my eyes when I saw that the smiling Maître d' was none other than MacIntyre, an old shipmate from the *Ocean Monarch*! We had heard rumors that he had a top-notch job in Bermuda, but I couldn't believe my luck!

He grinned at us and I greeted him, "Mac, you son of a gun! We heard you landed on your feet! These are my friends and perhaps you might find a table for us." I slipped him a twenty spot as we shook hands.

His savoir fare was as usual and he linked arms with each girl, and over his shoulder, "Follow me, my lucky lads." He strode down toward a four-table in the window with a view of the moon reflected on the shining sea. Of course, he was ladling the charm on the girls, his smile was framed by his white teeth and his black wavy hair. He seated the girls and said, in

Mac charm, "Bon appetit," with a wave of his hand, as he sailed across the dining room. As I sat next to Louise, it was my night!

While we scanned the menu, the wine waiter came to me and presented a bottle of Chateau Julian Burgundy, 1947, with the compliments of the Maître d'! Because we had ordered filet mignon and roast beef, everything was fine. Knowing Mac, I knew he knew we ordered red meat; he was "on the ball" as I knew him to be. After a marvelous meal with warm conversation and happy laughing and interchanging of information, we became more relaxed and had a good time.

I suggested that in about fifteen minutes the band would begin and perhaps the girls might re-fresh and we could get a table in the nightclub room and all meet at eight o'clock at the entrance of the lounge.

Everyone agreed, and in pairs we made our way to the dining room entrance where I thanked Mac for his hospitality and shook his hand. "Thanks for the wine, Mac. That was generous and made the meal special." Of course, as his normal ebullient self, he kissed each girl's hand and flashed his white smile, and replied, "Take care of these lovelies, it was good to see you again."

If ever twenty dollars had blessed a meal, this one did. So, we each went to find the toilets and refreshed ourselves before we emerged full of spirits for the evening. We met at the entrance as arranged where I requested a table for four and we found ourselves near the dance floor but not too close to the band. As I looked once again at Louise, so beautiful and so elegant with her smile and a whiff of her perfume, which I found was *Air de Temps*, I was bewitched or, in other words, I was at that moment "In Love," though I was not conscious of the fact. It was as if I had entered a *special space* that, through the evening, seemed to envelope me as though I could do or say anything. It was as if I was guided by a benevolent force that chose word or act.

In other word, whether waltz or foxtrot or tango, we synched as though we had been partners for years! Whether one or the other, the partners covered for the other. It was something I had not experienced in many partners in many evenings, because I was an average dancer, but what ever it was, I never forgot that evening. It was magical and I grew wings and danced on air.

Even now, after all these years, the happiness and *joie de vivre* that permeated my being that night and the following day remains impressed in my memory. She was as charming and easy to be with as anyone I'd known. We seemed to smile a lot and conversed easily about everything. When we didn't talk, it wasn't necessary.

It was as if Louise and I were what each had been looking for. When we parted on the moonlit terrace after the dance band had packed up and everyone had drifted off, it was with a promise to meet again the next day on the beach after lunch.

I returned through the winding lanes with their hibiscus and morning glory covered cottages, now softly muted in the in the moonlight, and for the first time in a long time, I was happy.

In the morning I learned that Johnny and Jean were meeting and planned to scooter around the islands and meet us at the hotel bar later. That was fine with me! The Elbow Beach was one of the premier spots in Bermuda. The sand is particularly fine and the beach is wide, a dazzling white in the subtropical sun, with the turquoise sea sparkling and splashing as the white surf breaks on the shoreline.

Striped umbrellas were spaced in lines below the cliff and as I walked down the stairway, an arm waved from under one of the umbrellas and there was Louise in her red swimsuit already wet from a swim. She took off her swim-cap and that raven hair spilled out as she shook it into place. She was beautiful and the welcome smile was evident and my world was complete.

That afternoon, between a swim and a leisurely afternoon's conversation and gentle banter, various kinds of information were exchanged which led to admissions of circumstances. I learned she took this particular vacation to get away in order to think over a proposal of marriage from a young lawyer in Wilmington, Delaware, whom she had known from her college days and who lived not far from her parents.

This news somehow did not affect me nor did it subsequently affect our relationship that seemed to grow more intense and personal by the hour. It was a fate accompli, having its own benign mind behind it.

Much of my adult education was life and movies: I had lived vicariously, in my mind, but I was sure I could read the signs that not only had I become enamored with this lovely woman but I knew she reciprocated my feelings. The fact of the matter was undeniable: *we were in love.*

The *Ocean Monarch*, which was to begin her return to New York, arrived and Louise came to the Hamilton dockside where we would depart. I managed to slip ashore and we went across the road up the stairs to the bar balcony where we could see the ship and know that the gangways were still connected to the ship.

We exchanged mutual assurances: I said I would send a letter from New York to reassure her when I would back in Hamilton, and she would be dockside when I returned. We embraced and kissed and I raced off before that last gangway was removed.

On Wednesday we returned and as agreed, she was on the bar balcony waiting for me. We embraced as lovers would and rented two motorized bicycles and wandered all the islands, had a wonderful lunch in a cafe by the water and wandered leisurely to Elbow Beach.

Of course the ship returned on Friday to New York and, since she would be leaving on Saturday, would have a look below for my ship as she flew to New York! I'm not sure that that happened but lovers reassured each other! However, my first letter was received as I docked in New York on Monday.

Whenever I could, I took a train at Pennsylvania station from New York at 5pm and arrived at Philadelphia about six-thirty. Louise would be waiting at the restaurant where we rendezvoused for a leisurely meal before I took the eleven from Washington back to New York. As the months went by we met as many time as we could and even met at Baltimore, since the New York strike meant we put in there, and another time we rendezvoused in New York for a couple of days.

By this time she knew of my separation from my previous wife and she knew I had contacted a lawyer friend in Philadelphia who arranged for my divorce. But Louise wanted me to write to the Pope and request that my marriage be annulled, since I was not married in a Catholic church.

As I came to know Louise those next few months, in our brief meetings between the trips, I discovered what an amazing woman she was. Her mother was Boston Irish, her father Philadelphia German, and they lived in Wilmington, Delaware, where Louise was born. She was instructed in pianoforte and obtained a scholarship to Moravian Woman's College in Bethlehem where she graduated with honors. She had studied voice along with the piano and performed in well-known cocktail bars and hotel lounges in New York. After taking business courses in typing and shorthand, etc., she came to Philadelphia and worked for Atlantic Refining Company, where soon she became the Chief Engineer's Secretary on the fifteenth floor of the Atlantic Refining Company's skyscraper.

It was evident when I visited her there that she was an efficient, well-respected, valuable secretary to the Chief Engineer, Sam Huff, whom I got to meet. I could see why Louise, with her sweet smiling face and cheerful engaging personality and quiet intelligence, would be so well regarded by all.

It was time for me to get my documents together and to get leave from the *Ocean Monarch* and the company so I could go to England and return with an offer of sponsorship by my friend Sam Johnson, my Philadelphia lawyer, as an immigrant through the US consulate in London.

It was in February 1952 that I learned of a shocking turn of events: my ex-wife's mother had been murdered by a burglar. I realized I should at least in some way support my ex-wife's grief, but also here was an opportunity to get to England and process my documents, get my visa as an immigrant and clear-up my divorce. More importantly, I could get to the US consulate and process my papers for immigration to the United States.

Between disbelief and shock, since I had not heard from nor seen Dorothy since our decision to separate following her sudden disappearance from "our so-called" Southampton home, I had mixed feelings about my obligations, but decided to take the opportunity to talk over the impending divorce face-to-face. There were, after all, questions unanswered.

I went to the Chief Steward and got permission to take compassionate leave, and as luck would have it, he was able to get me a berth for the next day on the *Queen Elizabeth*, sailing from New York from pier 90, only three piers from the *Ocean Monarch*.

I only had time to call Louise and apprise her of the situation and re-assure her of my processing my papers and backing from Sam Johnson, the lawyer. Her tears in anticipation of my returning as an immigrant and our impending union were evident. I would be back within a week if things went as smoothly as I reassured her. I asked her to pray a Novena for our quest.

The next day, I sailed on the *Queen Elizabeth*, went to the crew bar and got re-acquainted with some of my old friends who were agog at my news! In four days we were berthed in Southampton.

Let me not to the marriage of true minds
Admit impediments. Love is not love
Which alters when it alteration finds,
Or bends with the remover to remove.

O no! it is an ever-fixed mark
That looks on tempests and is never shaken;
It is the star to every wand'ring bark,
Whose worth's unknown, although his height taken.

Love's not Time's fool, though rosy lips and cheeks
Within his bending sickle's compass come;
Love alters not with his brief hours and weeks,
But bears it out even to the edge doom.
  If this be error and upon me proven,
  I never writ, nor no man ever loved.

William Shakespeare
Sonnet 116

A BRIEF ENCOUNTER AND A BRIEF EXIT

After arriving in Southampton, I took a room in a small hotel across the park and phoned Dorothy to let her know that I was in England. In the conversation, I learned that her mother had been buried the week before and that a suspect had been arrested and charged. I listened to the rambling recounting of events and could feel the distance that had grown between us.

    I arranged to meet with her at noon the next day at the Portsmouth Central station in the restaurant where we could share a leisurely lunch and talk. I took the local train from Southampton to Portsmouth the next morning at eleven for the twenty-one mile Journey.

The train arrived on time and I found the station restaurant. Dorothy was there, pale, cold and distant, as could be expected, but looking smart and attractive in a new suit. I hadn't seen her for over a year since her disappearance that last weekend when I had arrived after an Atlantic crossing on the *Queen Elizabeth*, after which, being confused by my then wife's disappearance and subsequent silence, I impulsively left the ship just before sailing.

Here, it was as if we were both playing out roles in a bad movie. The conversation was lifeless, as she explained in a monotone her reasons for leaving me when I was on the *Queen Elizabeth*: her wanting to have a different life; her mother's part in convincing her to leave Southampton and come and live with her and her sister, like the old days; the dancing on the pier weekends; and someone she had met (admissions of culpability that no longer hurt, a conclusion, a relief).

It was understood there would be no defense against the divorce. She would keep what she had and I would make no claims on her or hers. When we stood up to leave, she looked at me and for a moment she hesitated, "I'm sorry about..." but she did not finish. As I saw her wan face and thought about what had happened to her mother, I felt a pang of pity, but with my resolve to begin a new life long away from this dreary tragic scene, I stood up and I looked at her for the last time.

We offered our hands, perhaps in mutual regret, and I said, "I'm sorry about your mother, though we never got along. You know, this whole thing was wrong, somehow. I hope things will get better for both of us."

And we parted, she to return to her mother's house which she had inherited and I to return to Southampton, where the next day I would take a train to London to go to the United States embassy and finally get entrance to America and to begin a new life.

The parting was final. I did not look back; we never saw or spoke to each other again. I remember how perfectly calm I felt and how it all seemed totally abstract, without color or feeling, as though we were strangers making an agreement to change seats! I suppose we had never really come to know each other, we were parted so often.

The next morning on a cool, damp February day, I left the Polygon Hotel and crossed the Common to the Southampton Central Station and bought myself a return ticket to London, which luckily enough came puffing in among clouds of steam, screeching its breaks as it slid to a gradual halt along the "up-line" to London. It had come from the West: Plymouth, Torquay and Bournemouth, but was not crowded since it was winter and mostly business people and commuters were traveling rather than the vacationing families that packed in from their holidays in beautiful resorts in summer.

I only mention it now because that morning I felt acutely aware of my surroundings and was observing everything in a reflective way due, I suppose, to my feeling that I might not be back in England for a long, long time, if my journey to London was successful. (It was fifteen years, actually!)

In an hour and a half, I was taking the underground from Waterloo Station on the south bank of the Thames to Oxford Street from where I could walk to the American Embassy on Grosvenor Square off Duke Street.

After identifying myself and purpose to the first desk inside the door in the lobby, I was amazed at how quickly I was passed in sequence from one desk to another, where particular papers from the handful I was carrying were sorted, stamped, initialed and given back before I was ushered to another door and another desk!

By the time I had been fully processed, including my stripping and being examined by doctors and answering innumerable questions about my habits, hygiene, hobbies, and family history, etc., I found myself dressed and waiting outside in the lobby once more!

I looked at my watch and to my surprise, with much gone through, only an hour had passed since I had entered at 9am! After a short wait I was told to "go up to the third floor to room 301 for your final interview." I knock-knocked on door 301 and a clear voice called, "Enter."

The voice belonged to a smartly suited, bobbed-haired, self-possessed and attractive woman who introduced herself and smiled warmly as we shook hands, "I'm Olive Jensen. I'm your last obstacle in the rat-race,

Mister Harrison!" I immediately responded to her American warmth by mumbling something like, "It's not quite a race," or something equally inane, but I did feel a quick acceptance which, I confess, has been my good fortune to have in general with most Americans whom I encountered then.

She had all my papers in front of her on her desk and glanced through them, looked up at me, "Mister Harrison I do believe you have set some kind of record for being processed so far!" I smiled, congratulating myself on having worked so diligently over the last year collecting the necessary documentation and certificates, etc., but realizing my luck, too! "I see you are booked to sail on the Il de France in two days from Southampton," she noted. "Yes, I was lucky to get a berth on such short notice!" "Well, can you find something to do for a few hours while I complete your process? Say, be back here by 4pm?" "Oh, sure! I can find a lot to do here in London!"

We shook hands again and I left the embassy and went over to Oxford Street, had myself a limp thin sandwich and a weak tepid cup of tea (Oh, for a diner and a hamburger!) and began a long walk before I reminded myself that I'd better not get too far away from Grosvenor Square or get lost, so after a half an hours walk in the damp drizzle, I turned around and went to an Odeon cinema that I'd passed earlier on Oxford Street. Without even looking or caring what movie was showing that day, I paid the admittance, found a nice comfortable seat and, perhaps because of the tension or anxiety provoked by my sense of urgency and haste, gradually fell asleep!

I awoke suddenly, startled, straightening-up from my sideways slump in the aisle seat, fortunately towards the unoccupied seat next to me and not onto the aisle floor! I looked at my watch and heaved a sigh of relief. It was only 2:30pm! Though I watched whatever was playing on the screen, my thoughts were far away from that Odeon, speculating on my new life to come in America. To this day, I do not know what film it was! I was too occupied with my own scenario as well as attentive to time! I arrived at the embassy and took the elevator to the third floor. I knocked. "Enter!" Her voice welcomed me as I opened the door, and she smiled broadly as I walked to her desk. "Aha! Mister Harrison. On time." She stood up, lifted a manuscript-sized brown envelope off her desk and offering it with a bright smile, said, "Well, here it is! It is a pleasure to welcome you into the United States of America, Mister Harrison!"

I took it with my left hand, and pumped her hand with my right. "Thank you so much for your kind help in getting my papers through so quickly!" I was now filled with emotion. "Thanks, again," I managed, holding her hand just a second longer than protocol.

"It was my pleasure," she said, adding, "I hope you have someone waiting for you when you get there?" I turned around and looked at her, "Yes, I certainly do!" As I left, I thought, isn't the world a great place sometimes, when you are in love? I felt I was walking on air!

I took a train from Waterloo Station at 5:20pm and in one hour and twenty minutes I was in Southampton, got a room at the Polygon Hotel, had a meal in the dining room and retired to my room at nine o'clock exhausted from the busy and emotional day.

I wandered around in Southampton after a leisurely breakfast and, in a sense, said my farewells to my old haunts and favorite pubs and went down to the docks where I had sailed in the *Queens Mary* and *Elizabeth* and the *Mauretania* at the Cunard piers.

Reminiscing the years, as I went from one to another, I even went to find the orphanage, Saint Mary's, near the old football field, but the site of the orphanage was now a vacant lot full of weeds and the only vestige left of the building was the sand path leading to the worn steps, a few broken bricks and some charred beams hidden among the weeds.

I returned to the hotel and refreshed before dinner. I had a farewell drink in the bar and after dinner I retired to my room and went to bed.

After a good sleep and breakfast, I paid my bill and took a taxi to the docks, enquired where the Il de France was docked and boarded her with a sense of excitement, since in approximately four days I would be in New York, an immigrant legally living in America and I would be with Louise!

The trip was peaceful and the accommodations were good. I was in one of the cabin class cabins and the food, being a French ship, was French. It was good. But the only thing on my mind was getting to New York. I idled my time by reading a paperback book on the promenade deckchair for the cabin passengers. I could not get to see Louise quickly enough!

As we passed the welcoming *Liberty*, I felt a new emotion. I was an American, even if, when I opened my mouth, everyone would know I was English. But, deep inside I had a new feeling. I had passed the *Statue of Liberty* so many times over the years, but this was different.

Louise was there at the pier as promised, as she had always been since the day we met. Reliable and loyal, loving and constant, Louise. How blessed I was then. I can't tell you adequately what a blessing she was at that time in my life and how she gave back the confidence and trust I had lost in myself and in life in general. Following my letter to the Vatican to request that my marriage be annulled, I was finally able to set a date for my marriage to Louise in May 1952 in Philadelphia, of which more later.

In the meantime, I was in a new country and beginning a new life. How different that would be only time would reveal. But at that time, I was happy and feeling confident. Now my memories crowd time, many sad regrets fleet across the mind, but arriving to my love and my new country was a special experience. It was a memorable arriving, one I will not forget. I was home.

> He [Caesar] only, in a general honest thought
> And common good to all, made one of them.
> His life was gentle, and the elements
> So mixed in him that Nature might stand up
> And say to all the world, "This was a man!"
>
> William Shakespeare
> *Julius Caesar*, IV lb 71

CAESAR OF THE BARCLAY

As you might expect in the years that I was a steward on the transatlantic liners *Queen Elizabeth* and *Queen Mary*, and on the Mauritania and the *Ocean Monarch* cruising around the Caribbean out of New York, I met many interesting and friendly people, some of whom became longtime friends, though most are now only names on business cards in my study drawer!

One such friend was Jim Johnson, a Philadelphia lawyer, whom I had met when he was a passenger on a fourteen-day cruise in the Caribbean on the Mauritania in 1949. Among other things that he did for me was his expert and smooth handling of my divorce from Dorothy, my English former wife, who did not contest the issue. Jim invited Louise and myself out to his Valley Forge retreat one weekend, was a generous and goodhearted friend who instantly liked Louise and became a good friend and an enthusiastic supporter of my immigration to America, in particular introducing me to people in Philadelphia and so making my transition to America quite smooth and pleasant.

Although from Wilmington, Delaware, where her parents still lived, Louise was living in Philadelphia and was employed as secretary to the Chief Engineer at Atlantic Refining Company on the fifteenth floor on Broad Street, one of the busy main roads at the heart of the city. Louise introduced me to her boss when I arrived at the fifteenth floor one noon to take her to lunch.

Sam Huff was impeccably dressed in a dark blue suit and greeted me with a quick handshake and an easy smile on his tanned face. He was very gracious, and seemed to me then the epitome of an American executive, with a breezy personality but a quiet air of confidence about him, and took time off his executive duties to take his secretary and her English fiancé to lunch! I was well and truly introduced to democracy American style, and I really liked it!

I learned that Louise was not only obviously efficient as Sam Huff's secretary, but highly regarded by everyone I met on that fifteenth floor. She was what I had only seen portrayed in movies: a beautiful, smiling, secretary to the big boss! I felt I had arrived on a Hollywood set where a film was being made about Louise and Big Shot Sam Huff! I was definitely in America. I felt elated. I felt lucky! The fifteenth floor of Atlantic Refining was the Top of the World as far as I was concerned that day!

After the very pleasant weekend at Jim's place at Valley Forge, where among other enjoyable pleasantries I learned first-hand of his generous nature, we returned on the Monday back to Philadelphia where Jim had arranged a meeting with a well-known Hotel Maître d' and manager in the city who was known by all as "Caesar of the Barclay," in Rittenhouse Square. Later I learned there were many variations of his name according to language or level of acquaintance!

For instance, to prominent Italians in the city he was Caesar: authoritative, eminent, and dispenser of favors and in some cases, largesse. To his employees at the hotel, from the front office to the dining room staff, to the Banquet staff, waiters, headwaiters, bartenders and dishwashers, he was a legend.

If and when he appeared personally, as when a cardinal or a statesman such as Cardinal Spellman, or Senator Kennedy, or perhaps Maestro Ormandy or perhaps the Kellys with Grace and her sisters in tow, were attending one of his lavish lunches or dinners discretely sequestered away in one of the many tastefully appointed rooms in either the French,

German or English suites, as these private banquet rooms were called, it was considered a personal and appreciated coup by all concerned, and one that guaranteed the plaudits of the hosts and the unqualified success of the event. This man was apparently a unique well-known individual.

When Jim took me to meet Caesar at the Barclay, it was to introduce me in the hope that Caesar would see what Jim believed I had, and perhaps offer me a job. Little did I know then that Jim had already acted as my business manager during a previous lunch there and had said enough to get me this appointment with the great man.

As arranged, we arrived at 10am at the Barclay's entrance which was just a few doors away from the Curtis Institute, and a much less imposing facade than I had imagine, as far as hotels go. The entrance while elegant was quiet and unobtrusive. I learned later that it was precisely these attributes that earned the Barclay its privacy-oriented clientele. Unobtrusive and quietly dignified, that was the Barclay.

Jim and I were ushered up to the third floor offices and into the large three-windowed, tastefully furnished office that functioned as Caesar's planning and organization HQ. After an introduction and a brief but flattering description of both my background and Jim's perceived opinion of my personality and skills, Caesar, rimless glasses sparkling, asked if I had a tuxedo and could he see me in it? I assured him that I did and he could.

So it was the next morning that I traveled in my tuxedo under a raincoat, though the sun was shining and not a cloud in sight!

As I walked into Caesar's office that morning, I was beginning a new chapter of my life, and more importantly a more promising life, as I now gained opportunity and confidence as the result of Louise's unqualified love and trust in me that had led me to leave my sea-going career and immigrate to America, to Philadelphia, City of Brotherly Love, where my first job was now being offered. Being a headwaiter was no big thing, and in itself not really a change of job or of occupation. It was to where this first opportunity would lead me, and to whom it would eventually lead me that was the difference.

The Barclay Hotel, owned by John McShane, was a first class organization with a blue-book clientele and a favorite rendezvous for what was known then as "the Main Line." I would be under the direct supervision and tuition of a famous Maître d'Hôtel, Caesar, not only a unique individual from whom I would learn, but a warm hearted, generous enigmatic personality who ultimately blessed me with his personal friendship and benevolence.

He not only became Godfather to Louise and me at our wedding but also stood in for her father, when Louise's father declined to attend, though her mother Mary Everett did, graciously, in spite of John Everett's rejection of an impending English son-in-law. Actually, I never did get to ask him his specific objections or personal reservations about me, but having been through the English subtlety of bias, snobbery and class distinction, I was well able to provide my own observations and conclusions. After all, I knew that I was not what the Main Line would call a "catch." As an English immigrant, recently a steward on a passenger ship, a survivor of the Navy in the recent World War, with little or no education past the 11th grade, working as a delivery boy at 14 years of age, I was admittedly, an unknown nobody without credentials that would ensure his daughter's future.

When Louise had invited me down to Wilmington, Delaware just south of Philadelphia to meet her parents, John and Mary Everett, I had no intimation of his opposition to our intended marriage. At the modest house in a quiet tree-lined street in Wilmington where Louise had taken me, I thought to be welcomed into the Everett family, however, the atmosphere was polite but restrained as we sat around the small table set for lunch.

Her mother, of Irish and French background, was warm, smiling and welcoming, and we exchanged a few harmless bits of chitchat. But her father, of German parents, was quite another thing. Throughout the lunch his face was grim, lips set in a firm straight line and his remarks were gruff, his demeanor decidedly unwelcoming.

One remark that etched itself on my memory, "So, you were a seaman," was said not as a question of interest but more as an opening thrust. "Yes, after I was demobilized from the Royal Navy, I was employed by the Cunard White Star Line for five years, as a steward on the *Queens Mary* and *Elizabeth*." There was a silence. Then, "You were a seaman," in a flat tone that I could only interpret as an indictment! He relayed his obvious resentment that his one and only beautiful daughter should be contemplating marrying a mere seaman, and fired off his main armament, "What kind of a job would a seaman be getting in Philadelphia? I wouldn't think you'd be getting a law degree!"

Now I understood! Louise had been courted by a young lawyer from Wilmington when she took the two-week cruise to Bermuda to think over his proposal of marriage! Her father had probably bonded to the idea of a lawyer in the family and here I was, a seaman, a dummkopf seaman, an Englishman to boot, to take his little apple dumpling to God-knows where and for "*vat I gift the piano lessons und ze ladies college?*"

The meal was finished in total chill emanating from Herr Everett and, despite Louise and her mother's gracious efforts to fill in the gaps in the repartee, the awkwardness remained as a fifth guest at the table until Louise mercifully reminded her mother we had to catch the train back to Philadelphia. But a cloud had formed on my idyllic blue sky that was to bring future rain on my picnic.

I must say that I understood her father's coolness and obvious disappointment. His directness and blunt rejection of my past employment only served to sharpen my resolve to change things as soon as I could. Louise did deserve something better. I was blessed that she had seen in me what I was and what I might be. It truly was another awakening, albeit unflattering.

The chilling meeting, with Louise's father's unacceptance of me, was not a warm family event, although Louise's mother's blessing was given at the door as we embraced, and she gave smiling confidences as we left.

Her father's rejection of his intended son-in-law was on my mind, and on the return to Philadelphia I was determined to be a success and in time, have his approval of our family. I was resolved to be a success and to ask God to give me a way to become better and reciprocate Louise's love and loyalty.

The first few months working at the Barclay were fast and furious. The banquet department was huge and ever active. There were three headwaiters: one Frenchman, Pierre, (Caesar's chief assistant), one German, Gustav (Jawohl!) and one Englishman, me, Ken(t). The "t" was *accidentally* (or was it?) added by Caesar when I was introduced by Jim Johnson, "I'd like you to meet Ken Harrison, my friend from the Mauritania and the *Queen Elizabeth*." "Ah, Kent, so you are Kent!"

Being Caesar, none were offering to correct him, including me! I thought the mispronunciation of my name was the result of his accent, which was decidedly Italian, part of his persona, along with the big fat Havana cigar (Upman's Number One!) and his big solitaire set in thick gold on his ring finger, often waved obtrusively with his smoking cigar when punctuating some part of his presentation to a prospective banquet client.

So by fiat I became Kent of the Barclay along with Pierre and Gustav and Caesar. What a bunch of European-Americans, all with their personal idiosyncrasies.

When all the suites were fully booked for parties, dinner-dances, wedding receptions, formal debutante balls, and bar mitzvahs, it was a very busy place, but a well-oiled organization.

The French Suites was where Pierre and his Francophiles often gathered to savor hors d'oeuvres or various Chateaus of Burgundy or Chardonnays, etc. Gustav presided over the German Suites, where heels were clicked discretely *und ze fadderlandt toasted mit stein lager und bock*. As for me, I was to be found presiding over the English Suites and accentuated *ahs* and the *dahlings* and *luvly* and *How-do-you-dos. Gin and tonic or Pims or pale ale or a cup of tea*, the last resort! Often an individual having returned from a recent trip would show his trophies from Claridges or from Bond St., "...last London trip, don't you know." It was often a circus, but there were special times.

One day, Caesar was in his office as I was checking in to find the day's assignment. He waved his glowing cigar between his two fingers as he gestured me into his office. "Kent, I want you to be with me at 5 pm in the President's Suite after you've finished the Bishop's luncheon in the English Suite. Change into your best tuxedo and tie and I'll see you at five. This is a special cocktail, and Tony will be the bartender and you'll take care of the guests."

I was about to ask why I was serving as a headwaiter when normally a waiter would be serving. Then I remembered it was Caesar and that he had a reason for everything. So I smiled, nodded, and went about preparing the Bishop's luncheon.

These luncheons were monthly affairs where the Bishop and his monsignors and priests would quickly dispense with Diocese matters. When the Bishop had discretely slipped away, the coffee cups and brandy glasses cleared, the tables quickly stripped of white tablecloths, the tables were placed down at the end of the room, end-on to wall. The tables were quickly covered with green baize cloth, whereupon a set of dice were produced and a loud, noisy, craps game ensued!

I was surprised the first time I saw the priests and the monsignors, sans coats and collars and with some "rolled-up sleeves," enthusiastically blowing into their fists and clutching their dice before releasing them on the green baize as they muttered their imprecations, perhaps even a prayer!

No longer would I have the same sanctified image of Catholic clergy that I might have brought from my past impressions from England. Incidentally, the doors of our banquet rooms were soundproofed. No one outside would have a hint of what might be going on inside the doors, which probably added to the priest's carefree abandon which I observed.

After the Bishop's luncheon, I knocked on the door to the President's Suite. I was admitted by Caesar, who led me to the mobile bar where he indicated a tray of Martinis and a couple of Scotches on the Rocks. Caesar led me to two impressive gray-haired gentlemen in tuxedos, impeccably dressed, who each took one of the scotches, and then guided me to several beautiful women in their twenties, who apparently were the Martinis.

I smiled and, with vague recognition of the elegant blonde, realized it was Grace Kelly, the daughter of one of the elegant businessmen, Kelly, the millionaire. But, keeping my cool, I asked the two middle-aged women, who I surmised were wives of the two gentlemen, if they would like something from the bar. One said, "Bourbon on the Rocks," and the other asked for an Amontillado Sherry. When I delivered their choices, I realized Caesar had chosen me for this. From then on, I never questioned his motives. He had only one motive when it came to me: my good and his goodwill.

Once again I learned that God has His ways to work wonders. Earlier, I had been about to ask Caesar why I was serving cocktails instead of waiters, when I remembered that this was Caesar and he had a reason for everything he did.

One day, Caesar summoned me to the office at 9am and requested me to accompany him on Caesar's annual picnic with Charlie, his chauffer, in the black Daimler. We loaded a wicker hamper in the capacious boot, several French wines iced within a chest, three collapsible seats and a blanket.

Charlie was directed to drive west out of Philadelphia to the Amish area near Lancaster and York. Caesar being who he was looked for a particular field with a certain tree with a stream wandering through. Believe me, he found the particular spot with that tree and that stream! I learned that Caesar always had a plan in his mind and he executed it to the letter. In the event, we camped under the ancient oak, spread the blanket, placed on it a white table cloth, and spread the various dishes including a silver tray with dismembered chicken, crusty rolls, a dish of asparagus, and potato salad with sliced egg and mayonnaise.

It was a Caesar picnic with every condiment or every delicate complement you would wish. The white wine was Chateau d' Yquem, a Superior Bordeaux which I had served in the past on the *Queens Mary* & *Elizabeth* after the war.

Those hours are indelibly etched into my memory. Why Caesar included me in his company was a mystery. That day I found out that when he was in his thirties he was head chef on the famous beautiful Italian passenger ship, the Rex. The more I learned about Caesar, the more I admired and respected him.

In the few months my life changed. Caesar gave encouragement and, as time went by, he became not my boss but a mentor and gave me more than I ever expected. A blessing from God.

When he understood that my father-in-law was not accepting his role, Caesar not only volunteered to give the bride away but on that day he beamed his benevolence on Louise and, as he walked to the altar and gave her hand into mine, I knew God was participating.

At the reception Caesar stuffed four hundred dollars into my pocket. Again, Angels appeared in my need. Caesar was a blessing. It was a blessed wedding and a blissful honeymoon in which we bonded in love in Bermuda and recalled our meeting two years before.

> "But now being lifted into high society
> And having pick'd up several odds and ends
> Of free thoughts in his travels, for variety,
> He deem'd being in a lone isle, among friends,
> That, without any danger of a riot, he
> Might for long lying make himself amends;
> And, singing as he sung in his warm youth,
> Agree to a short armistice with truth."

George Gordon, Lord Byron
LXXXIII
From Canto III, *Don Juan*

GRACE HAD ARRIVED IN MY LIFE

In the next few months my life changed, beginning with marrying Louise in the Catholic Cathedral in Philadelphia, with Caesar as "Godfather." As I have noted earlier, Louise's German father was anti-English. An ex-sailor was not what he expected for his daughter. It took many months to reconcile him to the fact that his daughter's choice was based on her perception of my character and our compatibility but, more importantly, we loved each other and were meant to be partners.

My life in America was already challenging and exciting. John Everett was another unwitting catalyst. He, despite my crude attempts here to ridicule his attitude, made his point. I did feel he could have been more considerate of his daughter's happiness and her feelings rather than his own disappointment. But there it was.

Not until Louise's mother dropped dead of a heart attack on Atlantic City's boardwalk some years later when we were living in Phoenix would he communicate with his daughter. When Louise rushed back to the East Coast upon the news and helped him after the funeral, he relented and finally got to meet his two grandchildren, Heather and Colleen, by then five and two years old respectively.

One day, after two happy years at the Barclay, I awoke with a sore and quite swollen throat, and this was not the first time. The doctor told me I had strep throat again and he thought that something in my environment was causing repetition of the infection. In the discussion we felt that the tobacco smoke in the banquets and other social parties were the cause. When he ascertained that I did not smoke, he felt I should get away from Barclay Banquet environment.

The doctor's opinion was that within a year my three strep throats had put my health in serious hazard. His advice was to go to Arizona or South California to recuperate. It was a blow, because I had a lucrative position in a First Class hotel and moreover, I had success with Caesar and the Barclay.

However, my health was the important issue and I was exhausted, so Louise agreed we would go to Arizona for recuperation and perhaps investigate employment opportunities. We made the great leap to Arizona near Scottsdale, a beautiful area in Paradise Valley, where I recovered in several weeks.

We flew to San Diego and contacted several places regarding my résumé and with my experience at the Barclay and on the *Queen Mary* and the *Queen Elizabeth*, etc., there was interest. I got a summer position as the Maître d' in La Jolla at a well-known bar and restaurant and was then offered a job as Maître' d in the Hotel Adams, Phoenix.

It was a sad regret leaving Caesar, who was more than a friend. He understood my health and we continued to become friends. I once flew to see him in Philadelphia and he was the same Caesar, as urbane and gentlemanly as always.

We arrived at the Phoenix airport within the week as arranged. With help of the manager of the hotel we found a very nice two-bedroom bungalow a few blocks from the north end of the city not far from the hotel.

Louise soon found a job as a secretary to the chief engineer in Hughes Aircraft not far from Scottsdale. Soon Bobby Phael, a famous hotelier in Los Angeles, was looking for my style for a banquet for two hundred guests. He seemed to approve of the service of my waitresses and, as the speakers began to go to the podium, he came to speak with me at the main door.

"Maître d', I was aware of your smooth control off your staff, the service was superb and I admire your style." I smiled and thanked him for his graciousness. "Could we find the restaurant and share a coffee as we chat?" We found the restaurant and sat in a corner. In the conversation, Bobby Phael revealed his new hotel in Scottsdale and wanted me to be the Maître 'd of his catering department.

Again, changes were on the horizon. It seems I was beginning again! I was in Bobby's hotel in charge of his banquet department and his dining room and bar, which was a quite calm hotel compared to the Adams.

In fact, it was a downer and I began to regret Bobby's pitch. One day, I was having my lunch in the dining room when another hotelier, Jack Cogan, owner of the Manor House Hotel on Camelback Road, strolled into the dining room and came directly to my table.

"Do you have five minutes to listen to my pitch?" "Sure, Jack. Take a pew." I smiled as he a pulled up a chair. Once again, another a proposition by another owner. This was a more adventurous proposition. Jack's proposal was to take up a bankrupt restaurant and bar and partner with the manager who was coming from Cal-Neva, a well-known hotel on the boundary between California and Nevada. The basic was $500 a month plus 2½ % of the net.

Now, Jack owned an auto business in Chicago, but my instincts were not as sharp as my dollar need. So I became a partner to Doug who was the manager of a gambling saloon and instincts were blind in the dazzle of the bucks and the venture.

In months of long days without days off we worked physically and mentally to revive a profit venture. We gradually brought back the customers and around town the Manor bar and dining room was the place to be. Doug, with his contacts from the Cal-Neva saloon, was soon able to bring big names for one night at the Manor as they swung by on their way to the next contract.

One dramatic night a disgruntled husband of one of our waitresses brought trouble to the bar, the first since our opening. I had a glimpse of a revolver stuck in his belt as he sat at the bar. I let Doug keep his eye on the gun and we gradually let our customers close up the bar. Both Doug and I shepherded the reluctant as they finally said their "goo'-nites" and we gently ushered the last reluctant husband out the door.

We locked the door and let out our breath and within minutes we let the security know that an armed man was lurking around the premises. There was a scuffle and a crack of a gun and we were told by the police that an armed man had been shot. Later we were told he was dead. The reports noted that it had been the gunman whose revolver we glimpsed in the bar. Apparently he held resentment about his wife and had something on his mind that night.

After this incident, I was dwelling on my last few years and its rapid changes from the Adams, Bobby Phael and his hotel to my present situation, where I had not taken a day off in six months: seven days a week until 11 pm after the bar closed.

I resolved to take the next Sunday and accompany my wife and daughters to church. Little did I think that this decision would precipitate a storm of rancor from my boss, Jack Cogan, on the Sunday.

In the following several days after the shooting incident, we continued as usual with a few remarks from regular customers, though it dwelled on my mind and lingered in my memory.

I talked with Louise about the incident and we both felt it was a sign of direction. I had made several hasty decisions, particular the Jack Cogan Manor Resort with his deal and his taskmaster and no days off, no breaks since we began to restyle and refurbish the place. We had even gone to a Los Angeles Restaurant show to pick out crockery, silver, linen and kitchen equipment. In that few months of refurbishing, we had turned around a once-bankrupt business and made it into a popular spot on Camelback Road in Phoenix.

I felt inside me on that Saturday night that things had to change, and as I put the light out, I gave it to God.

A Prayer

"...Lo, children are a heritage and gift
of the Lord and the fruit of the womb is his reward.
As arrows in the hand of the giant:
even so are the young children.
Happy is the man that hath his quiver full of them:
they shall not be ashamed but they shall
speak with their enemies in the gate."

From Psalm 127
The Bible

TWO PRINCESSES AND A DREAM FULFILLED

My daughters, Heather & Colleen, who were two more blessings in our lives, were born two years apart.

Heather arrived in July, 1956, at a red-brick hospital in La Jolla near San Diego, where Louise arrived after I took her from Phoenix across the hot Mojave desert, driving at night to avoid the 100° plus temperatures of the blazing July sun to get her to sea-breeze cool La Jolla, where she could give birth in some comfort, I thought.

Once again in retrospect, I was a little foolhardy to drive her in her condition 400 plus miles overnight. But I saw her discomfort with the heat and thought I was doing the right thing to get her to the coast for the birth. God, I'll never forget that journey, as I'm sure Louise didn't! I drove all night and it was with some relief that we arrived in La Jolla in the morning where the cool sea air and the sound of surf was a soothing balm to our aching, tired bodies.

After making an appointment with a doctor referred by our Phoenix doctor, we slept most of the day. We learned that Louise would probably deliver the baby in about a week. But when the week came and went and a few more days passed, I was told that it was a late pregnancy and the doctor informed me, "I'll have to perform a Caesarian."

So, Heather, a ten + pound healthy girl, was born on July 15th, in the small red-bricked La Jolla General Hospital where Louise's room looked across the street into a little cove where locals and visitors played with their children in the sand and sea.

I had rented a small white-framed house in La Jolla for the summer and, after we returned from the hospital, as I looked into the bassinette in the-middle of that cool, linoleum floored, gloss-white painted bedroom, I felt for perhaps the first time a sense of culpability; a paradoxical blending of joy mixed with a pang of sadness, that I had participated in bringing a vulnerable human being into life and that whatever she would experience henceforward, the good and the bad, the joy and the pain, I would be responsible. I know it seems rather much, but that was the momentary insight that began my belated education of sorts: my maturity.

Colleen followed two years later on May 26, 1958, born in what was then Phoenix General Hospital, which of course was air-conditioned, though no view of a cove was available! We by then had become a little more accustomed to the heat and perhaps I, a little more circumspect! Colleen was also a ten-pound healthy baby girl, born on time as predicted. Though today they are and have been slim, trim and athletic, then they were chubby little children who bubbled over with squealing delight and momentary tears.

Both were a joy and a blessing to us. Like other families we accumulated many happy memories, and moments of anxiety as well of discovery and achievement, as parents and children alike discover more about each other as the years roll by. One thing lingers in my mind above all else: the love, the fun, and the pleasure we all shared in each other in those early years of the girls "growing up."

During the four years following Colleen's birth I was studying at Arizona State University. How I got there was another lesson on the unpredictability of people's actions and reactions when challenged by unforeseen circumstances or a crisis in their life.

The unpredictable arose one Sunday morning while I was preparing to leave our house on Flower Street in Phoenix to accompany Louise and the girls to church for the first time in six months, since my new job as catering manager at the Arizona Manor resort hotel, then on Camelback Road and Twenty-fourth Street. In renovating, redesigning and reorganizing the place, including physically remodeling the restaurant and bar, I had not been able to take one day off. But on this particular Sunday I was determined to at least go to church with my family for a few hours, before returning to work.

Just as we were about to leave, the phone rang. The familiar rasping voice with its New York accent assailed my ear. "Where the hell are you, Ken? The Greenbaum lady is here and she wans to go over her son's Bar Mitzvah wit' you'se!" I tried to be calm as I explained, "Jack, I haven't taken a day off for six months. Today I am taking my family to church, but I'll be back there after the service ends. Millie (my senior hostess) has all the details, and she can talk with Mrs. Greenbaum in the meantime."

Jack was not a reasonable man. Born in New York and living in Chicago, where he made his money in a Cadillac dealership and other ventures, he was apparently used to saying, "jump" and most people would not even ask "how high?" He immediately erupted into my ear, "She don't wanna' talk to any damn assistant! She wans ta talk ta you'se! So you'se better get back here right now. Ya' hear me?"

Normally, I did not have to listen to Jack since he kept out of the daily business, in the past trusting his catering manager (yours truly), whom he had enticed from his previous job as catering manager at Bobby Faehl's newest Scottsdale hotel, the Valley Ho, on the promise and agreement that I would be cut in as minor partner for 2 ½% of net profits from the bar and restaurant, plus a monthly wage that was more than I was receiving then at the Valley Ho. The enticement of the bonus at year's end was the deciding factor, though in retrospect, what a few judicial inquiries might have revealed! I might have been advised to be more cautious. I had regrets in leaving Bobby Phael who was not only a well-known, competent, and respected hotelier, but a gentleman as well.

In the event, hearing Jack's rasping aggressive voice with its belligerent undertones, I felt underappreciated and frankly, annoyed. After six months of sixteen-hour days building up a business to the successful operation that it had become, I felt some annoyance at his attitude and his seeming indifference to my personal sacrifices. I struggled to control my feelings. "Jack, I will be back in two hours. I understand Mrs. Greenbaum's concerns and I will take care of them when I return from church." There was a momentary pause before Jack's brain processed my reply and interpreted it as a challenge to his authority. "You get back here raht now or your ass is in a sling!" followed by a loud slam of the phone rammed with some force back into its cradle, preventing my eruption of pent-up resentment and reaction to the crudeness of his address. I began to seethe and, remembering my previous intent to attend church with Louise and the girls, I was hardly in a Christian mode of offering the other cheek, or indeed now in the right state to attend church.

So, in a voice with as much steel in it as Jack had tried to bludgeon me with, I said calmly, "Jack, you can take your job, the 2½% and your un-grateful self and stuff them all! I quit and am going to church!" Jack Cogan had unwittingly become the catalyst for an unlikely epiphany that changed my direction, and ultimately my life for the better.

Louise and I sat down and, after she heard my recounting of Jack's ultimatum and my release of frustration, asked me in a calm voice," What would you like to do?" In that brief moment, in what an epiphany must surely be, I saw in a flash that the years of futile, hard, personally unrewarding investment of time and struggle and commitment had all led to this moment, because it was not what I wanted to do, not what I was meant to do, not what I could do.

I spoke from my heart, not as a man with a family of needs, but with a voice that was really fourteen years of age: I was back answering my stepmother, answering the headmaster, and for the first time, speaking as a man with a vision. "I want to go to college to find myself, to make something of myself, to become proud of what I can do!"

I heard what I said as though listening to another voice, not my own. Louise, ever patient, ever supportive, reminded me that, "It won't be easy, but we can make it. You'll have to get some kind of a job that will enable you to take your classes during the day. But we can work it out." At that moment, I felt lucky and grateful to be married to such a supportive, understanding woman who encouraged my breaking away from the past.

She had already done that when she saw me as the man she loved. When one person invests his or her love in another, it is the greatest gift because it is a statement of worth, an appraisal of value, and a choice above others. In this case, I was trusting myself to begin an adventure with unknown consequences, but for the first time, perhaps, truly sensing that this was an opportunity to change what was unfulfilling into a truly enlightening venture: to go to college, to learn again, to know myself, perhaps. Little did I know, once again, how this would unfold.

THE PHOENIX

The mythical bird that built its own pyre
after fanning the flames with its own wings,
is reduced to ashes only to re-incarnate again.
In a way, I destroyed my so-called opportunity,
by changing my direction by becoming a student at ASU
and changing into a teacher which created a different life.

KHH

PHOENIX OUT OF THE ASHES

Here I was, finally back on my educational journey, enrolled as a thirty five year old freshman in Arizona State University in 1958. Actually it would be two years before Arizona State College became "University," but many changes were coming, particularly in my life and my perceptions as I began my goal to be a teacher and to develop mentally and spiritually as a result of my studies and understandings.

And so, here I was after two decades, two marriages and innumerable meaningless episodes around the world, standing in a room with mostly 19 and 20 year old high school graduates to discover who I was and whatever I could know.

The class suddenly quieted. In the doorway appeared a familiar tall, lanky man with tousled brown hair and a sobering mustache, Dr. Woods. I recognized him immediately because it was he who started this whole thing when I phoned him to pitch my quandary and ask his help. My mind mused on these pivotal events and my "guides," or in older times called "angels," people who by fate cross your path just when you need help with decisions or direction.

In desperation after being sacked by a Chicago boss from my last job as Food & Beverage Manager at the resort on Camelback road in Phoenix,

I reached the end of the line as far as the Hotel, Resort and Restaurant business was concerned. I had worked for sixteen hours a day for seven or eight months only to cross wills with the owner one day, when I came to the limit of unreasonable demands and untenable conditions imposed gradually by a hard, ruthless man with no regard for others.

After that phone incident, I went to church and prayed that whatever followed would be God's will. After church, I returned to the Arizona Manor to add a little of my own will to "God's plan!" After a tense face-to-face with the owner, where the irrevocability of both our positions was seen and re-affirmed, I was fired and subsequently given my severance check.

I was calm and, in a strange way, felt better than I had for some time, realizing I had been compromised by the lure of Cogan's promise of 2½% of the net profit. By the way, we had become the most popular bar and restaurant in Phoenix and every night was more packed and more and more popular. Our sales were higher each week and our efforts and hard work were being rewarded, and the future was rosy.

It was such a disappointment: a personal feeling of being screwed again just when my future was looking profitable and my confidence building.

When I broke the news to Louise, for a depressing minute or two it seemed as if our world had suddenly collapsed. In a moment of inspiration (or desperation?) I burst out with "Why don't I go back to school? I've always wanted to learn something, to be something else... to become.. 'SOMEBODY!'"

My outburst surprised me. I was at that moment in the grip of an idea with a mind of its own! It seemed to take over! Louise said, quite calmly, "Thank God, but you don't have high school transcripts! You have no records. You haven't been to school since you were fourteen!" Showing concern.

Then, when she saw that I was determined to follow my epiphany she, being the loving caring person she was, said in calm assurance, "But, if that's what you want, I'll go with you. It'll be hard, but we'll make it!" Those words, which I have never forgotten, were all I needed to put me into action. It is sad to know now that the new course would bring regret as well as success. But that was to come much later.

I seized the moment and I phoned the Art department at the soon to be Arizona State University in nearby Tempe to inquire if I could speak to the head of the department, Doctor Woods. Surprisingly, my call was connected without further question. I took it as a good omen and asked if I could invite him to lunch where I might avail myself of his expertise, since I was in need of advice. He replied that rather than leaving the campus, "Why don't you come over here and let me buy you lunch!" Of course, I was sure now that this was my lucky day and that, in some way, I was being guided. I was more certain later.

After explaining the situation as I saw it, between mouthfuls of tuna sandwich and French fries, and trying to connect the "last straw" nature of recent firing to my enlightenment about things, he asked several probing and succinct questions concerning my youth, my schooling in England. I tried not to clarify too much his apparent misunderstandings of my "English grounding," as he put it.

More like English dirt, I thought, as I recalled the old wood yard, rather than "grounding." But on the whole we seemed to hit it off and, he being a warm person with an alert mind, I felt as if I was being bathed in benign energy, just like a sailor would feel when he's on a good ship, with a good skipper and crew. I felt surprisingly comfortable throughout lunch.

The outcome of this meeting and luncheon was a visit to the Bursar in the administration office, prompted by Doctor Wood. His introduction and brief explanation of my circumstances, and a typical American reference to my English nationality, "Oh, a Limey, eh? I was over there in the last lot, on an airfield in Lincolnshire. Is it still raining?" was followed by hearty laughs all round!

When the war came up, they asked if my school records were still kept in Portsmouth. I told them that in the winter of 1940, German air raids destroyed the city hall and much of the city, possibly my old school. The Bursar suggested that I send a letter to the mayor to corroborate these historical events, since that letter would give me entrance as a special student. I followed the next day with a letter to his Honor. Within eight days I received a reply with the crest of Portsmouth (a quarter moon with a star in a background on a shield). I was excited and took it post haste to the Bursar at ASU. His Honor corroborated the events following the German fire raids in 1940, destroying the records in the Guildhall, which burned two days after the raids.

Keep in mind, I did not construe that my records were lost. It was given that the city records were destroyed after the November nights when the center of Portsmouth was set afire by incendiary bombs dropped and followed by high explosives which combined and gutted the center of the city. The Guildhall had burned for two days, and files were destroyed. My records were possibly not in the Guildhall, but the inference was enough!

However, the mayor understood my needs and was able to use his office and his authority to graciously give my authenticity as a schoolboy once living and studying in Portsmouth public school. Further, he closed "...It is uplifting and warm regards to one of our citizens who will take the road to higher education in the nation that served in our need and was our ally in the war as brothers. Good Luck in your endeavor."

With the crest and seal of the city, it was acclaimed another link between England and America and became my affidavit of admittance to Arizona State University. I enrolled as a "special student" and began as an Art Major. At that time, with the War only a recent memory, Americans were still allies to England and to ex-servicemen, which brought me like a dream to a freshman beginning, a much delayed emancipation and the road to enlightenment and a fuller life.

An epiphany of sorts, a rebirth. To begin back on the path of meaning and hope. As Professor Woods opening words, "We are here on a journey of discovery and understanding through our eyes, interpreted by exploration and history's artistic achievements."

My pencil began its first of many reams of notes. My dream was realized, though twenty years later! God works his miracles in wondrous ways!

"Imagination is a contagious disease. It cannot be measured by the yard, or weighed by the pound and then delivered to the students by members of the faculty. It can only be communicated by a faculty whose members themselves wear their learning with imagination. In saying this, I am only repeating one of the oldest of observations. More than two thousand years ago the ancients symbolized learning by a torch passing from hand to hand down the generations. That lighted torch is the imagination of which I speak. The whole art in the organization of a university is the provision of a faculty whose learning is lighted up with imagination."

Alfred North Whitehead
Universities and Their Function

THE ART OF SEEING

I stood behind the stretched canvas on the pine frame propped up on the dark brown, multi-colored, paint-sprinkled-all-over-it easel, feeling odd and out of place. After all, it was my first day, first class, first everything. It really was the beginning of a new me. From being always the observer... no, not from "being," I had not really *been* anything. Sure I'd had jobs. I had waited. I had served. I had bossed. I had opportunities and known what it was to be in the same room with celebrities: cardinals, generals, heads of state, film stars, and had a close-up presence to them but always as part of the furniture, so to speak, since I was either a waiter in a restaurant, a steward on ships, a headwaiter or a Maître d' hotel in plush hotels, or a catering manager in some banqueting department in a grand hotel.

I was joining the other world. Here I would not only be looking and seeing in new ways at new things, I would be part of it. It was a different point of view.

Alain Robbe Grillet emphasizes this point. His style of writing was to describe an action or series of acts repeatedly but each time emphasizing different details, as if seen from a slightly different point-of-view. It was the same scene, but viewed from a different observer. Funny how we seem to see things differently when we are forced or need to look at the situation again and again.

It was as if this decision to come back to school was not planned by me but was more the culmination of all that had gone before. The failures, the frustrations and lack of progress had, after all, led to my standing here behind an easel as one of the twenty four students in Dr. Wood's "Summer Workshop" in Tempe, Arizona, in June of 1958, after coming to a dead-end in my wanderings, inside the maze into which my stumbling had led me.

The ultimate realization that my *ignorance*, born out of not going on to a fuller, more exacting education, was probably responsible for most of my frustration and feelings of dissatisfaction in my lack of achievement, and it came like a light in the dark.

The years of blaming everything but myself for my failure at becoming somebody, at achieving *something* worthwhile, were wasted time and fruitless fretting. I was on my way. At thirty-five, I was back in school, studying Art! Art! What was "Art?" Up to that time, I knew of the *art* of subterfuge, the *art* of talk, of conversation, of perhaps, innuendo, and I had to admit, the *art* of evasion; but now, it was art with the capital "A."

I watched the young, recently graduated high school students, now freshmen at State U, sketching, drawing effortlessly, already with authority and fluidity, well beyond my present capability. A single undulating line would insinuate by delicate and subtle pressure on the pencil, graphite, or Conte crayon, a muscle or a bone, almost magically suggested along the curves of the line that appeared on the pristine white of the drawing paper.

In contrast, my lines were drawn as permanent borders that immediately defined space and arbitrary form, much like military fences, I thought: rigid divisions of fluid space as detractions from outside influences or invasions of un-disciplined forces. I could see the soft flesh of the model, even feel it in my lecherous recollections, though I could not seem to transfer what I saw into what could be intuited or felt; I had to admit, finally (in my new role as would-be-artist), that I lacked something quite indefinable at this time, evident, glaringly so, in my laboriously produced "sketches" and "drawing exercises."

My sketches of models were caricatures of the human torso, as opposed to the fluid lines of the already trained and talented young students around me. My lines seemed "metallic," with sharp edges, almost aggressive, one might say: imagine metal joints and steel rods rather than bone or muscle. Try as I might, I could not get the Conte crayon or the Faber soft graphite to "dance" across the huge void of white paper.

I found painting, however, something of a relief, and perhaps in the laying on of the oil, or acrylic, and blending of tones, calming and almost mesmeric. I suspected, however, that I would find expression in another media one day.

I remembered that as a young boy I learned to do cartoons and thereby was able to draw little cartoon people with exaggerated aspects of the human being: bellies overhanging belts, shoes with turned-up soles, hands that were larger than life and cumbersome or noses that were blobs or distorted beaks! I suppose that was not a good foundation for big "A" Art! Perhaps my doubts were stronger than my talent or determination.

The study of various artists' works, however, did fascinate me. Doctor Wood's History of Art was more than a chronological presentation of the great works. It was a work of art itself, with music of the period played in the background, along with his use of poetic lines as commentary as we stared at the wizardry before us.

"Maximum abstract?" A voice broke into my retrospective journey, fogged at first as though from a distance. "Huh? Oh," as I returned to the as yet completely blank canvas that finally focused in front of me. Doctor Wood's arched eye brow and wit conveyed me back to the present, along with the realization that I had not applied one brush to the canvas, as void of form or content as when I placed it on the easel fifteen minutes ago.

"I was thinking," I lamely answered, feeling rather stupid, as suppressed giggles floated around me to reinforce that impression. Doctor

Wood's retort, "It's time to act, not think. Paint! Let the eyes think for you!" brought more snickering from my fellow students around me.

I tried to get some inspiration by focusing on the rather obese Hopi woman that Doctor Wood induced to model for the Oil Painting - A 101 class that day, and the more I observed that mountain of Indian flesh draped in her black dress, weaving a little basket as she squatted on the stage against a backcloth of a brown and turquoise colored rug, the less inclined I became to use her as my subject.

I suppose, in thinking back, I had a different expectation when told we would be painting a live model. My reaction reveals more about my attitudes than anything else! After all, I was only just beginning that long process of what I hoped would be some kind of enlightenment: a college education!

I began to apply myself to the task when I found an acceptable solution to the problem of my negative reaction to the model. I stood back from the easel some time later, after working feverishly applying thinned down turquoise paint as a wash for my sky, with just a faint wisp of clouds over the distant mountains in the background, and a cluster of adobe huts to represent a Hopi village in the middle ground. Wild flowers and cacti accentuated the Spring in the desert overall. I painted a small, hardly discernable black Hopi woman squatting in a doorway with something in her lap.

As I stood back, admiring my ingenuity in creating such a pleasant composition out of my negative reactions to the model, I looked around to perhaps get acceptance, if not downright admiration for my creativity. But none was forthcoming. Doctor Wood, who periodically walked past each student's easel and in a soft voice made supportive or complimentary remarks, pointedly ignored my work and me. I could no longer contain the question of why he was ignoring me and my gnawing need for inclusion.

I stepped away deliberately as he came gliding by my easel the next time and, looking him in the eye, I asked, "Why have you not made any comment on my work, Doctor Wood?" He stared back through his black-rimmed glasses for a brief second and replied, "Because you are avoiding the problem, Ken," and continued gliding in his soft-soled shoes on his round of appraising students' work on their easels.

To say I was abruptly brought to a halt in my artistic (I thought) rendition of a tiny Indian squaw squatting in a Hogan doorway with the panoramic and picturesque pink mesa rising majestically in the background of the Sonoran desert, would be an understatement. I was momentarily nonplussed; but, I have to admit, his words went deep.

I knew he was right. I had shied away from the problem of artistically rendering what was given as a "subject." It was my first lesson in confronting my personal bias towards "fat," or heavier than what in those days was considered "normal." The Hopi woman was, I had thought, "gross." I'm sorry to admit her physique of rolling waves of fat had completely turned me off her as a model. I was judgmental.

I was perhaps even unsympathetic toward those who did not fit what somehow I had come to view as handsome or beautiful in a rather narrow, Anglo-Saxon way, if I may use that term. There is so much I could share about the blinkered, programmed, prejudiced views that swirled around me as a young boy growing-up in between the wars in England. Suffice to say that in that moment of rebuke by Doctor Wood, a crack appeared in the ignorant facade of attitudes and so-called values I supposed to be my veneer of sophistication gained from my background of simply *being* English.

One might have thought snobbery was the problem. But coming as I did from a naval lower-class background (or so I was led to believe), living in a naval town like Portsmouth, with its long history as home to thousands of carousing, drunken, brawling seamen and of shore patrols marching up and down the main street on a Saturday night attempting to keep a semblance of "law and order," was not conducive to breeding snobbery.

However, as young English schoolboys we were constantly reminded in school by the very fact that we had an empire, and that we (at that time) had one third of the world under our influence as a naval power, that we should be leaders, that we should understand our glorious heritage and our British character.

I must say, this false sense of pride in young schoolboys did show up as snobbery, particularly in those of the so-called "upper-class," who most definitely were taught to not only understand their God-given birthright to lead and govern others, but they often expected others to therefore give into them!

But that is a personal aside. Back to my first lesson, not in Art itself, but in the art of being true to oneself, and to one's chosen vocation or task. In a sense, to be aware of your own ignorance and therefore be more likely to learn when the occasion arises.

When Professor Wood stood me to task, I did not waste one more minute. I set to work furiously to white out all the irrelevant daubing that had betrayed my avoidance of the task and stared for a few more intense moments at the Hopi woman model.

For the first time, I saw how delicate her brown hands were as they manipulated the straw strands out of which she fashioned a perfectly round basket. At this stage, she had perhaps finished one third of the basket of dark walnut colored fiber with a ring of lighter color already woven into the base.

As I really looked at her face, I became fascinated with her eyes, her cheekbones, and her lustrous hair drawn back from her face and piled in a special way at the back, in a bun of some kind. I focused now on her hands and that completely peaceful face, eyelids drawn down, face fused; it seemed as one with her moving fingers and the gradually emerging basket. I began to etch very quickly, almost without looking at my canvas.

It was my first real epiphany in art. It was my first loss-of-self within myself. I was Zen. In my philosophy class later I tried to explain this epiphany to Professor Votichenko, who told me that I had experienced a "Zen" moment. Much later in life, I would be lucky to once again experience a "Zen moment!" in golf, when I forgot the *techniques* and just *played golf.*

Some time later, the voice of Harry Wood, (as I came to know his full name) came through my reverie as he called out "Class! Time to bring your work to the front and gather around for the viewing and commentary."

I hardly had time to stand back and appraise it myself. In the event, I took it and placed it against the model stage, towards the end of a row of different sized canvasses. As I walked back past the canvasses, I caught some very impressive work, and wondered at my temerity in being there among those eighteen and nineteen-year-old fellow Freshmen in the University. As Professor Wood worked his way along the row of student work, he both amused and enlightened us as he critiqued each work, drawing attention to subtleties and dynamic aspects as he did so.

"Notice the exaggeration of the hands in John's rendition. He gives a power to the hands that I presume he attaches to the act of creation. Notice his use of sepia and his suggestion of muscles through the paint."

"Look at how Betty has used impressionistic pointillism to bring in the variety of colors from the shawl and the bracelet on the model's arm."

"It seems Melinda has been focusing on the light coming from the skylight to the model's right and has rendered a beautiful study of light and dark much as in the Classical Dutch portraiture, with diffused background softening the contours…" and so he went on, both delighting us and encouraging us with his insights and warm, soft personality.

"Now, here is, I am delighted to say, an intriguing and successful composition!" I could hardly contain myself. He was speaking about my first painting!

He continued, "The artist has captured the almost mystical nature of creativity by painting the face of the model emerging, almost hovering above the two delicate hands above the whorl of the unfinished but powerfully depicted basket, with the fronds as almost as part of a meteorite in space, giving the effective of a dynamism emanating between the hands and the creation!"

Needless to say, his words went over my head, but the impact of his insight into my original avoidance of the "problem" and my subsequent facing it and overcoming it, was really more an epiphany than a lesson then, and has never been forgotten.

During my eighty-nine years of life, I have been privileged to have met and been guided by a handful of rare human beings. Harry Wood was one of them. Not, may I add, by or through his art, or artifices, or even his intellect, which was brilliant, but by his humanity and his understanding of his students, and of one in particular. I have never forgotten him.

Waiting for Godot

Waiting for Godot is an absurdist play by Samuel Beckett with two characters who wait endlessly and in vain the arrival of someone called Godot. I was looking for a perfect teaching job that would change my life. But I had to change, because my illusionary Godot was myself.

KHH

WAITING FOR GODOT

In June 1962, I graduated from four years of insights, learning and some understanding of the importance of literature, and the human mind and its possibilities. I found some enlightenment, latent and perhaps delayed by years of menial labor and circumstances!

I was anticipating becoming a teacher and changing my routine from attending classes at ASU in the morning and, in the afternoons somehow squeezing in time in the stacks at the library, reading not only assigned texts but many from the recommended lists, writing notes, thesis and so on, while keeping my eye on the clock at the end of the day, knowing I had to go to work by five, which meant I had to drive from Tempe over to Camelback and Central, where Navarre's was situated, about ten miles from the University.

I was a waiter at night for four years while I attended Arizona State University. I managed to get a waiting job at one of the best restaurants in Phoenix, since I was a friend of the manager. Navarre's was a classy watering spot with quiet decor and discrete table seating often frequented by the sports managers and baseball stars as well as notables from the city and visitors from LA or Hollywood.

If a notable were in town they would sooner or later show up at Navarre's, a nightclub atmosphere much like in the twenties in London, which served suppers late into the evening. I opened and prepared the restaurant for service because Jack Thomson, the manager, scheduled me early as a favor so I could get away by 10pm, with the exception of one night a week, generally Saturday, when I would be the late closer, since I had classes at 7am on the weekday mornings at ASU. This routine worked for both of us for which I was forever in his debt.

This amicable arrangement enabled me to carry a full load of credits each semester which in turn allowed me to complete the requirements and graduate on time four years later. There was one late night incident of note that was to have an important effect on my future, when I graduated in 1962. Another of those serendipitous occurrences.

It was in the spring of 1961 when I was the late-closing waiter. I greeted a late night customer at around 8:30pm as he sat down to order first a Scotch on the rocks and then his dinner. Relaxing with an after-dinner brandy, he called me over to ask several questions about Phoenix in general and we got into a talk of sorts, which, as the restaurant emptied, developed into a lengthy conversation during which he ordered another cognac.

This apparently predisposed him to make many inquiries concerning my reasons for waiting on tables and what was I studying at ASU, etc. He appeared to be sincere and interested in my explanations and about my developing ideas regarding teaching. When he rose to leave, after shaking my hand, he offered me his card with his invitation to call him when I graduated the following year.

I pocketed what appeared to be a usual business card of which I had been given hundreds over the years going back to my time on the Cunard passenger ships—the *Queens Elizabeth* and *Mary* and the *Mauretania*. Passengers and customers like this gentleman often enclosed their personal or business cards along with their envelopes containing gratuities, so I did not give it another thought and later put it with the random pile in my desk drawer.

I graduated in May and, having already sent résumés and letters to several San Diego school districts, moved my family out of the Phoenix heat in expectation of getting an offer from my contacts and my posted résumé. I had worked for several summers nearby in La Jolla and hoped that some of my contacts would perhaps reply in the affirmative.

In the event, when the days passed and the school year loomed on the horizon, I happened across the business card that was given to me by the Watsonville business man so interested in my background and my teaching career. I noticed he was chairman of the school board as well as the owner of his drug store! Since the summer was almost over, I phoned him and he not only remembered me, he immediately expected me to arrive today! He urged me to take a plane to San Francisco the next day and one of the faculty would meet me at the airport! His expectancy and the warmth in his voice and his sincerity bowled me over. Something inside told me to seize the moment.

So I said I would phone him later when I got the plane ticket.

That was how I began my career as a teacher in a small bucolic town, not as I hoped in some modern edge of technology in a big city! However, God has his invisible ways to perform his miracles! So be it!

The sky is torn across
This ragged anniversary of two
Who moved for three years in tune
Down the long walks of their vows.

Now their love lies a loss
And Love and his patients roar on a chain;
From every tune or crater
Carrying cloud, Death strikes their house.

Too late in the wrong rain
They come together whom their love parted:
The windows pour into their heart
And the doors burn in their brain.

Dylan Thomas
A Wedding Anniversary

MEA CULPA, MEA CULPA

As the semesters rolled into years students came and went, September Freshmen became June's Sophomores, and the Juniors promised to send me a card from Maui or London or wherever summer was taking them. Seniors shook hands and with smiles on their faces went out into the larger curriculum of college, university or into the harsher reality of their first "jobs" or their individual consequences of choice and circumstances.

Those first years of teaching at Watsonville High were a mixture of exploration, discovery and failure. I, like many other beginning teachers, went from "teaching as an instruction" with a rather stiff persona, probably assimilated from the residual effects of all the teachers I sat in front of ever since my English school days, from the Jesuits, who were authoritative, quick, and spoke from a loftier view than the low desk afforded me, to the more approachable teachers I experienced at Flying Bull Lane Senior Boys School where I ended my English school days at the age of fourteen.

The circumstances leading to the unexpected change from St. John's Catholic School to Flying Bull Lane Senior Boys School were brought about by my rebellion against the strict and punitive rules, part of the St. John's order of things. One Sunday, not feeling too well, I had declined to go to church and instead slept an extra hour. On the following Monday, I arrived in class as usual at 7:45am, fully recovered from whatever ailed me and refreshed by my extra sleep. Suddenly I was called up in front of the class by the priest-teacher.

"Harrison, why were you not at Mass on Sunday? You missed communion!" he asked me with his legs astride and his hands behind his back. "I was not well, Sir. My stepmother..." Before I could finish presenting the authority of a mother, albeit a stepmother, he reached from behind his back and with his left hand palm up appealing to God up in the ceiling, said, "Oh, Jesus! I've heard it all now! Now, young man, hold y'r hand out and take y'r punishment f'r not doin' your duty!" His Irish accent was not funny at that moment!

With this sentence pronounced his right hand came into view, clutching a thin cane, which he raised in the air ready to do his duty. My ire began to rise.

Bugles sounded. Somewhere in the misty distance through the harsh sound of enemy fire, I distinctly heard a voice, "Stand fast men! Don't blink... Hold your fire!" I raised my hand defiantly towards the enemy. There was a crack of a gun and the searing pain of a bullet as it struck my hand!

Through the mist, I saw the face of my teacher as he intoned, "Now ask God's forgiveness and be in church on Sunday!"

Everything exploded in me. "You don't know God! You don't know Jesus!" I dashed past his startled face, out the door and out of that place and I didn't stop until I found myself a half-mile up Edinburgh Road, almost opposite the Hippodrome theater, where I stopped to regain my breath and wipe my eyes and to get some kind of composure before walking the two miles to our house in Baker Street.

As I walked home, my thoughts were rebellious ones as the hot blood flushed my cheeks, *I'm not going back to that bloody place ever again!*

They can't make me go! I'll show him! As the anger abated, as the blood subsided and the flush ebbed, I began to face the consequences. *What will she say when she hears what I've done?* and as determination returns, *I don't care what she thinks! I'm fed-up with people ordering me around!*

I think it was the beginning of my true sense of becoming self, regaining what perhaps I had lost in the orphanage and the subsequent period of domination by my stepmother. I actually was quite calm by the time I got home and for the first time felt in charge of my life. It was about nine in the morning and for some reason Gertrude was not home and so, being hungry always, I looked the cupboard that functioned as the larder-come-pantry found a half-loaf of crusty bread, some margarine and a jar of marmalade and quickly spread dollops of both margarine and marmalade on a thicker than normal slice of that crusty bread. It was the best single slice of bread I could ever remember. I felt so good! Boy, I really felt I had in some strange way taken a step in a new direction. I was not quite sure what would happen, but I really didn't care!

Afterwards, as reality seeped back in, I carefully brushed up the crumbs and placed everything back in the cupboard and started to clear out the ashes from the cold fireplace. My mind wandered, *What happened to Beryl Bullymore?* I wondered if she was still on her way to Singapore or if she had arrived. The Bullymores had lived in 71 opposite our house in Bakers Street and when I was sick in bed upstairs, I used to lower a cord attached to a book out of the small bedroom window. l would swap the book with hers and I would pull the cord back up through the open window. Inside the books we would scribble little shy notes: "Hello, Beryl, I watched you go to school yesterday. I'm sorry I'm not able to see you. I've got asthma again. Thanks for the book. Ken." She responded with similar innocuous notes but, to our hungry eyes, there were signs of something we grew towards, but were not yet fully aware of, such was our semi-innocent immaturity in those days.

Beryl's father, a shipwright engineer, had been ordered two months earlier to accompany a huge dry-dock being towed to Singapore, where the Navy was looking ahead to prepare for possible emergency repairs to capital ships in need of a facility 10,000 miles from English ports. This was 1937 and the winds of war were blowing, fed by rumors from the continent.

How ironic, with the wisdom of hindsight 89 years later, when I recollect that two of our main battleships, the Repulse and the Prince of Wales, which might have been in mind when the dry-dock was moved to Singapore, were both sunk as the Japanese overran Singapore and its dockyard and dry-dock.

I never did hear or find out the fate of the family of Bullymores. This occurrence of lost connections was to become more the norm than unusual as war loomed over us, with its aftermath of dislocation, tragedy and upheaval.

But back to my present dislocation from Saint John's Catholic School and the uncertainty of my future: the sound of the front door opening and my stepmother's steps down the passageway as she came into the living room, startled somewhat by my presence there.

"What are you doing home this early? What's going on?" she asked all in one breath as she took her hat off and dropped a bag of shopping onto the table. "I left school because the priest caned me for not being at Mass yesterday!" I gritted my mouth in an attempt to show determination and resolve. "He caned you? Why?"

To my surprise, she seemed quite taken aback with the idea. "You must have said something. You were cheeky, maybe?" "No, I wasn't! He just wouldn't listen to me! He grabbed my hand and whacked it! It hurt! I told him he didn't know Jesus! And I rushed out of there, and I'm not going back, even if they drag me!" I gushed with still smoldering resentment.

After a long silence, during which she lit up a cigarette and looked out of the small window, tapping her right fingers on the window sill, she turned back and, to my further surprise, looked at me in a strange way, pronouncing her verdict: "Well, then, we shall have to enroll you in a council school, shan't we?"

I couldn't believe my ears! Inside, a faint intuition stirred. I believe I sensed a change in my stepmother's attitude toward me. I had stood my ground.

Later I was enrolled in the nearest council school, which happened to be Flying Bull Lane Senior Boys School, about four blocks away. I could still walk both ways, though it was a lot closer than St. John's, at least two miles away down Edinburgh Road at the back of the cathedral.

It was a better atmosphere, even though a boys only school. The teachers were friendlier and no one asked me if I had been to church, or mass, or confession. I quickly settled down though it took a little while to climb out of my "Catholic" shell and really open-up to my new schoolmates.

My memories at 89, are positive ones. They include being successful at my studies, 3rd in my class and offered a scholarship based on what the masters saw in my writing and English in general. Best of all, I got to play soccer, run in track, play cricket, and swim. It wasn't all rosy, of course, but a definite improvement in my school life, and I looked forward to going to be with my new classmates. Several teachers and one in particular, Mr. Gardner, my English teacher, were a positive influence on my interest and in my desire to become a teacher one day.

That day had arrived! I was a teacher at Watsonville High School in California where at the age of forty I, somewhat belatedly, graduated from Arizona State University with majors in English and Art. Being a beginning teacher held no qualms for me, perhaps due to maturity in years and being comfortable speaking and directing people during all those years on the ships and in the hotel business in general. So, once I overcame my rather formal, no nonsense demeanor in front of the high school kids, I began to smooth out my delivery and crack a joke here and there when I felt it appropriate.

I must say, I enjoyed my first ten years of teaching, including six or seven at Watsonville and the first three or four at the new Aptos High School outside of the Watsonville area, about seven miles along the highway towards what was once called Rio Del Mar but, as growth mushroomed, eventually became Aptos. I believe Aptos came from an ancient Indian tribe that lived in the area.

It was in Rio Del Mar, a small cluster of streets and a couple of roads meandering through oaks and pines on the Monterey Bay side of Highway One (which inevitably became the freeway) that I first was able to build a little house with two bedrooms, two baths, kitchen and living room on a nice lot among those trees. Though I was able to make a great deal of my house and lot, to my dismay I had to put up with Eucalyptus trees rather than oaks! They shed constantly, and if you are inclined to a flower garden, you are forever cleaning Eucalyptus droppings from your garage driveway, your garden path and what flowers you might have growing in the ground or in hanging pots. However, for $14,879, in 1969 we found ourselves living in an attractive shingled home in a nice community only half-a-mile from the beach shoreline! As a matter of interest, that same house sold for over $500,000.00 just 20 years later!

But in the 1990s, I was living in Seascape, a newer development a couple of miles along the shore. By then, we had sold the house on Hume Avenue in Rio Del Mar in the early 1970s for about 28,000.00 and parlayed some of the profit into a bigger gray three bedroom ranch style house with two and a half baths, kitchen, dining-room, study and an inside atrium around which these rooms were dispersed. A bigger house for growing family needs and a bigger mortgage, that was the norm in California then.

We had some happy years in that house on Beach Pines Drive, on a raised lot with large pine trees in the back. With two large floor-to-ceiling windows looking out on the pine trees and the big fuchsia bushes set in the garden box in front of each window, the view and setting was quite pleasant. We were now in an upscale community, with large pleasant houses on spacious lots. Quiet and peaceful and with mature pine trees.

A gravel path led from the side of the house around to the front two bedrooms, which had windows that opened out and sills that were only three feet from the floor. This was very convenient for both girls, particularly Colleen, who climbed out the window on occasion after having said, "Good night, Mum!" "Good night, Dad!" at 8pm. I suppose curfews were sometimes a little arbitrary. Parents were learning. We all learned together.

I had my own den, my workroom or office. After dinner it was routine for me to retire to the desk to read and comment on the students' papers and quite common to retire at eleven after several hours of this. Any serious, dedicated teacher of English would do as much in order to get feedback to the students concerning their efforts and their accomplishments. I was happy doing what I had dreamed of so long ago, when it seemed it might not be possible.

It was an ideal situation for a long time, but as life unfolds and time passes, things changed in unforeseen ways, though the Catholic shadow was ever in my life. Certain views came up that related to the girls religious indoctrination. Louise wanted both girls to get Catholic instruction by the nuns, to become officially Catholics and attend the nearby Catholic center for instruction and indoctrination. I felt they should find their own way to religion by making their own choice. We all went to a Catholic church nearby but I was not enamored and was not in the spirit, only the duty body for the family.

I really felt uncomfortable, somewhat hypocritical underneath, keeping my early experiences in mind. The girls were enrolled in a non-parochial school, Aptos High, where I taught. Heather never enrolled in one of my classes but Colleen did take my creative writing class and contributed to the Creative Magazine published by the class at term end. Aptos High was a well regarded school, which had been organized by a progressive, creative principal, Richard Cunnison, who had very modern ideas regarding the developing the curriculum and involving students and parents in the efforts to produce a qualitative teaching body, whose first consideration was the teaching of those young minds, instilling the verities and love of learning and accomplishments.

He put the students first and their minds second and teachers third. He was a new fresh breed of Educators, understanding the necessity of having the best teachers who were dedicated to the students' welfare and their understanding that their future was predicated on their studies and skills. He recruited the young, eager, creative teachers to Watsonville High School which at that time was overcrowded, functioning as two schools since the proposed new school, Aptos High, was behind schedule and not to be completed for another six months.

The general opinion among those interviewed as possible staff for the new school was that it was an exciting future for those chosen. Also, almost everyone was impressed with the new principal, Richard Cunnison.

Aptos opened in 1969, and my daughters attended several years: Heather as a senior; Colleen beginning her junior year. Both girls were intelligent, independent and talented and were happy there.

Louise continued to insist that the girls should be taught the Catholic catechism, and that they attend a Catholic seminary for instructions.

I had been enlightened by both my personal experiences and my four years of liberal arts and humanities study at Arizona State University, plus the many hours of postgraduate time studying philosophical works. Minds such as Locke, Kant, Regal, Jung, Freud, William James and Maslow, et al, piqued my interest in Philosophy 1 at ASU, and began my quest for, if not "the truth," at least to find alternatives to the kind of truths given to a naive and unquestioning boy by Catholic authority.

Without belaboring the crisis that developed between two loving parents who were possibly seen by others as an ideal couple with two charming, intelligent and talented daughters, the fact was that Louise was adamant that the girls be indoctrinated into the Catholic Church. I was cut-off by an invisible wall between us that became impregnable by reason or emotion. I was nonplussed and dismayed that once again Catholic influences would disrupt what on the surface seemed a bond of love and respect.

Reason had no sway on Louise or her dogmatic belief in her religion. And so, we actually went to a lawyer and began our separation, which finalized as a divorce. I must say with respect and love that this came suddenly, and I had not seen her Catholicism so cemented within her character, though I recollected her insisting I get my first marriage nullified by the Vatican before we wed.

So, seeds that are underground sooner or later grow and become weeds in your beautiful garden and you must remove them or they proliferate.

Louise was a beautiful intelligent woman, honest and warm and talented who was in thrall to the voices residing in her psyche and the dogma implanted in her since she was a little girl. It was a shock to find that my warm, kind, intelligent woman chose dogma rather than our partnership of twenty years!

It was a sad, regretful chapter in my life and as a father. Though my daughters throughout their lives have shown love and mature understanding of the both points of view of their parents and supported Louise always as they loved her and knew her as a loving and caring mother. I was devastated, and echoes of Catholic history from the past haunted me for some time. I paid for becoming un-Catholic: you pay for changing your mind. In the following years, Louise sadly developed emphysema, from when she was a secretary all those years among executives smoking one cigarette after another and, after some invalid years, finally succumbed to a weakened heart. She was buried in one of the last grave lots in the back of the Catholic Church, The Resurrection in Aptos that she faithfully attended and where Heather played her flute and participated in various duties.

At the funeral, Heather & Colleen went in front of the altar and gave their loving homilies and eulogies but I could only weep for a dear departed love whom, through hubris, I abandoned by divorce. Mea culpa. I never stopped loving her, and she was a model mother and warm-hearted woman. A tragedy unexpected. Both daughters have kept their faith and love and loyalty to their dad and they continue to keep in touch and visit whenever possible. Heather still teaches at Santa Catalina Catholic School in Monterey, where she has taught the first graders for 30 years. Colleen has taught Ballet and Modern Dance at two Junior Colleges in San Diego, where she has lived ever since graduating with a BA from California University at Erwin near Newport, California. Subsequently, she took a teacher's credential at San Diego State. She is well known as an excellent teacher of the dance and theatrics.

Her husband, Steve Shipkowski is a superintendent of police cars and vehicles as well as connected to the San Diego fire force. He and his son, Scotty, were active in the Boy Scout organization and both are avid outdoorsmen. Scotty is an outstanding young man who played football for his Catholic high school and was a junior fireman. As of now, Scotty is enrolled in San Diego University and in the San Diego Fire department, taking courses relevant for becoming a full-fledged fire-man, to follow his father's steps.

Both daughters inherited their mother's grace and intelligence and have given of themselves to countless students, and others in need over the years. I am ever thankful to God that I was privileged to be father to such warm, sensitive and intelligent human beings. Divorce did not diminish my love for their mother, Louise.

In the evening of my life, I remember the morning of hope and the dawn of love that was a new sunrise that lit my way to a new life. I have been doubly blessed, for my fate brought me to my final wife, Lupita, an-ex-nun disguised as an angel to teach me humility and the power of the spirit.

The irony of life is that after falling in love with Lupita, after eight years divorced, I discovered that she was a Catholic ex-nun who taught music at Marymount in New York State for fourteen year and then became a successful business manager for Nestle for 20 years.

God works in strange ways his miracles to wrought. He taught humility and forgiveness through Lupita.

But that is another chapter, which will end my third life in this narrative that might be completed with God's grace.

DEMOCRACY

Democracy is like the experience of life-always changing, infinite in its variety, sometimes turbulent and all the more valuable for having been tested for adversity. Free speech and opinion as part of free people.

KHH

THE NEW TEACHER LEARNS AMERICAN SPIRIT

I was met at the Oakland Airport by two high school faculty members from Watsonville, about an hour and a half south on the freeway, in Santa Cruz County, approximately eighty miles. "Hi! I'm Bill Combs, the Vice Principal," the big, tall one with black-rimmed glasses beamed, and, nodding at the overweight but sturdy looking older man with thick tortoise shell glasses, sparse grey hair, but thick Teddy Roosevelt mustache, "and this is, Jack Hamilton, head of the English department."

I shook hands, and noticed how big and firm they both were. No nonsense there, I thought. Especially with Jack, I noted as he nearly crushed my bony, uncalloused hand.

I was duly impressed and somewhat elevated that I should be accorded such a welcome and met by not only one faculty member but two, including the assistant principal and the head of English! This is going to be nice. They really seemed to be interested to have a genuine Englishman coming to join their staff. I was glowing in the warmth of my own interpretation when, after having been conducted to a rather shabby looking Ford station wagon, I spilled my gratitude all over them.

"Thanks so much for taking the time and trouble to meet me here at the airport!" I said jovially from the back seat as we swung onto the freeway south. They looked at each other for a moment, smiling, before Jack turned to look at me squarely in the face and gently pricked my balloon, "We were at a meeting over at UC Berkley and we were asked by the principal if we might pick you up on our way back to Watsonville," he said quietly, but with a twinkle in his eye he added, "Sorry the Rolls wasn't available, sir!"

I smiled, recognizing the good nature of the ribbing, and they continued to grin as we pulled into the parking lot of a large busy seafood restaurant on the fringe of Oakland.

Sitting at the bar between them with a scotch on the rocks charged to the expense account, I was regaining my aplomb and looking forward to the dinner I had been invited to share, also on the Watsonville School District account.

Now, this was more like it. I felt an important step was taken by accepting the phone invitation to come to Watsonville, California for an interview as prospective teacher of English at the high school.

I had flown from Phoenix a few days after graduation at the suggestion of a school board member whom I had met by chance in a Phoenix restaurant where I worked as a waiter by night while going to the University by day. The manager was a friend and associate when I was manager at the Arizona Manor, and the Westward Ho a new hotel, built by Bobby Phael, whose father years before had owned The Biltmore in Los Angeles.

"Come on, Ken!" Jack's voice brought me back from Phoenix. "For an Englishman you're a slow drinker. Drink up laddie," he lapsed into a Scot's burr to clarify both his pride in being of Scot's blood and his point.

"I didn't want to be a burden on the budget," I smiled. "Ohoo, did you catch the alliteration?" he asked Bill who was contemplating ordering oysters Rockefeller at the bar, since we apparently had a while to wait and by the look of it the budget was shot anyway.

"Oh, he's being British, you know. They all talk funny," was his way of not admitting he didn't know what alliteration meant, though he was an able, intelligent administrator.

He was an ex-PE teacher and basketball coach from North Dakota before being made vice principal at Watsonville High. His six-foot-three-inch height was probably an advantage for a disciplinarian at a high school with its quota of future football giants! That aspect of *teaching* had not been encountered by this novice as yet in my brief stint in *education*!

The three of us stumbled back to the station wagon some hours later and drove to Watsonville, arriving about 9pm in the late summer evening. As Bill was leaving the wagon in the school bus yard, where he had parked his car, he said, "You might take a brief look at the main administration building and your intended new classroom, should you be joining the staff," As we unlocked the back door, I caught a strong musty smell of old floor wax and other more vague odors which suggested old rather than new. Jack guided me down the badly lit hallway to an even more shadowy stairwell, lit by a single yellow light bulb in a wrought iron fixture on the stair wall below us. We stopped at a shabby wooden door, which I thought must be a janitor's closet, wondering why on earth we would be wanting to open the janitor's closet?

I stared at Jack's hand, turning a long antiquated metal key reminiscent of a jailor's key that one sees in costumed movies. As the key was turned, he actually pressed on a latched handle to release the door and as it swung open, he flicked the switch just inside.

Well, there it is!" He waved his hand, vaguely as if reluctant to be associated with it. Standing there in the dim depressing light of that shadowy basement room, redolent with ancient layers of well-worn floor polish and chipped paint mingled with vague vapors of stale sweat and perhaps chalk, I, for the first time, wondered what I was doing there! My false spirits buoyed by naive hope, desire, and two scotches-on-the rocks ebbed and sank to the thin soles of my shoes. It was the low point of my trip, which, I suppose was begun with more ignorance than knowledge, more faith than understanding, and a fervent desire born out of need.

It was my first lesson from that real world that I for so long wanted to join. *Expect the unexpected and deal with it,* I reminded myself. *Expectations that go beyond evidence always lead to disappointment.* It wasn't long before I returned to the fact that, after all, I did *have a job* and it *was* in California, and I was *out of the desert*, literally and figuratively!

Watsonville proved to be what it appeared to be on that first visit to interview for the teaching position at Watsonville High: a charming, friendly, peaceful place in which to raise and nurture a family. It was a small town then of twenty five thousand population, nestled in the Pajaro Valley at the base of Mount Madonna, the higher of several hills lying to the east of the valley which included the villages of Aromas to the southeast and Corralitos to the north, nestled among the apple orchards just a couple of miles from the Monterey Bay coast.

Its industry was mainly market farming and apple growing, evident from the large and profuse orchards outside of town which I delighted in driving past and through whenever I made visits to Corralitos, particularly in the Spring, when the air was filled with white and pink apple blossoms as far as the eye could see.

Sadly, some of them are gone: trees chopped down and the more profitable multiple harvest strawberry fields often draped in plastic sheets replace them; the harsh facts of bottom-line labor costs and upkeep of the one-crop-a-year orchards eventually doomed the apple business in Watsonville and unfortunately changed the landscape around the town drastically.

Once orchard-wooded hills that cradled the pretty, peaceful town have become flat, plastic-covered strawberry fields that shimmer in the spring sun like mirages, suggesting lakes where there are none. Then, the rains come and the banked rows of loamy soil and sand are eroded and sometimes flooded away leaving strips of plastic mingled and mangled along the furrowed, eroded hills, like grey bandages falling away from the wounded body of the land.

I think about those stately, upright rows of pink and white blossomed apple trees that once graced the foothills of this valley of the birds, this Pajaro Valley, and know that beauty is not only in the eye of the beholder, but, as I look at the photos on the walls around my study, it is also transient.

After breakfast at Bill McComb's he suggests we should meet our principal. I thought we would go to his house, but he smiled and said,

"Let's go outside and meet our Principal." I couldn't believe what I was seeing: a principal and a neophyte would-be-teacher meeting in the middle of the street with a scotch on the rocks in his hands, as if gathering a party on a patio!

I felt like I was in a Fellini movie. By his bearing and his abrupt, direct and blunt delivery, I immediately got the impression of a military man. His six-foot plus height added to that impression, though I didn't really know the man. "So, this is the *Limey*?" "Jason, this is Ken Harrison, the English teacher from Phoenix who might join us. He's an Englishman... from England!" he added unnecessarily (being ex-football coach, he understandably knew nothing about tautology) but I rather liked his openness and warmth.

He reached forward to shake my hand and left no doubt as to his confidence, or his welcome, as he pumped my hand a couple of times. I was surprised by the familiarity of the slang term, particularly coming from the new principal of my intended school and I suppose, my naive expectation of entering a more professional, formal environment of education. But I quickly accepted the greeting as a friendly ice-breaker, no doubt the tinkling glass helped me in my association, as did my several sips of Bill's scotch.

"So," I countered, stressing the adjective, "You're the Big Principal I've been warned about! I'm pleased to meet you." He squeezed my hand a little bit harder. "A smart ass Limey," he chuckled. "Has he met Jack yet?" turning to Bill. "Oh yes. He's met him. We picked him up at Oakland after our Berkley conference yesterday."

"Well, Ken. Welcome to the Watsonville High team! But remember, we speak American around here!" His rimless glasses glinted in the setting sunlight as he turned abruptly and called to Bill over his shoulder, "Take care of... the Englishman!" I caught the hesitation and smiled. It was going to be all right. I had a good feeling and it wasn't all scotch. Watsonville was my first teaching job, and I'd already had a lesson in one-upmanship. Smile a lot when you're testing the ice!

Apparently his taste of scotch, acquired when in England as an American army officer during the war, carried over when he re-entered the civilian life, as I witnessed now as an educator in this bucolic small town. We retraced our steps across the road to Mr. McComb's house where our glasses were refreshed, as if it were normal around here.

The lesson was applied that evening as I was introduced to the department heads around the well-extended dinner table in Bill's crowded dining room. As I listened to the conversation and observed the personalities around that table, I realized I had brought a false expectation of what I would encounter based on my student teaching and long ago memories of my experiences in English schooling in a rather more autocratic environment.

I had a vague feeling of suddenly being odd, not quite out of things but not in, either. But I pushed such thoughts away as I finished my scotch, and switched to a glass of Californian chardonnay from Napa, I was told, though they didn't give the vineyard, but by then I didn't really care. I was beginning to like being a teacher more and more. But this was before I learned how little I was going to be paid!

The next morning before I was to go to the Oakland airport, I was driven by Bill to the high school where we met Jack in the principle's office. Jason was not there and for a moment I was surprised, I didn't know why. "Well, Ken, there's just a couple of details you will need to know before you give your decision. Jack will explain your probable class assignments first." He gestured towards Jack who laid down some papers he had been perusing.

"Ken, you'll be teaching one remedial English class, two freshmen and two Junior English Literature and Composition classes. I'm also going to give you..." He paused to dramatize the gift, "the special responsibility for the Pippin, our creative writing book that is composed of the best work from the students." Jack adjusted his glasses, "Being English, from England, I mean." He seemed to be fumbling and taking his glasses off, he cleaned them with his handkerchief put them back on and finished, "I thought you'd do a good job."

"Thank you, Jack. That was good of you to offer that." I, too, was caught in the moment. "Now, Ken, about the salary," Bill broke in, "Since you are a first year teacher, our district scale shows that to be four thousand, eight hundred a school year."

My ears heard but my mind was flashing back to Philadelphia, The Barclay Hotel, and Caesar Innocenti, speaking, "Ken, you will be paid four hundred dollars per month, and you will get a full share in the gratuities which will be paid weekly based on the week's business." My first week's gratuities amounted to over two hundred dollars that first week and later went often to plus three-or four hundred; so that I was earning with raises, one year later an average between five hundred and six hundred dollars a month, around seven thousand dollars that year.

That was ten years ago! Here I was being offered as a teacher, after four years study and training and more studies and training to come for my secondary credential, forty-eight hundred a year with a wife and two girls to support. "Do you accept the conditions?" Bill's voice broke into my comparisons. "Oh, 'er, I, well, yes. I was not expecting (there I go again!) such a low salary. Will there be increases or changes?" I was clearly not aware of the reality of educational finances and of being a burden to the public taxpayers. "Well, yes, of course things could change." Bill looked over at Jack for support. "Oh, yes, the union is constantly reviewing the situation." *He couldn't really sound more phony or unassuring*, I thought. But there I was. It was late August. I wanted out of Arizona. I wanted a teaching job. I needed a teaching job. So, standing up, I extended my hand to Bill, then to Jack, "I accept. Thanks for your hospitality and your kindnesses."

After signing the contract, which had been filled in in expectation of my acceptance, I was given the green copy. "When will you expect me here?"

"First meeting of teachers is… "Bill consulted the large calendar hung on the wall to the left of the principal's desk around which we had been sitting, "…let's see, we open September 4, teachers meetings are August 27th and 28th. So, we'll see you on the 27th, Ken. If you can get here earlier you might find it more convenient to get yourself and your family settled. You'll need to find a place to rent I expect. "Give me or Jack a call if you need anything, Jack will take you to the airport after lunch. What time was your plane?"

Three hours later I was on the Hughes Air West on my way back to Phoenix with a contract to teach in Watsonville High School in a small farming town for four thousand eight hundred a year. Somehow, the contract seemed worth more than that to me. I was beginning a new direction, a new path, but an old quest. I would be searching for something that, though still not clearly perceivable, I felt was coming more into view.

A GOOD MOVE

And so, the well-worn carpets up,
And privacy's print curtains down,
More space than we had remembered,
In naked, more revealing light
Stripped, we stood, once again exposed
Upon the bare-board reality,
Staring at the wall's negatives,
As pictures chosen with great care,
Remembering the positives.

The world crammed with goods then,
Well plundered with our dollars,
Our lusts, we shoulds, oughts and musts
Of child-deep commercial longings.
Now tightly packed in sealed boxes,
Some in cardboard coffins aboard
The big white mover's mobile dicker,
Waiting to carry our goods and
Not-so-goods to another state.

Kenneth Hugh Harrison

FROM CACTUS TO APPLE ORCHARDS

We arrived from Phoenix in August, 1962, a week before school was scheduled to begin, and stayed the first night in a motel at the entrance to town. The great moving van containing all our furniture and belongings arrived the next day. What followed on that day provided positive proof that my decision to accept the teaching job in this small, farming community was the right one!

I met Jack that morning and as results to my requests for help in locating a place to stay, a car to drive and a loan to tide me over to payday, (I really needed help!) the following arrangements were made in swift succession:

The principal knew of an apartment available across the street(!), above Dr. Christy's office in a large white-framed two-storied house! I took one look at the spacious apartment with four windows and a wall bookcase for my books, two spacious bedrooms, a nice light bathroom and a light kitchen, and I was hooked! Next I was taken by Jack down to the Ford dealership on Main street and introduced to the manager who in short order arranged a suitable second car on credit!

Finally, we arrived at a small office in a home on Martine Road where several of the administration lived and, in fact was a rather attractive tree-lined area of substantial homes I would later get to know as friendships grew.

I was introduced to a union man who was the secretary. There in that home office, I was swiftly provided with a loan that allowed me to retrieve our furniture and belongings from the removal van and have them delivered to our new apartment!

A car, a home, and a loan in one day!

I felt it was an omen that this new venture was blessed. We moved in that day and by seven at night we were at home: Louise, Heather, Colleen and I were home. We felt blessed and, around the table that evening we were a family and we thanked God.

The high school was opposite the house on the road, and the girl's school, called Minty White, was two blocks from our apartment, which meant the girls walked to school with ease and in safety.

Mr. Martinelli's house was next door with a pretty flower garden and his cider business, recessed in a back acre. Soon Mrs. Martinelli heard a knock on the door and two little girls, with a bunch of her own flowers, introduced themselves as their new neighbors, the Harrisons! Mrs. Martinelli, being a warm understanding person, took it all in good humor and even gave them a red Delicious apple! However, the girls soon understood that they should not pick a neighbor's flowers even though they thought it would be nice to introduce new neighbors!

I was to teach English for seven years at Watsonville High, including evening classes for foreign students, and started and coached a soccer team, permission for which took two years of cap-in-hand pleading with the long entrenched, football-obsessed athletic director!

Watsonville High had been and was a football dynasty! To speak of "soccer" was to speak sacrilege. It was then in the minds of most Americans a non-American game, though it was played in almost every country in the world!

Because Watsonville had many Mexicans, Guatemalans, Hondurans, Nicaraguans and a sprinkling of Caribbeans as part of its farm labor pool, it was not long before I noticed them playing soccer here and there.

Also, it was a proven healthy sport since it was built around constant running and athletic movement when played at its best. I finally convinced the coach that his football players, especially the wide receivers and defensive cornerbacks, could improve their speed and dexterity through soccer training and playing.

It took President Kennedy's passing of a bill to promote minority participation, including girls, in sports, to finally allow the formation of a soccer program, which the director reluctantly acceded to by offering me a $100 budget for the first year. This bought the team 15 pairs of soccer socks, shorts, and shirts, two balls and the logos for the school, "thrown-in without charge."

Unfortunately, the Iranian friend who accommodated me, Fred Nourzad, an All-American soccer player from San Jose State now a businessman at West Coast Soccer Supply, was not American born, thus not savvy to colloquial usage or the implications of historical abbreviations. So his "no charge" embellishment of our brand new Watsonville Soccer Club uniform resulted in two letters in black on the yellow shirts and shorts: WC! I leave it to your imagination what put-downs might have resulted from this faux pas! All my plans as a new coach were down the toilet as they say! Adversity breeds something, I guess, for we had a winning season and my thought is that the kids took it out on the other teams as they went 8-2 that first year. The fact that some of my players were newly from Mexico probably had something to do with it! I enjoyed those early successes but the winds of change were blowing up.

As the years passed and as growth was spreading, Watsonville High School and the others were bulging at the walls, so we split the school into two halves while the new plans were being financed and accomplished.

One school began at 7am, and finished at 1pm and the other began at 1:30pm and ended at 7pm. Of course, this was not a good situation but it was what we could do given the situation. Thank God it wasn't long before the building of Aptos High began and we had a half high school with freshmen and sophomores.

It was traditional that new English teachers be "thrown to the wolves," so to speak, and the "wolves," though not canine, were quite capable of tearing to shreds a young teacher's confidence and credibility if one was not up to it. Hence, the blooding of the neophyte!

So it was that I found myself in September of 1962 in my dismal room down in the basement facing a motley group of short and tall and a couple of huge and rather untidily attired boys. I say boys because this was my so called remedial class, freshmen or sophomores I supposed to be in need of more tutoring in the intricacies of English grammar than the regular students. So my first class was not brilliant, bright and eager students, but somewhat jaded young minds.

My opening remark that morning was made with a rather forced smile in an attempt at American style, warm and friendly looking. "Good morning students! I am Mister Harrison. I will be your English teacher for this semester." There was momentary silence as though they had been tranquilized. Sadly, though, it was not so. They erupted into such aping and mocking utterances as I might imagine coming from a Marlon Brando motorcycle gang making fun of some poor dupe!

But I was not Marlon Brando, nor was it, contrary to their behavior, a gang of hoodlums in front of me; it was my English class! One of the larger, uglier boys was punching the back of the smaller one in front. I fastened my steeliest gaze upon this big simian bully and in my iciest delivery, pointing at him with a rigid finger at the end my fully extended hand and arm as if I were shooting him with a pistol, I snapped, "You, there! What is your name?" And as I stood there and kept my authoritative finger extended, my arm pointing in accusation, the ape looked up from his pummeling, and the rest of the class suddenly hushed to a few titters here and there. His brows furrowed as if concentrating, and he said, "You mean... me?" He tapped his chest with a finger as if to verify his being. "Yes, I mean you. What is your name?" "Dickerson, that's my name," he smirked all around the room. "Come here, Dickerson!"

I lowered my arm and I walked to the front of the room, ready to face him squarely. There was an audible letting out of air, some gasps, some titters.

As Dickerson stood up, I realized two things I might regret: 1) he was not just large, he was huge, he was simian: 2) I should never have called him out! His desk hung around his hips like he had squeezed into a child's desk. The punch-bag in front helped Dickerson to extricate himself from the embraces of the desk and this huge man-boy ambled down the isle to tower over me. At that moment I learned another paradoxical lesson. Authority is given but you can't assume it unless you already have it. Arnold Schwarzenegger, I was not! I was all of one hundred and sixty pounds spread about my six-foot frame. Light-in-weight, light-in-authority.

I looked up at him, took a measured breath and, in my best impersonation of Mr. Chips said, in carefully enunciated steely no-nonsense words, "Young man! Let there be no more *wasting of my time!*" Pointing as I did so with that same *not-to-be-messed with finger* back to his desk.

Miracle among miracles! The completely bewildered behemoth turned and stumbled back up the aisle to his baby-desk, punching a couple of arms on the way. Never call a student out to be embarrassed and particularly a 225 pound all county tackle on your high school football team who was perceived by all as an all state left guard. And I had had him up in front of all his idolizing troop of astonished fans.

The amazing thing was, as I entered the classroom the next morning, I was welcomed by the chorus of footballers, "*Good morning, Mr. Harrison!*"

I was not expecting such a welcome but, reacting with the same cheery replay (in my English accent!), "Good morning, Class!" From then on my classes were what I as a teacher would wish for: malleable and attentive from the rest of the semester, and I larded positive reinforcement from Bill, Tom and Greg!

"I heard you disciplined young Dickerson, today!" Sam Schulburger, the football coach mentioned at lunch in the cafeteria. "Well, actually... "I was about to define "discipline" when the coach cut me off, "Good for you, Ken, Just make sure he *passes* all his *tests*. Y' know what I *mean*?" He punched me on the arm. I discovered that football was King there, and as to "English," it was an archaic subject that got in the way of catching a pass and carrying it on lumbering thighs into the end zone.

I was beginning to know not necessarily what everyone meant, but I certainly was getting to know everybody. I also made a mental note of the arm punch reassurance, which I now concluded to be a local macho bonding ritual. That is not to say that those were the only punches exchanged and the only part of the anatomy to which they were delivered! It would be quite some time before physical displays of anger or aggression would become rare in my daily teaching experience.

Here in Watsonville, a small town steeped in agricultural pursuits, one was never very far from the smells and residuals from the farms and ranches or the animal world, so to speak. It was in a remote area of California and a long away from the grammar school I graduated from in 1938! But it had new things to learn and understand, this new home in the beautiful bucolic Pajaro Valley where I landed from Arizona, by chance and luck.

At the end of that semester, I learned more than my students! They were not the intellects that I was to be blessed with later, but I believe the toil I experienced made me a better teacher. I certainly developed more patience and learned to leaven my instruction with humor and ways to get the students interested in the material. Actually, of the footballers, most earned a "C" and two got "Bs."

I was a better teacher because of this class. They gave me one of the shirts from the football team as a gift. I still don't know if the coach was the catalyst for that trophy. But, for me, it was better than anything else they could give me.

The coach stopped hitting my arm and I appreciated his restraint! My bruises on my arm had healed, Thank God!

HIPPIES

A young person, especially in the 1960s, who
who rejected accepted social and political values
and proclaimed a belief in universal peace and love.
They also wore unusual attire that proclaimed
they were different from the main stream.

KHH

BEADS, BANGLES AND BONGOS

The 70s were in unrest as the United States continued large-scale bombing raids against N. Vietnam, battles with Vietcong in Cambodia and fighting in Indochina, after years of violence between Catholics and Protestants in Northern Ireland: 467 Northern Irish killed in a year.

The War in Indochina finally ended when a cease-fire was agreed upon. North Vietnam combat deaths during 1965-1973 were horrendous, in the hundreds of thousands. Estimates of the number of casualties vary, with the Vietnam government suggesting as many as 3.1 million violent war deaths: Vietnamese, foreigners and soldiers included. A detailed demographic study calculated between 791,000 and 1,141,000 Vietnamese deaths, both soldiers and civilians, from 1965-1975. 84,000 children were included in the deaths.

The young survivors of the carnage and the psychical effects of war came to a changed world, and a different country and often were our students children of those service-men whom war had changed.

Change was the order of the day. Exactly what "change" we had yet to discover. This was later to be quite symbolic of not only the times (the 70s) but also of the new attitudes and activities which we were to discover and of necessity cope with as we went forward blithely to build our brave new world of Aptos Half-High! That phrase was to have added significance as we moved with the aid of the Beatles and the "new society" in what was hip to call "the Grasslands of Freedom, man."

Yes, not *all* students (but *some* faculty, I found) were "half-high." When an assistant principal was taken to a "hidden" marijuana patch up the hill among the redwoods, it became clear that what was rumored was now fact: "I get by with a little help from my friends," "Lucy in the Sky with Diamonds," and such terminology as Mary-Joe, Horse, Uppers 'n Downers became known to us. I, for one, could see things changing before my eyes in such a way that I thought of *Paradise Lost* and knew we would never be the "Way We Were."

It didn't happen overnight, but you could see it just as surely as the hair grew long and the clothing got loose. The ties disappeared and quasi-ethnicity, being bare-footed, wearing beads, having a Huron crested haircut or letting it become a tangled mass perhaps held in check with an "apache" sweat-band, became "normal."

Clothing as seen on "Laugh-In," wide angled pant-legs, Bishop-sleeved ruffled collar blouses, garish colors, larger cleavage and strange marks appeared on the student bodies. Beads, bangles and Indian feathers, leather waistcoats, T-shirts emblazoned with the Grateful Dead or Zappa or just a grinning skull, it all became a circus.

But, I still came to class with my briefcase full of the student compositions and essays, corrected and marked with appropriate notations as per usual. The pressure to "loosen-up" was subtle at first but eventually came into the main-stream when young, new-method "specialists" were brought in to demonstrate their "new-approach" to teaching these new breed of hipsters and would-be Beatles, Gypsies, Nomads and Minstrels, what they wanted.

This inculcated in us a sense of antiqueness or archaism in that correct grammar, clarity of statement, learning to acquire a critical appraisal of literature or assimilating even the fundamental skills were questioned in the light (?) of *new directions* and a *desire for change*, or using a sophomoric *non sequitur*, let go of in, "the need to produce a kinder world," or "to teach students with more empathy for his less fortunate third-world fellow inhabitants of this one world." As if literacy was an impediment to empathy and foggy logic a key to change!

All this time I had the impression that I was a teacher of English, trained to do that and willing to do that to the best of my ability. I even believed after a reasonable period and fairly objective review by me and those whose job it was to evaluate my work, and results of that work, that I had become a successful teacher according to my peers and students opinions, but I taught what was erroneously called, "English." The fact is that I was able to assimilate the modern language called 'American" but still taught clarity of thought and logic as insight into the prose and poetry. I had to honestly accept actually becoming more "American" than I was "English," although to my colleagues, I was "obviously" English! But, reading and enjoying Emerson, William and Henry James, Walt Whitman, E.E. Cummings, Emily Dickinson, Gertrude Stein, Hemmingway, and Steinbeck and the rest, finding and discussing the American spirit of openness, the "up-and-at-'em" frontier courage, optimism and, above all, the American spirit, its confidence and easy-going generosity that I experienced personally beyond the books and theorists, gradually began to have a profound effect on me.

I began to enjoy my being American and happy being free and privileged to teach; to delve into my subject matter and teach from this new understanding of intellectual freedom and to touch the new spirit within myself I supposed I had extrapolated from all the wonderful American voices I listened to as I worked my way through American Literature!

Part of my year's curriculum was to teach American Literature. I was to learn beyond the books; to learn from my own life once again. I became more in touch with myself through getting in touch with others: my students, and of course, my family.

It is easier to say now what I could not earlier, when still psychologically in the process of discovering myself and, as the Bhagwan's words told me later:

Hate exists with the past and the future—love needs no past, no future. Love exists in the present. Hate has a reference in the past: somebody abused you yesterday and you are carrying it like a wound.

I had much to learn before I could profess to teach. Though I had the job, the credentials were a license rather than true preparation, as any teacher knows, emerging in the turgid and incredibly insipid conglomeration of trivia and crap that was the curriculum for Teacher's Education Courses.

I found that my one semester as a "student teacher" in a high school classroom was more insightful, more valuable than all the neo-Victorian morality, the post-Dewey theory, post-Skinner behavioral psycho-babble wrapped in the dullest minds and therefore presented, I thought, as dull fare for a hungry mind. Thank God for whatever preserved my drive to become a teacher in spite of the preparation and the lack of financial incentives (though I question my lack of acumen and a not-yet "American" nose for the money!) for I was, from some deep-rooted desire, determined to become a teacher. In retrospect, and with whatever the experience endowed or left me with, I now say it was for the first ten or fifteen years a delight and a privilege; but after that, as society found within the constitution its right to pop, smoke or inject its choices of uppers, downers, marijuana, LSD or whatever "turns you on," I sadly found more often that it turned my students "Off' rather than "On!"

Thus ended that intangible thread of magical umbilical cord that connected a student to his teacher, doctor, priest and parents: trust, believe and it will be so. The miracle, the magic, was puffed away as illusions filled the day. For this dad, this teacher born in a far-away-place with its own illusions far-nobler and worthy of some sacrifice, teaching as I understood it and learning as I could understand, became more and more instruction, then imposition and, finally, impossibly absurd.

My few years at Watsonville High and my first few years at Aptos Half-High were a privilege, and I learned much as I struggled to teach and, I believe, became a teacher after several years of parading knowledge as the result of my learning, rather than eliciting it from students. I learned to lead them to their own understanding rather than needing to show mine and, as I became more creative with presentation and less concerned with administration and image, shrugging off my PTA armor, becoming Zorba, I taught.

I was paid to teach "English," which of course is nigh impossible if you understand "English." Consider, in my classes in Watsonville, the first two or three years I had 30-35 young girls and boys from the following ethnic groups: Mexican, Spanish, Slavic, Serbian, Croatian, Italian and Japanese. Watsonville was then a primarily white community with no Afro-Americans, since field work or other work associated with the tilling, growing, and harvesting of crops was not popular with Afro Americans around Watsonville with few exceptions.

But to get to my main point: to teach "English" as the phrase might imply, was neither possible nor practical. What I did teach was the love and power of learning itself. Oh, Yes! I followed the guide-lines in the curriculum and week by week we worked our way through the grammar book exercises, developing clarity and sense of meaning by relating phrases and clauses, both independent and subordinate within sentences, simple, compound and complex as we developed understanding of the language and adopted techniques. But the reading of archaic, decrepit English Literature books with stories from eras long gone and language so remote from these students' needs or understandings, became a labor without love or comprehension.

So, I bought two sets of paperbacks: one, Hemingway's *Old Man and the Sea*, and the other, Harper Lee's *To Kill a Mocking Bird*, and told the students that we were switching to American Lit as a teacher elective! They not only read the assignments, but also were eager every day to discuss them. Some bought their own copies after I told them I could get copies for those who wanted them. Atticus, my alter ego, in *To Kill a Mocking Bird*, became their hero.

This success was followed in the Freshmen classes with *The Old Man and the Sea*, where the relationship between Santiago, the old fisherman, and the young Mexican boy was understood and empathized by all the young students whether of Mexican, Slavic, Italian, German or Irish descent: the qualities of love, faith, honesty, fortitude and courage were clearly presented and understood by all. The discussions were lively and the exchanges were revealing, none more surprising than my own recollections of such fortitude and courage in the face of many of my shipmates in dire circumstances, which I shared quite freely in the five minutes before the bell at the conclusion of the class.

After a while, I was aware of a change taking place within myself at the same time I was noticing attitudes changing in the students. I had begun as an eager new teacher crammed with book learning and an intellect sharpened to a razor's edge by four or five years of unrelenting study of other peoples' words and ideas. I was organized, disciplined and I talked less, but guided the students into their insights and understanding. It was a mutual pleasure to share the lessons.

WAITING FOR OPPORTUNITY

For years I had been patient for the day when I could be teaching. When I dreamed as a young boy, I idolized my English teacher, Mr. Gardner, who taught me the magic of words and ideas in 1936, in Flying Bull Lane School. In 1962, I was fulfilling my dream.

APTOS HALF-HIGH

Things had changed. It was 1968, Robert Kennedy and Rev. Martin Luther King were assassinated, United States was in the Vietnam War and there were clashes between Catholics and Protestants in Ireland. The world was changing and my own change was taking place and the students changed too. Young minds were choosing new things and unfortunately smoking pot and taking pills to excite the senses, or dull them, as they took both uppers and downers, we had to learn.

When Aptos High, the long awaited new high school was finally built, a new principal came to town to interview and select some of his staff for the new high school out of town and down the coast towards Aptos and Rio del Mar as it was known then, a cutting edge of society.

Mr. Cunningham was a man with a mission to change the long established focus of education from authoritarian teaching and strict disciplinarian orientation towards "problems" to a more "enlightened" Democratic approach, where the student's problems and his difficulties in his attempts to learn were to be the focus of our efforts to change our attitudes and perceptions of what we wished to accomplish.

In other words, we were to not only creatively re-shape our curriculum, but also to re-think our commitment to teach. We were being given an opportunity to put new ideas into operation that might improve our teaching. He told us we would be "encouraged to incorporate new technology and methods" into our teaching, to challenge the status quo, it seemed!

For a fairly new teacher, though not young since I was now forty-seven, it was a challenge, and one which most of those chosen by Cunningham were ready to accept. Though, as time would show, some would resist and some would find the changes untenable and therefore drop out.

When the new high school was ready it turned out to be only the first half of the eventually completed school. For instance, and I find this rather ironic, there was no library built in this first half. There was a gym, of course, actually the most imposing building so far! There was also an administration building complete with principle and vice principle offices. There was also a large office for the secretaries and bookkeepers etc.

But there was a football field and a baseball diamond already cut into the hillside. The classrooms were in four timbered buildings, arranged like a reversed L, with two on the ground level and two raised-up on wooden pillars on ledges cut into the hillside. On the ground-level was one building for Business and Foreign Languages, one for Mathematics and Science; on the upper level were Social Science and English in one building and mixed usage rooms, such as Mechanical Drawing, Phys-Ed and Health, and one classroom set aside for the "Library." At that time I could see no visible evidence of "a new curriculum" or even a "modern high school."

The architecture was innovative in that its appearance was suggestive of a radical turn from the California Spanish red tile stucco of Watsonville. In fact it seemed much more in tune with the trend of Junior-college designs prevalent in that part of California at that time. The nearby Cabrillo College, a terraced row of heavy beamed "ranch style" buildings with decks acting as outside corridors connecting each classroom, built several years after I began teaching at Watsonville, and the new Aptos High School, could well have been built by the same architect.

It, too, was on a hillside recessed from Freedom Boulevard, with expansive and imaginative use of huge laminate beams and posts erecting those classrooms up on the hillside, with decks and stairs guiding all traffic between classrooms on the outside of the buildings. Some touches suggested optimistic uplifting of appreciation of aesthetics expected from the new breed of students: a fountain built in front of the administration building was soon removed after students put a jumbo packet of Duz detergent into it, causing a soapy bubble-flood at the entrance to the office!

Well, it was only a half-a-high-school and we were told the second half would be built later, which it was, including a large fully equipped modern library, and a small auditorium as the Music Building. In the meantime, we learned to "make do." For instance, the "Library" was situated in what was destined to be a science lab in the second phase.

Once in an English class, having given a test based on several chapters of the current reading, I found unusually low scores and I was surprised, since that particular class was of above average intelligence and responded well. I decided that this particular test was an anomaly.

So I stood in front of the whole class and took it upon myself to wave the papers above my head saying, "Class, I am surprised at the low response to the last test! It is below your normally good responses. Can you tell or enlighten me as to why it was not your best work?"

There was a moment of silence, and one particularly mature and confident young student blurted-out, "I wasn't prepared. Didn't get to finish the assignment. Sorry, Mister H."

Another young girl whom I knew was a diligent student, spoke up, "I also wanted to talk about the main character, whom I really found complicated. And I did not finish the chapter, Mister H." Several students gave their various and similar comments, and it occurred to me that perhaps I had not given my usual interpretation of the subtleties within the chapters.

I listened to the students and knew this group were serious about their studies and assignments, so I waved the abnormally low scores results above my head and asked the class, "If I tore up these results," doing so, I ripped them asunder, "would you go over the two chapters tonight and re-take the test Friday?" The whole class erupted in cheers and clapping that warmed all hearts, including my own! When the burst of enthusiasm faded, I told them, "Let's open our books, and form your questions for me to elucidate... if I can," I added, being somewhat humbled by the openness of the students.

It is a two-way street, this "education:" the students gain knowledge and learn about the teacher and how to communicate their thoughts. The lesson I learned that day was to be an honest teacher, to know when you had accomplished "teaching," and when on odd days you might not have, you might have stimulated the students' thirst for knowledge and confidence in their understanding... not only of themselves, but confidence in the teacher.

When I lost my lucrative job in Phoenix, and in a moment of serendipity, or if you wish, a fateful decision to go back to school after 26 years of wandering over the world from one tenuous job to another, I thanked God for that insight and a loyal, wonderful wife who immediately saw that I had to remake myself, or reclaim myself, for even as a young student in England, I had dreamed of going to college and becoming a professor. Now I was determined to reclaim that dream. For that moment I was unburdened of a weight within that had tethered me to a slave of unfulfilling jobs, chasing money like a donkey, going round and around chasing the hay. Teaching freed me from a Sisyphean task that was the result of ignorance and losing my young dream.

I hope my delight in the privilege to teach young minds was evident in my efforts. Thank you, God.

Shall I compare thee to a summer's day?
Thou art more lovely and more temperate:
Rough winds do shake the darling buds of May,
And summer's lease hath all too short a date;

Sometime too hot the eye of heaven shines,
And often is his gold complexion dimm'd
And every fair from fair sometime declines,
By chance, or nature's changing course, untrimm'd;

But thy eternal summer shall not fade,
Nor lose possession of that fair thou ow'st;
Nor shall Death brag thou wander'st in his shade,
When in eternal lines to time thou grow'st:

> So long as men can breathe, or eyes can see,
> So long lives this, and this gives life to thee.

William Shakespeare
Sonnet 18

THE CIRCLE HAS BEEN MENDED

One day I was invited to a union social gathering in Pajaro Dunes on the coast not far from Watsonville. I was teaching at the new Aptos High School, built northwest on Freedom Boulevard, about 5 miles from Watsonville. It was modern architecture, designed as single buildings on the slope of a hill with outside steps and paths and a large patio at the foot of the hill. The classrooms were next to each other California style, with large windows that let in the light and the traffic flow went around the decks that connected each building.

It was a Friday and it was my habit to use all the machines and facilities after the staff normally left by 4pm with the weekend in mind. I was asked to attend by 4pm at Pajaro Dunes and, as an added lure, I was told there was a special woman whom I must meet. Having been busy making copies for my Monday's tests and printing my class assignments and schedules, I glanced up at the clock and to my dismay I found it was 4:35pm. Remembering the invitation, I put the stacks next door in my room and locked the door. I raced to my Z car and really sped to the Pajaro Dunes gathering. I got there in about fifteen minutes, risking a ticket!

As I entered the hall, I noticed there were only about fifteen or eighteen people scattered around and I went to the table where about a dozen bottles were uncorked, a small amount of Chablis, Chardonnay, Sauvignon Blanc, Merlot and Burgundy.

So putting three bucks into the union collection, I took a small amount from one of the Chardonnay bottles and topped it with Chablis, thinking it might become a lighter Chardonnay!

I turned from my alchemy and taking a sip of my concoction, I began to cross the room towards the host, when I almost bumped into a petite, slim girl with beautiful eyes and a glass with a strange chateau wine with an amber color. As I glanced at her glass, I queried (rather flip!) "What chateau is that stuff?" Without hesitation, she smiled, "It's Chateau Martinelli." I wheeled about and we both laughed, because Martinelli was a local apple cider producer whom everybody knew.

We exchanged pleasantries and in five minutes I was entranced by this petite intellect with a wonderful smile and I felt a connection without rationalizing and so I asked, "Could we have dinner together tonight?" and without blinking an eye she agreed, "Yes, that would be nice."

Impulsively, I kissed her to tie the bargain! Unfortunately the host, a Mensa member who had invited me to come to the wine tasting at Pajaro Dunes, rounded up the small group and announced that we were all going for a Chinese dinner in Watsonville. So much for my intimate dinner date!

When we got to the Chinese restaurant, I maneuvered so I was sure to sit next to my "date!" When the dinner was over I drove Lupita to her house and made sure from that evening that I never let her out "of my sight," because I made sure that she was never out of my mind or my sincere best intentions. I was intrigued by her beautiful eyes, her warm personality and her serene character, so I was not about to lose her, nor was I flirting with her. I was attracted immediately as though it was fate, as we seemed to understand each other without the need to explain. Lupita was taking care of her mother in her house in Watsonville, so I knew I would have to be patient. One day after calling on her and chatting together I was about to kiss her when her mother opened her door and before she could see us (her sight was not very good), I pulled Lupita under the dining table where we lay while her mother walked with her cane across the dining room to go into the kitchen. She came back with a glass of water and went back into her room and shut the door.

I learned that she was a formal lady with old-fashioned ideas about propriety and, indeed, the next time I came to see Lupita, her mother insisted that the front door be left open while I was in the living room! Of course, I did not go under the table again!

As I got to know more about Lupita and her family and her sister and her family who lived near Washington, in Alexandria, Virginia, I instinctually was attracted, having noticed their intelligence, humor and warm kindness. It was an invisible bond that developed almost from the first meeting and it cemented my love for Lupita and her family.

We saw each other almost every day except when she was scheduled to take a trip to Nestlé's headquarters in White Plains, New York. Sometimes we rendezvoused on her trips: once to St. Thomas in the Caribbean for a week, and another time to Spain where we visited a Nestlé's factory.

One day I proposed to Lupita to be my wife but said that I would wait for as long as it was necessary since she was taking care of her mother. She agreed and for two years we did things together as partners.

After an illness her mother passed away and I went with Lupita and her family to Spain with her mother's ashes, which were to be interred in the crypt where her father was buried near Colombres in Asturias, where they had a family home. We stayed with Lupita's sister, Carmelina and her husband, Jose Antonio Roca, in their family's big house at the edge of Colombres, and I found them warm and accepting of this Englishman.

The house was large and looked out over the hills and fields with cattle grazing nearby, and where the cows were brought in by young girls to be milked. As the years passed, this routine ended as Colombres changed in some ways. Tourists and growth changed farms and the area became more about catering to visitors and tourists. Of course, the area still was sustained by farming and fishing, in particular in Saint Vicente de la Barquera, Llanes and Gijon and other small towns on the coast of Asturias. I found peace there.

Of course the highways developed and it was easy to go from one place to another on the new roads. It used to be several hours to go from Santander where we arrived on the overnight boat from Portsmouth to get to Colombres.

Several years later we took a plane from an airfield nearby Southampton in England, not far from Romsey. We flew with Bill and Mavis Smith, longtime friends from adventures in the Caribbean and Hawaii, to Spain where we had a wonderful vacation in their son's villa in a lovely community near the coast. We landed in the Valencia airport on the southeast coast of Spain and spent a couple of weeks at Javea near the coast, where they had developed a nice community of villas with white and pink walls and red tiles and flowers everywhere in each garden.

We have been to Spain several times, staying in the Roca's family house on the north coast of Spain in Colombres, Asturias. We also spent time there with other members of the family, especially their children: Carmen Mari, Aurelio, Diana, Denise and Lupi. The family of Jose Antonio and Carmelina is quite a large, happy group! They seemed to accept this Englishman who loved Lupita, who was Carmelina's sister, and she was a favorite aunt to the children of the Roca tribe and loved by all. Jose Antonio was the patriarch and the head of the family, a warm generous individual and physically strong. He was a dental physician and well skilled, with a large practice in Arlington.

Diana and her husband, Jose Lara, and their two daughters, Maite and Ana, spent some time one summer in a small house nearby, a mile or so outside of Colombres. It was a peaceful, quiet place to rest and walk along the paths across the fields and hills. Their home at the time was in Navarra, Spain, but later they moved back to Colorado, when the girls were getting ready to choose a college.

We visited Virginia when the Rocas lived in Arlington and later when they moved to a high rise apartment in a new complex in Falls Church, where they joined two apartments so they could have an extended dining room and an extra bedroom for visitors, it being a busy city not too far from Washington and its politics and commerce.

Lupita's sister and brother-in-law had six children who were adult and married with children when I met them. One Christmas a couple of years after Lupita and I were married, we were invited to share Christmas with the Roca family in Arlington. Jose Antonio and Carmelina gathered the extended family! There were six Roca children, their spouses and some more children: Carmen Mari, her husband, Jaime Gutierrez and their two sons, Mark and David; Aurelio, his wife Beverly and their children, two boys and a girl, Adam, Caleb and Alison; Diana and her husband, Jose Lara, and their two girls, Maite & Ana Maria; Denise and David Curry and three children, Galen, Devin and Tess; Lupi and Ted Crowley and two children Patrick and Abby; and Sergio and his daughter Kristina.

Now the older children have since married and have their own children, you can imagine how astonished I was at the fertility of the Roca dynasty, being an only son without my mother!

Without my enumerating the individuals that have been added to this loving and close family, you can imagine the number of the relatives and offspring. It reminds me of the Old Testament where patriarchs multiplied their progeny to where tribes were all relatives of each other! One Christmas I noted 12 children which, when totaled with the adults, made 26 around the tables in a family convention for Christmas! I won't bore the reader with the mathematically multiplying Roca fertility cult, but by my reckoning at this time (almost 90 years old) the Roca progeny has amassed a regiment of 30 or more, from two original parents who escaped from Castro's Communistic State of Cuba (with Lupita's help to whisk three children away to America and in Catholic sanctuaries) and with lucky help from one of Castro's associate, who allowed them at the last moment to fly to Mexico, from which they were helped by Lupita to get visas to America.

Lupita found a haven for the three children whom Jose and Carmelita wanted to get away from Castro's communistic Cuba. At the time, Lupita, as a Catholic nun, used her connections to help the Roca family. Jose Antonio went to a Catholic school and used to play basketball with Castro. Although Jose Antonio had been a professional dentist with full credentials, as a refugee from Cuba he was forced to be a temporary recruit for two years as an American socialistic medical for the coal miners in West Virginia as a quid pro quo in order to get his USA dentistry license to practice in Virginia.

With determination and skill he built a successful practice and was esteemed by his peers as not only a professional but also a caring and warm-hearted man. Carmelina, in her own right intelligent and caring of all her children, was not only the matriarch of this family but loved by all. Their father and mother regularly visited or kept up communications and as the years went by, Carmelina and Jose Antonio became Grandmother and Grandfather, as their children had their own children, and as the older children became adults, they also had their own children.

I could not herein list this remarkable family that is a testament to love and courage and will power, keeping close their progeny through love and unselfish caring throughout their lives. Since I was in an Catholic orphanage at three, not knowing my mother or having even a photo of my mother, I give thanks for Lupita, my loving wife, who was brought to me as a gift by God and Fate to mend the circle of love and faith, bringing me into God's grace and his mercy. She has been a light that chased away the shadows and doubt that followed me through a long period of my adult life.

I think back on her entering the convent as a novice right out of college, determined to follow God and give her life and caring to the needy and to search for a meaning beyond her own life. Her musical talent was particularly known and she earned her Masters by playing a concert in Washington as part of her degree.

Lupita spent thirteen years at Marymount in Tarrytown in New York State, teaching music and pianoforte as a nun, until Pope John modified the order and, like others, she was determined to come out to the world where she felt that her faith and training could be followed in ordinary life.

When I met her at the end of my teaching career at Watsonville, it was an epiphany, part of God's plan for my enlightenment. Lupita was a supervisor in a Nestlé's office in Watsonville, California, where she transferred from White Plains, New York State. She was promoted by the retiring manager, a good friend to us, Pete and Madge, his wife, and she became the new manager of the staff of about twelve salespersons with the responsibility for eighteen states in the west.

As I write now, I am coming toward ninety years of age. One can only feel that God had his finger on me for his purpose. I regret that I did not accomplish what I might have but perhaps whatever small or slight transgressions I may have done, God knows I was not a paragon of piety, but I know, because his mercy is infinite, I have been blessed and forgiven for my omissions and perhaps selfish acts when courage might have won the day.

Louise and Lupita were angels in women's bodies. Louise, who saw my heart and my potential and loved me and gave me two loving beautiful daughters who, following in their father's steps became teachers for thirty plus years.

Lupita was God's gift to me after wandering around for eight years after a tragic divorce. She more than anyone gave me the courage to face my broken faith and realize how blessed I have been, and to ask God's forgiveness. She brought happiness and humor and humility back in my life. I love her and know that God has his reasons, for the circle has been mended. I was afraid of nuns as a child but as I was enlightened as I matured, I saw their mission.

An irony and a gift, when I found my nun, Lupita, who taught me humility by her patience and earthly realism. Her spiritual goodness and sensitive and wise intelligence diminished my egotism and I understood how blessed I was when we met. She healed my hurts and made me whole, able to give and know that I have been blessed.

My life has also bee blessed by the love and acceptance of the Roca family but most particularly by Lupita's warmth and love and caring, which I'm sure healed me. I'm amazed at her grit and will power in that slight body and the intelligence she showed in times of stress or emergency! However, we both have had a rich life together, sharing so much and living with many interests and active minds. We particularly share Lupita's love of music and talent and sixteen years of participation in the Carmel Bach Festival, where she has sung in the chorus over the years. When she is on the stage singing I notice a glow on her face and know that she is doing what she loves and is connected to her deeper self, which brings contentment beyond words. After all, she was trained as a small girl and was talented and had public performances on the piano. She is older now with rheumatism in her fingers, so singing is a link with her soul and mind that keeps her happy and perhaps in touch with her greater love and faith.

What can I say, when I need to give my personal understanding of what my life was lived for? I have been loved, blessed, saved in so many ways: close to death, in the war, illnesses, accidents and operations upon my body, as well as the mental anguish we all go through regarding loved ones and friends. However in my later years, for some reason of God's, He has given me time to understand that He has His reasons for forgiveness and His love.

I have not accomplished all I dreamed of being, perhaps attaining my goals in my youth, but I have strived to be a helper, a friend, a lover, and to share whatever I could, and I finally reached my goal.

When I found my youth's dream to be a teacher, I was finally happy doing what I should have been doing all along. Others, particularly my students, must render my verdict as a good teacher, but I have been happy to be a guide to the light we all look for in our lives: to share, to love, to give help and skills for the greater good.

AMAZING GRACE

"Amazing Grace, how sweet the sound,
That saved a wretch like me.
I once was lost but now I'm found,
Was blind, but now I see."

John Newton

P.S. Every day that the ship left port the radio officer played this old hymn to let all know that the ship was the *"Amazing Grace."*

THE SHIP *AMAZING GRACE*

In 1985, I was offered a pre-retirement bonus as a planner for pre-college exams for seniors, giving me three terms as exams planner and a $5,000 bonus. I could begin to ease away from my heavy load of 5 periods of English composition, including two classes of advanced English preparation for college, which meant much more preparation and planning.

I accepted and for the next three years worked with the vice-principal preparing and correlating the exam results and preparing records for each student, and following-up for absences, etc.

This eased my retirement for which I was duly grateful, as part of my personal plan was to compile a book of poems from my fifty years of writing.

I retired in 1989 at 65 after teaching 25 years, and had been employed since 1938 at the age of 14 years and two months! At the time of my retirement, Lupita was still a manager for Nestlé at Watsonville. She supervised a staff of 12 women and one man who were responsible for 18 states in the

West. I traveled with her on business trips, including New York State and Saint Thomas in the Virgin Isles.

It was not all business and we had some pleasant and special experiences. We had the taste and leisure for travel again and we found a small boat that could accommodate 80 passengers to sail out of Freeport on what was called the Grand Bahama off the Florida coast.

It was built in Scotland and designed to supply the lighthouses around the Scottish coast, which were in Argyll and Bute, Ayrshire (South), Dumfries and Galloway, Grampian, and Highland, Lothian, Fife and Borders, Orkneys, Fair Isle, Shetland Isles. As you can visualize, Scotland has many isles and headlands with crenulated shores and bays on an infinite coastline. So without numerating each lighthouse, note that I have given areas that contained one or more lighthouses.

But back to the ship that was designed to supply and take mail to the major lighthouses: it was bought by the Windjammer Company. It was no more than 2,000 tons. She had lovely lines with a single raked funnel and a forecastle, a hold in the foredeck, with about 14 cabins extended at the stern and connected to the super structure, and about fourteen other cabins in the center. She was our yacht! And so much fun we had on that little boat. Such simple things such as crab races or costume night using your whimsies or imagination out of a chest of hats, clothes, cloaks, brick-a-brac and notions.

In the late nineties, Lupita and I went on the *Amazing Grace* for three cruises. On one of the trip, we met the Smiths, Bill and Mavis from Romsey, England, and Berkley and Cynthia Cooke, who to this day are close friends.

We taught Bill and Mavis our latest card game, "Moon," which they both loved and when they come to our home, we all play "Moon!" We have gone to their home in Ramsey, near Southampton, which was where I was as a child in the Catholic orphanage and where my father was born. Both the Smiths and the Cookes became our shipmates and over the years we have visited them several times.

Both couples had a sense of humor and free give and take in verbal exchanges. Bill and myself particularly, being both British, gave each other as good as we got! Berkley was more subtle and urbane but joined in the fun. In the event, we shared not only the card games, but also the tomfoolery and the "dress-up nonsense" that was a part of the cruise activities.

A particular theme was, "Pirates, Priests and Prostitutes!" A raunchy theme for sure. Cynthia became a rouge cheeky in high-heeled spikes, swaying her hips, with a swing handbag and a cheek full of bubble gum blowing up bigger and bigger balloons as a climax. I found a costume for a quasi pirate with a drooping mustache, a cutlass and a patch over one eye. I found white cotton trousers and shredded the legs and bared my feet, and Lupita found a miscellany of wild Gypsy colors and came close to being a Carmen with big earrings. Not sure which category she found herself in, but she had a cardboard pistol and a Spanish shawl! We were in the three best costumes! I must say, we were something out of an Errol Flynn film! A lot of fun and nonsense!

Being a supply ship, the *Amazing Grace* was often a mother ship for the fleet of barques, schooners and a couple of yachts adapted for sails and jibs, etc. This miscellany of ships was positioned along the string of the Antilles from Freetown to Trinidad. The *Amazing Grace* was the link for all of them and in three voyages we got to see all the tall-masted ships and once in a while got to go aboard some of them. Their names were as varied as their ships: the *Flying Cloud, Polynesia, Yankee Clipper, Mandalay* and the *Fantome*. A motley of assorted crafts, each with its personality.

However one year, the *Fantome* was off Belize when the captain had a warning of a hurricane building up between him and his route to the destination of the south of Mexico. He set the passengers off in the nearest port and set sail to race the hurricane. Unfortunately the hurricane suddenly veered and the *Fantome* was not fast enough to race out of danger and she was lost with all of the crew. At least he put the passengers off! The young captain was very popular and it really hit the group, who were very close, as well as the company, which did not survive the tragedy. When you realize how old those ships were, they had to have problems sooner or later. It was an adventure that had to end one day.

Those lovely islands are beautiful and romantic with their pristine beaches and azure water and their chain like a string of pearls, strung along the Leewards and the Windwards, from the Virgin Islands, Anguilla,

Netherlands Antilles, Antigua, Guadeloupe, Dominica, Martinique, to Saint Lucia, Saint Vincent, Barbados, Grenada, and Trinidad and Tobago, and smaller islands that I have not mentioned.

On one trip we asked the steward if he could set up a poker table for six of us. He was not only eager but we found he would run the table, and he was so eager that he made a plate of sandwiches and paid for our after dinner drinks! Apparently, we were the "boobs" who would be fleeced by this card sharper!

We began at 8pm and by 10, Lupita and I had big piles of chips representing three quarters of the pool. At this point the hotshot ordered another plate of sandwiches and another a round of drinks! To soften up us boobs!

The steward loosened his tie and tried his best to get our money! At ten-o'clock, he asked if we would play until 11pm. Sure we would play for another hour, we assured him. Well, sandwiches all gone, the drinks all empty at 11pm, the "sharpie" steward finally paid us our fifty bucks each and we thanked him for his hospitality. We each gave him ten bucks, at which he was very surprised! It was a nice evening. He did not ask for us on the way back to Freeport!

By the way, there was a small island called Palm Island. There was one house on top of a small mount. A millionaire owned that house and the *Amazing Grace* brought him some equipment, so we frolicked on the small island. I believe the island was only half a mile long. That's a mite too small for me, particularly with hurricanes being much bigger!

The crew brought an ice chest full of beer and Cokes and sandwiches. It reminded me of Robinson Crusoe, but he didn't have sandwiches and beer!

The *Amazing Grace* was an important link with some of the remote islands. Those days were precious because we were all getting a little older. In the 90s, I was twenty-four years younger! As I sit here at my computer, I feel every joint and know that I'm *becoming* ninety next year! We were so full of fun and jolly times.

In fact, we still play the card game called "Moon!" which is an exciting game. We start with one card and progress to ten and then reduce back down to one. The up-card is trumps and you can call 50 points during the first four cards, after that, you bid whatever your hand suggests.

Lots of fun! Whenever Bill and Mavis visit we reprise of those fun days and adventures! Also, Berkley and Cynthia remained friends, though sadly, after Alzheimer's disease had occurred for Cynthia, and after several years of gradual losing her memory, she died last year. A sad loss, for Berkley, and us.

We should go back in our minds and thank God that we had so much fun, pleasure and good companions: Bill, Mavis, Berkley, Cynthia, Lupita and me (Ken): it was a blessing... an *"Amazing Grace."*

I recall in the orphanage so long ago... the voices of children singing that old song... *"Amazing Grace...."* An historical memory that reverberates today, reminding me how God's grace is unending.

MY RANDOM MEMORY & BLOOD TYPE

It was as if I was living in two worlds. The one I felt beneath my ass, the seat, the pressure up from the floor, I could feel in the tension in my legs coming from the combined forces of gravity and the hundred and sixty pounds weight, give or take, of my six foot body sitting at this moment of consciousness, and the whirling, ever-moving, never static, constantly changing atomic miraculous dynamic energized force fields of my invisible inner world that sometimes came to my attention when doctors drew me to some evidence of quantum change below or above the *norm*.

That last blood test was an example of my other world, as a boy. Then, when I had a blood "test," it was simply to find out if I was anemic since the doctor had observed that I was half-starved, pale, and listless.

"Yes," he said, turning his face from the report to my stepmother, "Your son's blood is thin and he could do with some iron," and I wondered how I was going to tell him, or anyone, that she was not my mother and I was not her son. I was diagnosed as "anemic," possibly a lack of adequate food, the lot of many families in those pre-war poverty years, particularly on a seaman's wages. Today we would understand my needs, but that was 1937.

The question about "my blood type" re-appeared when I was about thirteen and sprouting up on long gangling legs and about a hundred and forty thin pounds and probably uncertain of my lack of vitality.

I mused why my blood was "thin," that my problem was more mental... in a moment of epiphany, I realized I was not loved as a son, with a real mother, but was an odd inconvenience, a burden... I realized our conflicts arose from each of our needs, which had become incompatible. In life, we have insights that take us to where we see our direction and God's plan.

After reading a book in the library by Sigmund Freud on Mental Ills and Psychoanalysis and later, on Neurosis, I was able to "trace" my early "below the norms" and sometimes "above norms" to my fear and loathing of my step-mother, who was not the wicked stepmother of fairytales, obviously evil, but, like others, had her own demons. She lived between two worlds, scraping a living without a husband in the house and who was God knows where in the world, and the unknown tomorrows that the war might bring. She was, after all an immigrant learning her alien society's customs and foibles.

However, she was intelligent, wily, and more German than she was Belgian, since she had lived in and liked her Cologne connections. But more to the point, she was not unreliable, as I found out, later, when her two sons Ernst and Erik from her previous marriage to a German came one day to see her in June 1938. They cycled from Dover where they crossed from Antwerp to visit their mother.

"The Reich was marvelous and their ships so 'vunderful' and the German sailors so 'schmart' in their uniforms, so much better than the sloppy 'Anglish'!" I anguished silently, telling myself, "Wait 'til the *Hood* shows them!"

It was not a pleasant visit because in the two days they were there, I was shunted into the kitchen and ostracized as a pariah, not included in any conversation or meals that were lovingly prepared by their real mother with such enthusiasm that I could not believe a person could so suddenly morph into a different person. I was like a mute piece of furniture that took up space, not included in the conversation or the social niceties. Meals were given to me alone in the kitchen. It was a wake up call for independence, and I understood that I was an awkward appendage that did not belong in that body from the past and so, ignored. However, it clarified my status between my stepmother and her priorities, and I grew overnight in the sense of understanding of my position and knowing more of my stepmother's complex character. The fact that there were handsome blond Germans in the house was made known by my stepmother in her pride.

She was a statuesque, complex, intelligent woman who was fluent in Flemish, French, German and English. She was socially adroit and very manipulative. She was an accomplished whist and bridge player and of considerable charm to many and was a somewhat exotic mystery to the beer and chips variety that lived around her.

In the dull, industrial red brick rows of miniscule rabbit hutches like number 10 Bakers Street off Sultan Road, Mile End Portsmouth, she stood out as an alien misplaced. When the two boys returned to Germany by way of Dover on their "Churman" bicycles, she lauded their praises wide and far, but it wasn't long before she vented her spleen on good ol' Ken, her albatross, as part of a bargain she probably rued.

Now, my latest blood test was more complex than that one to determine my anemia or lack of energy or why I was asthmatic when I was eleven. In those days, I ascertained the obvious....Now I receive the result of their taking some of this eighty-nine-year-old's blood and doing a wide-spectrum chemistry test that included Lipids, PSA, Hemoglobin and Urinalysis and concluded on page five with a Hematological alphabet code with quantified percentages alongside on the right. The Norm for each category was a far cry from the "thin blood and iron" age; which probably got me on this "two-worlds" thing.

In the event, I came out of my contemplation of things past... and heard the doctor asking me, "Ken, what is your blood type?"

"The same as my father's I expect!" Which was not a scientific answer, but in my mind I understood my answer and to peace with it and the past.

ANGELS WHO APPEARED AS PEOPLE

The memory. now at its eighty-ninth year of use, frayed and somewhat embellished, having been rather hedonistic and apt to focus more on the present pleasure than on the past, is probably not as acute as it was. During my life I have changed other states of mind, such as temporarily trying to be existential, having read Albert Camus' *The Stranger*, and in college contemplating Kierkegaard's view that "truth is subjective," and dwelling on Sartre's philosophy of "anguish and despair," as he shows the meaninglessness of modern existence, and the absurdity of proper "choice" when equal evils are part of decision.

When I read Kafka's *The Castle*, with its ominous and insidious overtones of despair and futility, combined with my own long held jaundiced doubts about the Catholic views of an absolute authority with undeniable truths for the faithful believer, it led me into a period of almost daily existence devoid of plan or purpose. My so-called "faith" was being shaken in those student days at the university.

Now in my maturity, or older age, I will attempt to recall as many angels and friends who supported me, loved me and smoothed the path of life. To begin with, the first three years of my life is a mystery to me, since I have no recollection nor any photos to give me any help in knowing where I was or with whom. I have no picture nor photo of my mother Hilda Gladdis Harrison. After searching the records in London the only reference I've seen was her name on the copy of the marriage certificate as wife to my father Victor Hugh Drummond Harrison dated 1923.

No photos or memorabilia from my life under my stepmother, from 1931 to 1940 have ever survived. In his own way my father tried to give me a comfort and protection when he took me to the orphanage because he was on active duty in the Navy and there was no one to take care of me. When he was able to find another wife, he took me out of the orphanage in an attempt to give me some normal care, though ironically, my care was less than nurturing under my step-mother's manipulations and her self-serving pleasures while my father was away.

Mr. Gardner, my English teacher in 1938 was one of my first angels who began my odyssey in English as a student. He also recommended me for a scholarship, but my stepmother refused on grounds that I should seek work.

Stan Thomas was my first friend who shared my love of ships and the sea. In school we designed our ideal ship on scraps of paper and sent them desk-by-desk.

When I was 17, after my first six months of service during my year and a half stationed in Freetown, in Sierra Leone, West Africa, I was chosen to open and manage canteen, which was only a shed with a flap that opened in such a way that the ratings could stand there and be served with beer or cigarettes or sometimes "nutty," as they termed chocolate. It was on an edge of a cleared area that was being built as a shore base. I had many cracks about my baby face at seventeen! An early "Angel" was my immediate manager, the Chief Petty officer, an angel when I needed him. I'm sorry I have forgotten his full name, but I always called him "Chief." His laconic, casual personality was what I needed. He was more of a quasi-parent, keeping an eye on me but letting me get on with it. It was my first inkling that someone could rely on me, thus he let me have my head, as they say. He was one early angel who saw my potential for responsibility.

When my substitute was posted on the daily announcements, having been eighteen months in West Africa, I began to sweat and tremble and almost collapsed. My friends told me not to go to the sick bay, because I'd be held back from going back to England. So they packed my duffel bag and more or less heaved me onto the rope ladder by using their shoulders to support my weak legs. If ever there were angels, those two casual mates were two.

Ironically, when I recovered a month later from malaria, and (God forbid!) dysentery and concomitant bronchitis, I mentioned to the drafting officer that I hoped I would be in cooler climates when I recovered and fit to be shipped. In the event, he sent me to a destroyer whose duty was Russian convoys! No angel he!

After the war, I met an ex-RAF mechanic who became a close friend, Don Pink, who added to my life in many ways as did his wife, Pat. Both were witness to my first marriage. Sadly, he died of cancer as a result of his life long cigarette habit. He would ironically say, as he coughed his life away, "It's a small comfort, mate." Another angel. I miss him.

Mr. William Harrison who gave me the job on the new *Ocean Monarch* was an angel who gave me a chance to change my life by giving me the last job on a beautiful ship. It was on the *Ocean Monarch* that I met and subsequently fell in love with a real angel, Louise, who became my second wife and mother of my two daughters, Heather and Colleen, dare I say angels too? Every dad probably says that! But, they grace my life and carry their mother's love.

Another angel appeared in the guise of a lawyer whose name was Jim Johnson, whom I met on the Cunard ship *Mauretania*. We became friends and he handled my divorce from Dorothy in England from the USA, a remove you might say! An angel indeed!

He introduced me to another arch-angel, Caesar Innocenti, who gave me an opportunity and became my Godfather and gave away the bride, Louise! A man of generous proportions and great generosity. Deo Gratias!

Later I was recommended to relocate to the dry climate of Arizona for my health, where I met another angel called Bobby Phael, the son of a well-known hotelier in Los Angeles and who saw merit in me. He offered me an opportunity as his catering manager in his new hotel, the Valley Ho in Scottsdale, Arizona.

The next angel was professor Harry Woods, in charge of the Art Department at Arizona State University, who was able to get me enrolled as a special student, based on a letter of certification of lost records due to a 1940 German air-fire raid, another serendipity that allowed me to pursue my love of literature and art.

Another angel was in the guise of a late diner in a Phoenix restaurant where I worked as a waiter while a full-time student at Arizona State University. He turned out to be a Chairman of the Watsonville School Board, and proposed to me that when I graduated, I should get in touch with him. A door was opened for me. Life changed almost magically and it was not long before an angel appeared as the Head of the English Department, Jack Hamilton, who, although American, still rolled his "rr's" and affected his Scottish ancestry! He seemed to respect me, even though I was an Englishman! He was a generous mentor.

While I was teaching at Watsonville an other angel in the guise of Dick Cunnison, the new Principal of the cutting-edge new high school, a new approach to curriculum and teaching. He surreptitiously slipped into my room, finding a seat at the back. Apparently, he was impressed by my style, whatever I was teaching, because he later sent for me and asked if would I join him in the new school.

Again all through my life these angels appear to guide me or put me on new paths! My close associates in the Aptos faculty were Mike O'Brien, Jack Jones, Norm Hagen, Matthew Miskic & Bob Hestand. The first three were English colleagues. Matt was French teacher, and Bob was a Social Studies teacher. Jack Jones taught next door to my class for many years and we shared many things, but most of all the love of teaching and students and shared ideas. Michael O'Brien was a light that illumined us all in our department, Irish to the end. Norman Hagen was another luminary and a friend who overcame his handicap illness with spirit and love of teaching. Bob Hestand, diminutive in statue but a giant in his love of his students and his warmth to all, and his apples! Matthew Miskic, Croatian, mysterious, lover of life and building, bilingual, big appetite beyond mortals, bon vivant, dreamer with many femme fatale!

Friends all, compatriots looking for the Holy Grail but sipping out of a common glass, dreaming. For me, they were comrades in arms with books and pencils, scaling the walls of ignorance with love of the word and its enlightenment.

Finally, I must include friends who have gone before me: Professor Lochar, a friend and angel who gave me a Danforth Scholarship, enabling me to get a Masters degree in Liberal Arts over three summers at Reed College in Oregon, a delightful sojourn that furthered my love of poetry and of Baroque music. I would be remiss if I did not mention an angel with whom I shared much, Anne Wright, at Reed.

There is one unusual late literary friend, Dick Kilham, who corresponded with me quite regularly for four or five years and enlivened my life with his urbane wit and insouciance and bonhomie. A delightful companion who sadly succumbed to a sudden illness.

Sadly, Louise was lost to us due to a fatal lung ailment. A tragic loss followed by eight years of rudderless wandering, but with one brief friend, Betty De Jesu, who helped for a while when we both were in the desert without direction and real purpose.

Until one day, by the grace of God and Fate, by chance and serendipity, I met Lupita, a true angel, an epiphany beyond my earthly understanding, so blessed was it. She has enriched my spirit and joy and continues God's blessings.

God had his own plan, but I did not let Lupita get out of my sight. I intuited that she was a special angel sent to heal my loneliness and need. My final angel, whom I love and who has blessed my life. So much love and happiness a man could have in his maturity!

I've mentioned the Smiths, English friends who have added to our lives in many ways, and whom we have visited in Ramsey, their home near Southampton, and they have reciprocated by visiting us many times over the years. Bill and Mavis Smith have been friends since we met as fellow passengers on The *Amazing Grace* in the nineties. We sailed twice and have shared time in Hawaii several times. Shipmates and travelers.

My oldest friends are Geoffrey and Geraldine Thornber and who, thank God, are still gracing the earth, still sharing meals, a game of Moon and whatever else friends do. Geoff was a bon vivant, a business man with his own company, not only a capable mechanic with a complicated but agile mind, but also a well-paid consultant! Geraldine is a multi-faceted, capable and intelligent woman who, in my opinion, had the best garden in Santa Cruz County!

Two other friends that share some of our pleasures are Lloyd and Barbara Wells here in Del Mesa Carmel. Both have graced my older-self and my wife, Lupita, and both add to our joi de vivre! Lloyd is a wit and a Yale grad, a good fellow and a Samaritan. Barbara is an ornithologist, intelligent, and both are most delightful companions, particularly when playing cards! We are enriched by them.

What can a man add that has not been said or remembered? Why has God allowed me so any blessings and for such a generous period of life? I hope in my little way that I have given half as much as I have been given. I pray that I gave love and forgiveness and charity to my students and some smiles on the way.

As a teacher, I was given the opportunity to shine a light upon my student's shadows, and perhaps even enlightened their hopes, which I fervently hope I did. It was a privilege.

"Knock on the door, and ye shall enter." Many doors have been opened to me, as opportunity for enlightenment and for love and forgiveness.

An important door was the one I went through in the Church in the Forest on the campus of Robert Louise Stevenson School in Pebble Beach. I met the new pastor, Bill Rolland, just arrived from Minnesota by way of Dunfermline, Scotland! When he found that I had been in Dunfermline during the World War, in 1943, we began a friendship that has not ended. His warmth, energy, intelligence, wit and kindness are well known far and wide. We golf once and a while, too.

I participate as a regular lector and over the years, Bill has been an exemplary pastor, not only in his sermons but also in his actions and guidance of the church. He is a humanitarian at heart with wit and bon ami. I must mention Charles Anker and our new addition Ken Fiske, who now make an imposing triumvirate of the spirit! Over the years their contribution to the services and good deeds are part of their characters. Charles has been Bill's able and intelligent partner over the years.

To conclude, Lupita and I, in our evening of life, have been blessed by family and friends and by decisions over the years that have allowed us to retire in Del Mesa Carmel, where we reside today. On Thursdays I participate in a poker group, and on Tuesdays and Fridays I bowl on the green with convivial friends and have fun, and know how blessed we have been.

"Let the circle be unbroken," as the hymn says.

I can say without qualification, that my circle has mended and my life is fulfilled by God's love and forgiveness and a loving wife, indeed a friend, who, if there are such angels, she is one, thanks be to God.

THE END

A LUCKY LIFE PHOTO ALBUM

1. Colleen
2. Roca-Sanchez Family
3. Ken & Lupita
4. Bill, Ken, Mavis & Lupita
5. Ken, Pat & Don
6. Mary, Kingsley & Lupita
7. Colleen & Steve's Wedding
8. Heather & Don's Wedding
9. Dick
10. Scotty
11. Ken & Dennis
12. Ken & Pauline Galloway
13. Lupita & Ken
14. Berkley & Cynthia
15. Ken in Norway
16. Ken with Heather & Colleen
17. Carmelina & Lupita
18. Harriet, Ken & Lupita in Hawaii
19. Ken & Lupita's Wedding
20. Louise, Ken, Colleen & Heather in Arizona
21. Heather & Colleen in Arizona
22. Don & Pat in America
23. Lupita & Ken on a Cruise
24. Ken Arriving in Philadelphia
25. Colleen & Heather in Amsterdam
26. Mike, Sandy, Lupita, Dylan & Jack
27. Lupita, Geraldine & Geoffrey
28. Madge & Pete
29. Lupita (Sister Marie Borromeo, RSHM)
30. Lupita
31. Hotel Barclay Banquet Trio

1

2

3

4

5

6

13

14

15

16

17

18

19

21

20

22

23

24

25

26

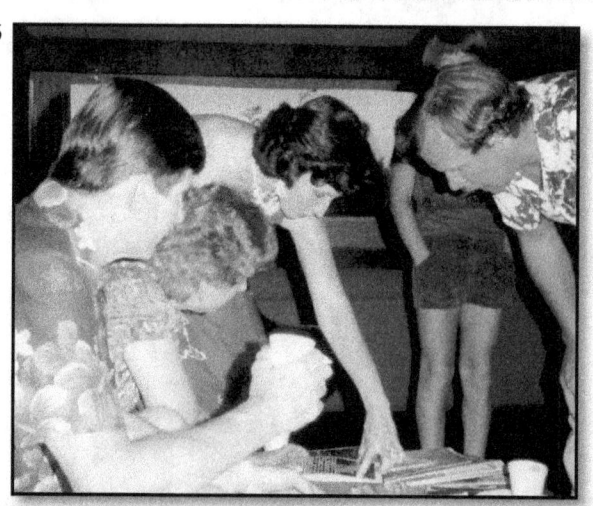

27

29

28

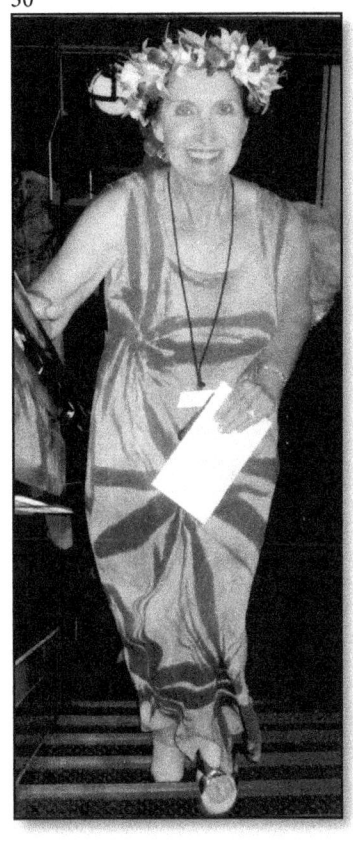
30

31

www.ingramcontent.com/pod-product-compliance
Lightning Source LLC
Chambersburg PA
CBHW071155300426
44113CB00009B/1217